VIRTUAL CHEMLAB
ORGANIC SYNTHESIS AND
QUALITATIVE ANALYSIS V.2.5

BRIAN F. WOODFIELD
MERRITT B. ANDRUS

BRIGHAM YOUNG UNIVERSITY

Upper Saddle River, NJ 07458   Provo, UT 84602

Media Editor: Michael J. Richards
Editor In Chief, Science: Dan Kaveney
Executive Editor, Chemistry: Nicole Folchetti
Executive Managing Editor: Kathleen Schiaparelli
Assistant Managing Editor: Karen Bosch Petrov
Senior Managing Editor: Nicole M. Jackson
Production Editor: Ashley M. Booth
Supplement Cover Manager: Paul Gourhan
Supplement Cover Designer: Christopher Kossa
Manufacturing Buyer: Ilene Kahn
Manufacturing Manager: Alexis Heydt-Long

© 2007 Pearson Education, Inc.
Pearson Prentice Hall
Pearson Education, Inc.
Upper Saddle River, NJ 07458

Printed in the United States of America

10 9 8 7 6 5 4

ISBN 0-13-238827-8

Pearson Education Ltd., *London*
Pearson Education Australia Pty. Ltd., *Sydney*
Pearson Education Singapore, Pte. Ltd.
Pearson Education North Asia Ltd., *Hong Kong*
Pearson Education Canada, Inc., *Toronto*
Pearson Educación de Mexico, S.A. de C.V.
Pearson Education—Japan, *Tokyo*
Pearson Education Malaysia, Pte. Ltd.

Table of Contents

Overview

Introduction

Welcome to *Virtual ChemLab*, a set of realistic and sophisticated simulations covering general and organic chemistry laboratories. In these laboratories, students are put into a virtual environment where they are free to make the choices and decisions that they would confront in an actual laboratory setting and, in turn, experience the resulting consequences. These laboratories include simulations of inorganic qualitative analysis, fundamental experiments in quantum chemistry, gas properties, titration experiments, calorimetry, organic synthesis, and organic qualitative analysis. This Instructor's Manual contains an overview of the full capabilities of the site license version of *Virtual ChemLab v2.5*, installation instructions, and the answers for the laboratory assignments provided in the student laboratory workbook. You have received this Instructors Manual if you have purchased the site license version or if your students are using a student version of the software.

Virtual ChemLab is sold as a site license version and as a single user or student version. The site license version is intended for institutions and the student version is intended for individual student use on a single computer, although they can be used together as will be described later. The site license version, in addition to allowing multiple installations of the software at an institution, is the only version that includes the stockroom or *Instructor Utilities* which is the management side of *Virtual ChemLab*. *Instructor Utilities* allows an instructor to establish classes, make assignments, and view the results, grades, and lab books of the students. The site license version also includes an option to install the software in an electronic workbook mode that is designed to be used in conjunction with an accompanying student laboratory workbook. Details on the various software configurations are given in the next section.

The general features of the organic simulation include the ability to synthesize products; work up reaction mixtures and perform extractions; use nuclear magnetic resonance (NMR), infrared spectroscopy (IR), and thin-layer chromatography (TLC) as analytical tools; purify products by distillation or recrystallization; and perform qualitative analysis experiments on unknowns using functional group tests with actual video depicting the results of the tests. The simulation allows for more than 2,500,000 outcomes for synthesis experiments and can assign over 300 different qualitative analysis unknowns.

The student version of *Virtual ChemLab* and the accompanying workbook are intended to be used in conjunction with *Organic Chemistry* by Paula Bruice and *Organic Chemistry* by Leroy Wade or other mainstream organic texts. The virtual experiments in the organic simulation can be used to demonstrate important reactions, reaction mechanisms, product selectivity, spectra interpretation, and qualitative analysis techniques. This workbook contains the nearly 90 assignment worksheets that correspond to these experiments. These worksheets may be used as an effective practice tool for students or may be assigned by the instructor. Several student assessment experiments have shown that using *Virtual ChemLab* improves student performance by as much as 30%.

Many of the assignments contained in this workbook involve performing synthesis experiments where the student is expected to choose the correct starting materials, reaction conditions, and reagent for the assigned product. After the reaction is started, the student is then expected to perform Thin Layer Chromatography (TLC) experiments to determine when the reaction is complete. (The first assignment, VCL 1-1, demonstrates how TLC works and how to use it to determine when a reaction is complete.) The student is then expected to wash or work up the reaction with the appropriate aqueous reagent and to analyze the product or products using IR and NMR spectroscopy. The cumulative effect of these assignments is to test the student's knowledge of the reaction mechanism and appropriate reaction conditions, give the student experience in working up reaction mixtures, and provide practice for interpreting IR and NMR spectra.

Other assignments in the workbook allow students to gain significant practice interpreting IR and NMR spectra by accessing the spectra library containing over 750 IR and 750 NMR spectra. There are also several qualitative analysis assignments where students can be given unknowns containing specific functional groups, and the student must deduce the structure and name of the unknown from functional group tests, C-H analysis, and IR and NMR spectra.

Software Configurations

Although the *Virtual ChemLab* simulations can be used as an exploratory activity or tool for students, the true power of the simulations is realized when students enter the virtual laboratory and perform assignments or experiments given to them by the instructor just as they would do in an actual laboratory setting. Because these laboratories are virtual, a wide variety of experiences can be provided ranging from very basic and guided to very complex and open-ended. It is up to the instructor to decide the best use of the laboratories, whether it is as a pre-lab, a lab replacement, a homework or quiz assignment, a lab supplement, or a lecture discussion activity. Because each instructor will have a different comfort level using software in the classroom or laboratory and will have different levels of technical support available, several different methods of implementing the simulations at an institution have been provided. Brief descriptions of these are listed below. Details on actually installing the software are given in the installation instructions.

Individual Student Versions. Individual copies of *Virtual ChemLab* can be packaged with Prentice Hall textbooks, purchased by students and installed on personal computers, or installed on institution computers using a site license version. In the student version, an electronic workbook is provided at the beginning of the simulation that allows students to select experiments that correspond to laboratory assignments in the accompanying workbook. Students can also enter the laboratory, bypassing the preset experiments, to explore in the laboratory on their own or to perform custom experiments designed by the instructors. This version of the software, when initially installed, is configured to have the full functionality of the various simulations, but it cannot receive nor submit electronic assignments. This version is the most simple to install and use and requires almost no oversight by the instructor. Since this version cannot receive nor submit electronic assignments, assignments are expected to be given using worksheets. This version, however, can be enabled to use the Web Connectivity Option for transferring electronic assignments. (See the Electronic Assignments and Web Connectivity Option section below.)

Direct Access Computer Lab (A Network Version). In this implementation, a centralized database is installed on a network drive accessible to all client computers in the local area network, and the *Virtual ChemLab* software is installed on any client computers needing access to the simulations. This installation is called a direct access installation since the client software accesses the database containing the class lists, assignments, lab books, and scores directly using a mapped or named network drive. This version allows instructors to give assignments and receive results electronically. This is a simple installation for computer labs and allows multiple instructors to use the software, but there is some network security issues associated with this type of installation. The electronic workbook is not available in this installation.

Web Access Computer Lab (A Network Version). This implementation is very similar to the direct access installation described above, except in this instance, the assignment and lab book data are passed indirectly to the database using a servlet engine running on a TomCat web server. This installation does not require a local area network but, instead, only requires a simple connection to the Internet. This installation also corrects several security issues associated with a direct access connection. Details on setting up and using the web connectivity feature is given in the *Instructor Utilities* user guide from the management perspective and in the various simulation user guides from the student perspective. It is strongly suggested the user guides be reviewed before trying to implement this version. Most questions and problems can be avoided if the user guides are studied carefully.

Web Access Student Version. The student version of *Virtual ChemLab* described above can be activated to a full web version when students are provided with a user name, password, and the URL address for the servlet engine. After the web functionality is activated, the software is no longer configured with the electronic workbook and access to the laboratories is gained solely through the General Chemistry door or card reader. This option allows students to install individual copies of the simulations on their personal computers and then perform their assignments and submit their results electronically over the web. This option has all the advantages of the Web Access Computer Lab installation but relieves the instructor from having to maintain the software on institution computers. In all respects, this installation is identical to the workbook version, except the workbook will not be available.

Electronic Assignments and the Web Connectivity Option

As was described previously, one of the key features of the *Virtual ChemLab* simulations is the ability to give assignments to students using either worksheets out of an accompanying workbook or electronically. Although worksheets are a convenient method to give assignments to students, electronic assignments offer the largest variety of activities and the most control over them. The purpose of the *Instructor Utilities* component of *Virtual ChemLab* is to allow instructors to create electronic assignments, submit them to students, retrieve the student lab books, and assign scores. The ability to give assignments and retrieve results is only available when students running the software have access to the *Virtual ChemLab* database (see the *Database* section below). Installing a direct access version in a local area network is one way of doing this; however, this generally limits students to working in a computer lab.

A more flexible approach has been developed where the necessary information for assignments from the instructor and the results from students can be passed indirectly through a servlet engine running on a TomCat server. (Details on installing and setting up the servlet engine can be found in the installation instructions below.) This method of passing data is called the Web Connectivity Option or Web Database Access. The advantages of this method include (a) it allows an institution to still setup the software in a computer lab without requiring read/write privileges on a network drive (a moderate security hole) and (b) students can install their own copies of the software and still have access to electronic assignments wherever they are as long as they have access to the Internet. The general principles upon which the Web Connectivity Option is based are described next.

1. The database containing the class lists, assignments, lab books, and scores must still be maintained but it can now be stored on a local computer if only one instructor will be using it or it can be stored on a network drive if multiple instructors will be using the same servlet engine to pass data to and from the students. See the *Database* section below for more details.

2. The Web Connectivity Option works by using the servlet engine as a vehicle to receive data from both the instructor and students and save it temporarily on the server. The instructor will send (update) data for each class (from the main database), which the students can, in turn, retrieve and download to their own computers and incorporate it into their own local databases. In a like manner, students submit (update) their results for an assignment to the server; and the instructor, in turn, will retrieve those results and incorporate them into the main database. This synchronization of the instructor and student databases is the responsibility of the individual users. If regular synchronization is not performed by both the students and instructor, then unpredictable results can occur.

3. For *Instructor Utilities*, the Update and Retrieve functions can be performed at two locations. First, the *Class Roll* folder for each class has an *Update Web* button and *Retrieve Web* button. Clicking these buttons performs the indicated action for the selected class. Secondly, the *Utilities* drawer contains a *Web Tools* folder where multiple classes can be selected and the Update and Retrieve functions performed for the selected classes.

4. When a student version is first installed, the software is *not* initially configured to receive electronic assignments. The Web Connectivity Option is activated by going to the *Web Options* button in the lab

book, enabling the *Web Connection*, and adding the user. The information a student must have to add a user is his or her user name, password, and the URL address for the servlet engine. The user name and password are assigned when a student is added to a class. Once a local user has been added, entry into the laboratories is only allowed by providing a password at the card reader, as is the case for a direct access installation. After the first user has been added, other users can be added by using the *Add New User* button on the card reader. It is useful to note that the student side has the ability to enable automatic updates and retrieves. This option is mandatory for computer lab installations and highly recommended for students with continuous Internet connections. Details on using the student side of the Web Connectivity Option are given in the individual laboratory user guides.

5. Before the Web Connectivity Option can be used, the Web Connectivity Option must be enabled and the URL address for the servlet engine specified in the Web Tools folder. Details on configuring the Web Connectivity Option and other important web functions are found in the Web Tools section.

Database

The database that contains the classes, students, assignments, scores, and lab books is kept in the *Data* directory inside the main installed *Virtual ChemLab* directory. The database is stored as encrypted text files and cannot be accessed or modified without the encryption key. All login information is stored in a separate file; and student lists, assignments, and scores are stored in files for each individual class. A separate subdirectory is created for each student inside the *Data* directory and contains the data for each student's lab book. In a direct access network installation, the database (and other common files and directories) must be kept on a mapped (PC) or named (Mac) network drive that all *Virtual ChemLab* client computers can access with read/write privileges. In a web access network installation, the database can be stored on a network drive if several instructors will need access to the database; or it can be kept on a local drive, even on a portable computer, as long as there is an Internet connection to allow for the update and retrieval of the web data.

System Requirements

Minimum system requirements are as follows:

PC
Pentium 500 MHz (Pentium II or better recommended)
128 Mb RAM (256+ Mb Recommended)
CD-ROM drive (for installation only)
200 Mb of free disk space
Display capable of **and** set to millions of colors (24 bit color)
Minimum resolution 800 x 600 (1024 x 768 or higher strongly recommended)
Windows 2000 Professional or Windows XP
QuickTime 5.x/6.x/7.x

Macintosh
PowerPC (G3 or better recommended)
128 Mb RAM (256+ Mb recommended)
CD-ROM drive (for installation only)
200 Mb of free disk space
Display capable of **and** set to millions of colors (24-bit color)
Recommended minimum resolution 832 x 624 (1024 x 768 or higher strongly recommended)
OS X (any version)
QuickTime 5.x/6.x/7.x

Server (network installations)

For a Direct Database Access network installation or common database sharing among instructors, a file server running an operating system capable of mapped or named drives accessible to all clients in the local area network is required. The clients must be running an operating system compatible with the *Virtual ChemLab* software (see above). Linux, OS X, Windows, and Novell file servers have all been successfully implemented to host the *Virtual ChemLab* database.

Note: The above requirements are the recommended minimum hardware and system software requirements for reasonable execution speeds and reliability. However, it should be noted that the software has been successfully installed and used on computers with significantly lower capabilities than the recommendations given above with corresponding reductions in execution speed and media access time.

Installing Virtual ChemLab

Locate and run the program "Setup ChemLab" on the CD-ROM drive then follow the prompts. The following installation options are available:

- **Single Student Installation.** The student version of the software, when initially installed, is configured to have the full functionality of the various simulations but is configured to use the electronic workbook and worksheet assignments. This version is the most simple to install and use and requires almost no oversight by the instructor. This version can be enabled to use the Web Connectivity Option for transferring electronic assignments. *Instructor Utilities* is not installed with this option.

- **Full Local Installation.** This installation provides a fully functional standalone version of the software. This installation does not include the electronic workbook for student use, but it does include *Instructor Utilities*, which allows the management of electronic assignments using a Direct Database Access or Web Database Access configuration. The software is initially configured to access a local database, but this can be changed within *Instructor Utilities*.

- **Network Installation.** This installation provides options to install *Virtual ChemLab* in a number of different network configurations for both the instructor and student computers. An option is also provided to create a Client Installer at a network location to make it easier to install *Virtual ChemLab* at different locations within the local area network. Some of these options can be selected simultaneously but most are mutually exclusive. Given below is a description of the various network installation options.

  - **Install Database to Network Location.** This option will install the *Virtual ChemLab* database to a user specified location (usually on a network drive). This option is used to create a common database that all client installations on a network will use as part of the Direct Database Access option. This database installation can also be used for instructors who need to share access to a common database for a Web Connectivity configuration.

  - **Install Client Installer to Network Location.** This option will create a Client Installer at a user specified location on the network. The Client Installer is intended to facilitate the installation of *Virtual ChemLab* clients on network computers without the need of the installation CD. The Client Installer allows the installation of clients with either the Direct Database Access or the Web Database Access options. If this option is selected, the user will be requested to provide (a) the location for the Client Installer on the network, (b) the default web address for the servlet engine (optional), (c) the default network database location (optional), and (d) the default location for the client installation (optional). These default values are used to streamline the client installation process during later client installations using the network installer.

  - **Install Client to Local Location with Direct Database Access.** This option will install *Virtual ChemLab* on a client computer and configure the installation to use the Direct Database Access option. A *Virtual ChemLab* database must first be installed at a common access location (usually a network drive) before this installation will function properly. The user must provide the location of the network database during the installation.

  - **Install Client to Location with Web Database Access.** This option will install *Virtual ChemLab* on a client computer and configure the installation to use the Web Database Access option. The Web Connectivity Option servlet engine must first be installed before this installation will function properly. The user must provide the web address for the web servlet engine during the installation.

- **Install Instructor Utilities with Client.** This option will install *Instructor Utilities* along with the client installation for a Direct Database Access option. *Instructor Utilities* is required for assigning and retrieving electronic assignments either through Direct Access or Web Access.

All users who will be running *Virtual ChemLab* where they will be accessing a centralized database on a network drive must have read/write privileges to that database directory (including subdirectories). This does not imply that users must be given access to these files and directories but only that they have read/write privileges to enable the software to run correctly. Multiple users access the same database in a direct access installation and when multiple instructors manage classes with the Web Connectivity Option but using a common database. Further installation instructions can be found in the Installation and Overview Guide found on the CD.

Getting Started with the Student Version

After the student version of *Virtual ChemLab* has been successfully installed, the *VCL* icon used to launch the program will be located on the desktop, in a Program Group on PC machines, and on the Dock for Macintosh machines. Clicking on the *VCL* icon will start the simulation where you will be brought to a hallway containing three doors and a workbook sitting on a table (see Figure 1). Clicking on the electronic workbook opens and zooms into the workbook pages (see Figure 2) where you can select preset assignments that correspond to the assignments in the laboratory workbook. The *Previous* and *Next* buttons are used to page through the set of assignments, and the different assignments can also be accessed by clicking on the section titles located on the left page of the workbook. Clicking on the *Enter Laboratory* button will allow you to enter the organic chemistry laboratory (see below), and the *Exit* button is used to leave *Virtual ChemLab*.

From the hallway, students can also enter the organic laboratory by clicking on the Organic Chemistry door. Once in the laboratory (shown in Figure 3), students have access to a lab bench, reagents, glassware in the drawers, a stockroom containing starting materials, IR and NMR spectrometers, and other useful items. Mousing over an object in the laboratory displays popup text that identifies the object.

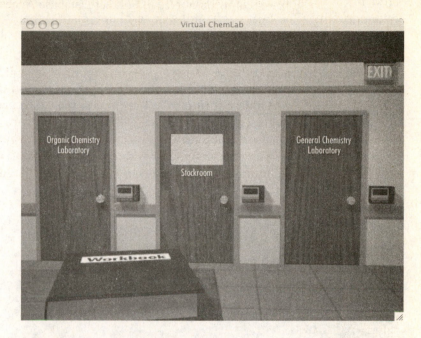

Figure 1. The "hallway" leading into the different virtual rooms in *Virtual ChemLab*. The organic chemistry laboratory can be accessed by clicking on the Organic Chemistry door and the electronic workbook is accessed by clicking on the workbook.

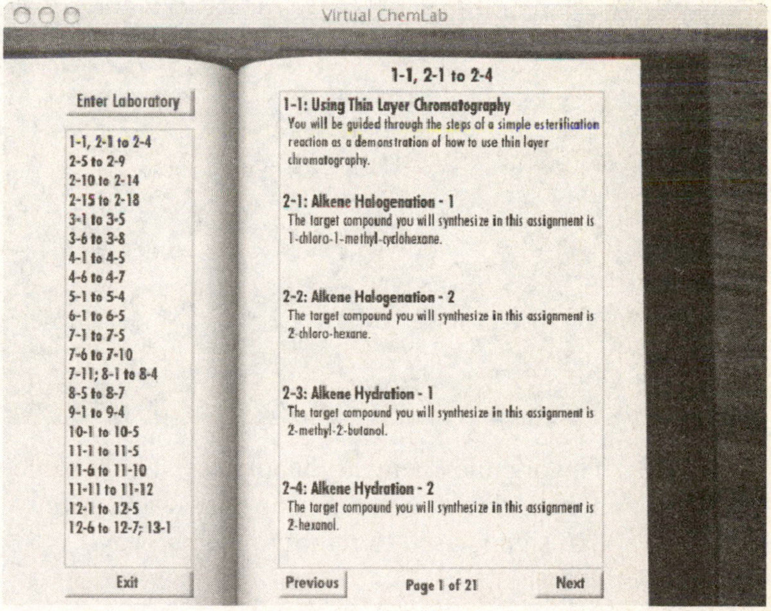

Figure 2. The electronic workbook. Preset laboratories corresponding to assignments in the workbook are accessed by clicking on the assignment.

Experiments are started by going to the stockroom, using the clipboard to select a reaction or unknown type, selecting starting materials or an unknown, and returning to the laboratory. While in the organic chemistry laboratory, the full functionality of the simulation is available, and students are free to explore and perform experiments as directed by their instructors or by their own curiosity. The Exit signs in the general chemistry laboratory are used to return to the hallway.

Detailed instructions on how to use the organic simulation can be found in the User Guides Folder located on the *Virtual ChemLab* CD. This same user guide can also be accessed inside the laboratory by clicking on the Pull-Down TV and clicking on the Help button. The TV can also be used to access the Spectra Library.

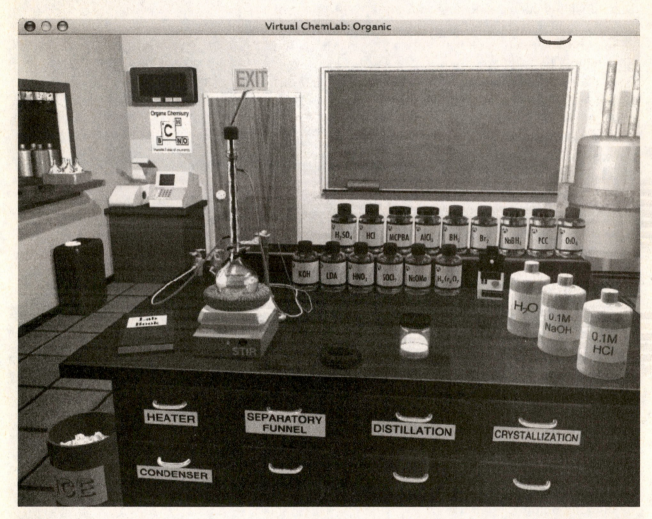

Figure 3. The organic chemistry laboratory. The organic chemistry laboratory contains the lab bench, stockroom, reagents, glassware, spectrometers, and other useful items. The exit sign is used to return to the hallway.

Important Installation Notes and Issues

1. The graphics used in the simulations require the monitor to be set to 24-bit true color (millions of colors). Lower color resolutions can be used, but the graphics will not be as sharp.

2. When installing *Virtual ChemLab*, you must be logged in as an Administrative User in order for all files and folders to be installed correctly and to have correctly configured file permissions; otherwise, unpredictable results such as hard crashes and other errors can occur during installation and running *Virtual ChemLab*.

3. Occasionally when installing on the OS X operating system, the system fails to copy over the VCL icon for aliases created on the desktop. There is no known cause for this. Aliases with the correct icon can be created manually inside the installation directory or by copying a VCL icon on to an already existing alias.

4. When installing on the OS X operating system v10.4 (or Tiger), selecting the option to place an alias on the dock causes the dock to be reset to its initial installed state and any dock customization is lost.

5. In the directory where *Virtual ChemLab* is installed, the user must always have read/write privileges to that directory and all directories underneath. This is the default state for all Administrative Users (both Mac and PC), and this condition has been set by the installer for Standard Users in OS X as well. However, if users will be logged in as Restricted Users in Windows (such as in a computer lab), then the privileges for the *Virtual ChemLab* directory must be set manually to "Full Access" for everyone. The installer attempts to set these permissions for Windows installations, but for unknown reasons it is not always successful. In addition, if the system crashes hard while running *Virtual ChemLab* (either on Windows or OS X), these permissions may have to be reset to read/write for everyone.

6. The installer does not allow installation and other directory paths to be typed in directly, but all installation paths must be identified or selected by browsing to the desired location. When installing on the OS X operating system, browsing to a folder using aliases occasionally causes the installer to spontaneously shutdown. Consequently, it is recommended that aliases be avoided when browsing. There is no known cause for this.

7. All users running *Virtual ChemLab* where they will be accessing a centralized database on a network drive (Direct Database Access) must have read/write privileges to that database directory (including subdirectories). This does not imply that users must be given access to these files and directories but only that they have read/write privileges to enable the software to run correctly.

8. When installing *Virtual ChemLab* onto the OS X operating system, the user must have read/write permission for the folder into which *Virtual ChemLab* will be installed. In the vast majority of cases, *Virtual ChemLab* will be installed into the Applications folder, but in order for this to be successful the user must be an Administrative User. In some cases, however, the permissions for the Applications folder have been modified by other software installed on the machine, which will prevent *Virtual ChemLab* from being

installed in the Applications folder. These permissions can be reset back to their default state using the *Repair Disk Permissions* function in the Disk Utility program located in the Applications folder.

9. QuickTime 5.0 or later is required for the software to run properly. The most recent version of QuickTime can be obtained at http://www.apple.com/quicktime/

10. When the simulation software has been installed on a Windows 2000 Professional operating system, users will experience better performance and better system stability when the Windows 2000 Support Pack 2 has been installed.

11. For unknown reasons, on some machines the QuickTime videos will not play properly if the system QuickTime settings are in their default state. This can be corrected by changing the Video Settings in QuickTime to Normal Mode.

VCL 1-1: Using Thin Layer Chromatography

Thin layer chromatography (TLC) is a simple and relatively fast analytical tool that is used to measure the extent of a reaction or measure the relative polarity of a molecule. A TLC plate is a sheet of glass that is coated with a thin layer of adsorbent such as silica (or occasionally alumina). A small amount of the mixture to be analyzed is placed or spotted near the bottom of this plate. When monitoring reactions, it is common to place the starting materials on one side of the plate (or in the left lane) and the reaction mixture in the right lane. The TLC plate is then placed in a shallow pool of a solvent (20% ethyl acetate/hexanes) so that only the very bottom of the plate is in the liquid. This solvent, or the eluent, is the mobile phase, and it slowly rises up the TLC plate by capillary action.

As the solvent moves past the spot that was applied, it carries the spotted mixture up the plate where a competition occurs between the solvent carrying the mixture and the silica on the plate. Since the silica adsorbent is polar, polar molecules in the mixture will rise very little up the plate, but nonpolar molecules will have little attraction to the silica and will consequently rise to the top. Molecules of intermediate polarity will stop somewhere in between these two extremes. When the solvent has reached the top of the plate, the plate is removed from the solvent, dried, and then separated components of the mixture are visualized by exposure to a UV lamp. The positions of each spot on the TLC plate are identified and recorded by assigning R_f values from 0.0 to 1.0, where a 0.0 indicates the spot is at the bottom of the plate and a 1.0 indicates the spot is at the top.

In this assignment, you will be guided through the steps of a simple esterification reaction as a demonstration of how to use thin layer chromatography as a tool to monitor a reaction until it reaches completion. This assignment will also serve as a tutorial to teach you how to utilize the various parts of the organic simulation that will be used in later assignments.

1. Start *Virtual ChemLab* and select *Using Thin Layer Chromatography* from the list of assignments in the electronic workbook. The lab will open in the Organic laboratory. You should see a lab bench containing reagents on the back of the bench, aqueous reagents on the right, drawers containing necessary laboratory equipment (clicking on a drawer will open it), a red disposal bucket for cleaning up the lab, and the organic stockroom on the left. Other pieces of laboratory equipment will be used in other assignments.

2. Enter the stockroom by clicking inside the *Stockroom* window. Click on one of the round bottom flasks located on the stockroom counter and drag it to and then drop it on the cork ring near the box of flasks. Now select the starting materials for the reaction by first clicking on the bottle containing 2-phenylacetic acid (PhAcOH) and dragging and dropping the scoop on the mouth of the flask. Now do the same for 3-methyl-1-butanol (PentOH) except this time a syringe will be used since this starting material is a liquid. Starting materials can also be added by double-clicking on the bottles. Click on the green *Return to Lab* arrow to return to the laboratory.

3. The round bottom flask containing the two starting materials should now be on the stir plate. Click on the handle located in the upper right corner of the laboratory to pull down the TV. The TV should already be in *Tutorial* mode and the two starting materials should be listed. Mousing over the listed starting materials will display their structures on the chalkboard. Help on using *Virtual ChemLab* can also be found on the TV by clicking on the *Help* button.

4. In order to perform an esterification reaction, sulfuric acid (H_2SO_4) must be added to the starting materials. This is done by clicking on the H_2SO_4 bottle on the reagent shelf on the back of the lab bench and dragging the syringe to the round bottom flask. The acid can also be added by double-clicking on the H_2SO_4 bottle. The TV should now show that the acid has been added to the reaction mixture.

5. Before the reaction can be started, we must be able to heat the reaction mixture so the reaction can proceed at a suitable rate. This is done by adding a heating mantle to heat the reaction mixture, adding a condenser so the mixture can be refluxed, and then adding nitrogen gas to maintain an inert atmosphere and to prevent pressure buildup. Click on the *Heater* drawer to open it and then click and drag the heating mantle to the round bottom flask to place it on the stir plate. Now open the *Condenser* drawer (you will need to close the *Heater* drawer first) and place the condenser on top of the round bottom flask. Finally, click on the nitrogen gas hose to the right of the stir plate and drag and drop it on top of the condenser. Now click on the *Stir Plate* button to start the reaction. You should see the reaction mixture stirring in the round bottom flask.

6. Before waiting too long, perform a TLC measurement by clicking on the TLC jar (located to the right of the cork ring) and drag the TLC plate and drop it on the round bottom flask. A window should now open showing the TLC results. In the starting material lane (the left lane) you should see two large spots near the bottom and in the reaction lane (the right lane) you should see the same two spots.

   Why are the spots the same for both the right and left lanes? _____

   _____

7. Close the TLC window and now advance the reaction forward 15 minutes (or you can just wait 15 minutes) by advancing the time on the laboratory clock. This is done by clicking on the appropriate button under the minutes, tens of minutes, or hours digits on the clock. Now perform a new TLC measurement on the reaction mixture.

   *What is the new spot?*_____

   What has happened to the size of the starting material spots? Why? _____

   _____

8. Close the TLC window again and now advance the laboratory time forward until all of the starting materials have been consumed. You will need to monitor the reaction with TLC measurements until you observe that the starting materials have been consumed.

   How much time did it take to complete the reaction? _____

   What are the R_f values for the starting materials and product? _____

   What can you say about the relative polarities of the starting materials and the product? _____

   _____

   _____

9. When a reaction is complete, the reaction mixture is rinsed or "worked up" by adding an aqueous reagent of an appropriate pH to the reaction mixture in a separatory funnel. After you shake the funnel to thoroughly rinse the reaction mixture, the water-soluble products will be in the aqueous phase and all others will be in the organic phase. Open the drawer containing the separatory funnel and click and drag it to the round bottom flask. The reaction mixture should now be in the funnel. Now select the HCl aqueous reagent and drag it to the top of the funnel to add it. There will now be two layers, the top being the organic phase and the bottom the aqueous phase. Click on the organic phase to extract the product and drag it to the cork ring on the lab bench. Perform a TLC measurement on the solution in the flask to confirm that it is the same product produced in the reaction.

VCL 2-1: Alkene Halogenation – 1

For this assignment, the target compound that you should synthesize is **1-chloro-1-methyl-cyclohexane.** This will be an electrophilic alkene addition reaction where the π-bond is broken and two new covalent bonds are formed. Examine the product carefully to determine the new functionality. Keep in mind the mechanism and form the more stable, most substituted carbocation intermediate.

Synthesis Procedures

1. Start *Virtual ChemLab* and select *Alkene Halogenation – 1* from the list of assignments in the electronic workbook. After entering the organic laboratory, go to the stockroom by clicking inside the *Stockroom* window. Next, select a round bottom flask and place it on the cork ring on the stockroom counter. Using the available reagents on the stockroom shelf, identify the appropriate starting materials required to synthesize the target compound and add them to the round bottom flask. Now add ether (Et$_2$O) as a solvent and click on the green *Return to Lab* arrow to return to the laboratory.

2. The round bottom flask containing the starting materials should now be on the stir plate. Click on the handle located in the upper right corner of the laboratory to pull down the TV. The TV should already be in *Tutorial* mode and the starting materials and solvent should be listed. From the group of reagents found on the lab bench, select the correct reagent to synthesize the target compound and add it to the flask on the stir plate. Now attach the heater, condenser, and N$_2$ gas to the round bottom flask so the reaction mixture can be heated.

3. Start the reaction by clicking on the *Stir* button on the front of the stir plate. You should be able to observe the reaction mixture stirring in the flask. Monitor the progress of the reaction using TLC measurements as necessary until the product has formed and the starting materials have been consumed. You can advance the laboratory time using the clock on the wall. With the electronic lab book open (click on the lab book on the lab bench), you can also save your TLC plates by clicking *Save* on the TLC window.

4. When the reaction is complete, "work up" your reaction by first dragging and dropping the separatory funnel (located in a drawer) on the flask and then adding H$_2$O to the funnel. Extract the organic layer in the funnel by clicking on the top layer and dragging it to the cork ring on the lab bench. Your target compound should now be in this flask.

List the starting materials, solvent, reagent, and products formed: _____

_____

How long did it take to finish the reaction? _____

What are the TLC values (R$_f$) for (a) Starting Materials: _____ *(b) Products:* _____

Write a mechanism for this reaction:

Chapter 2

IR and NMR Spectra

After completing a reaction and working up the products, it is still necessary to confirm that the correct product was formed. The most common tools used for this analysis are Infrared (IR) and Nuclear Magnetic Resonance (NMR) spectroscopy. In the virtual laboratory, only ^{1}H NMR spectra are available. Details on interpreting IR and NMR spectra are found in your textbook. Your instructor may or may not ask you to perform this section depending on how your class is structured.

5. To collect an IR spectrum of your product, click on the IR spectrometer located underneath the laboratory clock and drag the salt plate icon to the flask on the lab bench. A window containing the IR spectrum for your product should now open. Identify the relevant peaks in the IR spectrum and record the position and associated functional group for each in the IR table below. The IR spectrum can also be saved to the lab book for later analysis.

IR List position (cm^{-1}) & functional group	4.
1.	5.
2.	6.
3.	7.

6. To collect a ^{1}H NMR spectrum of your product, click on the NMR magnet located to the right of the chalkboard and drag the NMR sample tube to the flask on the lab bench. A window containing the NMR spectrum for your product should now open. You can zoom into various portions of the NMR spectrum by clicking and dragging over the desired area. The *Zoom Out* button is used to zoom back out to view the full spectrum. Identify all of the peaks in the NMR spectrum and record the chemical shift, the splitting, and the number of hydrogens for each peak in the NMR table below. The NMR spectrum can also be saved to the lab book for later analysis.

^{1}H NMR	Peak	Chemical Shift (δ)	Multiplicity[†]	H[‡]	Peak	Chemical Shift (δ)	Multiplicity[†]	H[‡]
Structure:	1				7			
	2				8			
1-Chloro-1-methyl-cyclohexane	3				9			
	4				10			
	5				11			
	6				12			

[†] Specify the multiplicity as a singlet (s), doublet (d), triplet (t), quartet (q), or multiplet (m).
[‡] Specify the number of hydrogens associated with each peak.

7. *Do the IR and NMR spectra you measured and recorded in the tables above confirm that you synthesized the assigned target compound? Explain.* _____

_____

_____

_____

4

VCL 2-2: Alkene Halogenation – 2

For this assignment, the target compound that you should synthesize is **2-chloro-hexane.** Again, this is an electrophilic alkene addition reaction. Examine the product to determine the new functionality. Keep in mind that multiple starting materials may give the same product, but not with the same selectivity. Remember to form the more substituted carbocation intermediate.

Synthesis Procedures

1. Start *Virtual ChemLab* and select *Alkene Halogenation – 2* from the list of assignments in the electronic workbook. After entering the organic laboratory, go to the stockroom by clicking inside the *Stockroom* window. Next, select a round bottom flask and place it on the cork ring on the stockroom counter. Using the available reagents on the stockroom shelf, identify the appropriate starting materials required to synthesize the target compound and add them to the round bottom flask. Now add ether (Et_2O) as a solvent and click on the green *Return to Lab* arrow to return to the laboratory.

2. The round bottom flask containing the starting materials should now be on the stir plate. Click on the handle located in the upper right corner of the laboratory to pull down the TV. The TV should already be in *Tutorial* mode and the starting materials and solvent should be listed. From the group of reagents found on the lab bench, select the correct reagent to synthesize the target compound and add it to the flask on the stir plate. Now attach the heater, condenser, and N_2 gas to the round bottom flask so the reaction mixture can be heated.

3. Start the reaction by clicking on the *Stir* button on the front of the stir plate. You should be able to observe the reaction mixture stirring in the flask. Monitor the progress of the reaction using TLC measurements as necessary until the product has formed and the starting materials have been consumed. You can advance the laboratory time using the clock on the wall. With the electronic lab book open (click on the lab book on the lab bench), you can also save your TLC plates by clicking *Save* on the TLC window.

4. When the reaction is complete, "work up" your reaction by first dragging and dropping the separatory funnel (located in a drawer) on the flask and then adding H_2O to the funnel. Extract the organic layer in the funnel by clicking on the top layer and dragging it to the cork ring on the lab bench. Your target compound should now be in this flask.

    List the starting materials, solvent, reagent, and products formed: _____

    _____

    How long did it take to finish the reaction? _____

    What are the TLC values (R_f) for (a) Starting Materials: _____   (b) Products: _____

    Write a mechanism for this reaction:

IR and NMR Spectra

After completing a reaction and working up the products, it is still necessary to confirm that the correct product was formed. The most common tools used for this analysis are Infrared (IR) and Nuclear Magnetic Resonance (NMR) spectroscopy. In the virtual laboratory, only ^{1}H NMR spectra are available. Details on interpreting IR and NMR spectra are found in your textbook. Your instructor may or may not ask you to perform this section depending on how your class is structured.

5. To collect an IR spectrum of your product, click on the IR spectrometer located underneath the laboratory clock and drag the salt plate icon to the flask on the lab bench. A window containing the IR spectrum for your product should now open. Identify the relevant peaks in the IR spectrum and record the position and associated functional group for each in the IR table below. The IR spectrum can also be saved to the lab book for later analysis.

IR List position (cm^{-1}) & functional group	4.
1.	5.
2.	6.
3.	7.

6. To collect a ^{1}H NMR spectrum of your product, click on the NMR magnet located to the right of the chalkboard and drag the NMR sample tube to the flask on the lab bench. A window containing the NMR spectrum for your product should now open. You can zoom into various portions of the NMR spectrum by clicking and dragging over the desired area. The *Zoom Out* button is used to zoom back out to view the full spectrum. Identify all of the peaks in the NMR spectrum and record the chemical shift, the splitting, and the number of hydrogens for each peak in the NMR table below. The NMR spectrum can also be saved to the lab book for later analysis.

^{1}H NMR	Peak	Chemical Shift (δ)	Multiplicity†	H‡	Peak	Chemical Shift (δ)	Multiplicity†	H‡
	1				7			
Structure:	2				8			
Cl	3				9			
2-Chloro-hexane	4				10			
	5				11			
	6				12			

† Specify the multiplicity as a singlet (s), doublet (d), triplet (t), quartet (q), or multiplet (m).
‡ Specify the number of hydrogens associated with each peak.

7. *Do the IR and NMR spectra you measured and recorded in the tables above confirm that you*

    synthesized the assigned target compound? Explain. _____

    _____

    _____

    _____

VCL 2-3: Alkene Hydration – 1

For this assignment, the target compound that you should synthesize is **2-methyl-2-butanol.** Again, this is an electrophilic alkene addition reaction. Examine the product to determine the new functionality. Keep in mind that multiple starting materials may give the same product, but not with the same selectivity. Remember to form the more substituted carbocation intermediate and place the electrophile at the terminal position.

Synthesis Procedures
1. Start *Virtual ChemLab* and select *Alkene Hydration – 1* from the list of assignments in the electronic workbook. After entering the organic laboratory, go to the stockroom by clicking inside the *Stockroom* window. Next, select a round bottom flask and place it on the cork ring on the stockroom counter. Using the available reagents on the stockroom shelf, identify the appropriate starting materials required to synthesize the target compound and add them to the round bottom flask. Now add water (H_2O) as a solvent and click on the green *Return to Lab* arrow to return to the laboratory.

2. The round bottom flask containing the starting materials should now be on the stir plate. Click on the handle located in the upper right corner of the laboratory to pull down the TV. The TV should already be in *Tutorial* mode and the starting materials and solvent should be listed. From the group of reagents found on the lab bench, select the correct reagent to synthesize the target compound and add it to the flask on the stir plate. Now attach the heater, condenser, and N_2 gas to the round bottom flask so the reaction mixture can be heated.

3. Start the reaction by clicking on the *Stir* button on the front of the stir plate. You should be able to observe the reaction mixture stirring in the flask. Monitor the progress of the reaction using TLC measurements as necessary until the product has formed and the starting materials have been consumed. You can advance the laboratory time using the clock on the wall. With the electronic lab book open (click on the lab book on the lab bench), you can also save your TLC plates by clicking *Save* on the TLC window.

4. When the reaction is complete, "work up" your reaction by first dragging and dropping the separatory funnel (located in a drawer) on the flask and then adding H_2O to the funnel. Extract the organic layer in the funnel by clicking on the top layer and dragging it to the cork ring on the lab bench. Your target compound should now be in this flask.

    List the starting materials, solvent, reagent, and products formed: _____

    _____

    How long did it take to finish the reaction? _____

    What are the TLC values (R_f) for (a) Starting Materials: _____ (b) Products: _____

    Write a mechanism for this reaction:

7

IR and NMR Spectra

After completing a reaction and working up the products, it is still necessary to confirm that the correct product was formed. The most common tools used for this analysis are Infrared (IR) and Nuclear Magnetic Resonance (NMR) spectroscopy. In the virtual laboratory, only ^{1}H NMR spectra are available. Details on interpreting IR and NMR spectra are found in your textbook. Your instructor may or may not ask you to perform this section depending on how your class is structured.

5. To collect an IR spectrum of your product, click on the IR spectrometer located underneath the laboratory clock and drag the salt plate icon to the flask on the lab bench. A window containing the IR spectrum for your product should now open. Identify the relevant peaks in the IR spectrum and record the position and associated functional group for each in the IR table below. The IR spectrum can also be saved to the lab book for later analysis.

IR List position (cm^{-1}) & functional group	4.
1.	5.
2.	6.
3.	7.

6. To collect a ^{1}H NMR spectrum of your product, click on the NMR magnet located to the right of the chalkboard and drag the NMR sample tube to the flask on the lab bench. A window containing the NMR spectrum for your product should now open. You can zoom into various portions of the NMR spectrum by clicking and dragging over the desired area. The *Zoom Out* button is used to zoom back out to view the full spectrum. Identify all of the peaks in the NMR spectrum and record the chemical shift, the splitting, and the number of hydrogens for each peak in the NMR table below. The NMR spectrum can also be saved to the lab book for later analysis.

^{1}H NMR	Peak	Chemical Shift (δ)	Multiplicity[†]	H[‡]	Peak	Chemical Shift (δ)	Multiplicity[†]	H[‡]
	1				7			
Structure:	2				8			
	3				9			
2-Methyl-2-butanol	4				10			
	5				11			
	6				12			

[†] Specify the multiplicity as a singlet (s), doublet (d), triplet (t), quartet (q), or multiplet (m).
[‡] Specify the number of hydrogens associated with each peak.

7. *Do the IR and NMR spectra you measured and recorded in the tables above confirm that you synthesized the assigned target compound? Explain.* _____

_____

_____

_____

VCL 2-4: Alkene Hydration – 2

For this assignment, the target compound that you should synthesize is **2-hexanol**. Again, this is an electrophilic alkene addition reaction. Examine the product to determine the location of the new functionality. Keep in mind that different starting materials may give the same product, but not with the same selectivity. Remember to form the more substituted carbocation intermediate.

Synthesis Procedures

1. Start *Virtual ChemLab* and select *Alkene Hydration – 2* from the list of assignments in the electronic workbook. After entering the organic laboratory, go to the stockroom by clicking inside the *Stockroom* window. Next, select a round bottom flask and place it on the cork ring on the stockroom counter. Using the available reagents on the stockroom shelf, identify the appropriate starting materials required to synthesize the target compound and add them to the round bottom flask. Now add water (H$_2$O) as a solvent and click on the green *Return to Lab* arrow to return to the laboratory.

2. The round bottom flask containing the starting materials should now be on the stir plate. Click on the handle located in the upper right corner of the laboratory to pull down the TV. The TV should already be in *Tutorial* mode and the starting materials and solvent should be listed. From the group of reagents found on the lab bench, select the correct reagent to synthesize the target compound and add it to the flask on the stir plate. Now attach the heater, condenser, and N$_2$ gas to the round bottom flask so the reaction mixture can be heated.

3. Start the reaction by clicking on the *Stir* button on the front of the stir plate. You should be able to observe the reaction mixture stirring in the flask. Monitor the progress of the reaction using TLC measurements as necessary until the product has formed and the starting materials have been consumed. You can advance the laboratory time using the clock on the wall. With the electronic lab book open (click on the lab book on the lab bench), you can also save your TLC plates by clicking *Save* on the TLC window.

4. When the reaction is complete, "work up" your reaction by first dragging and dropping the separatory funnel (located in a drawer) on the flask and then adding H$_2$O to the funnel. Extract the organic layer in the funnel by clicking on the top layer and dragging it to the cork ring on the lab bench. Your target compound should now be in this flask.

List the starting materials, solvent, reagent, and products formed: _____

_____

How long did it take to finish the reaction? _____

What are the TLC values (R$_f$) for (a) Starting Materials:_____ (b) Products: _____

Write a mechanism for this reaction:

IR and NMR Spectra

After completing a reaction and working up the products, it is still necessary to confirm that the correct product was formed. The most common tools used for this analysis are Infrared (IR) and Nuclear Magnetic Resonance (NMR) spectroscopy. In the virtual laboratory, only ^{1}H NMR spectra are available. Details on interpreting IR and NMR spectra are found in your textbook. Your instructor may or may not ask you to perform this section depending on how your class is structured.

5. To collect an IR spectrum of your product, click on the IR spectrometer located underneath the laboratory clock and drag the salt plate icon to the flask on the lab bench. A window containing the IR spectrum for your product should now open. Identify the relevant peaks in the IR spectrum and record the position and associated functional group for each in the IR table below. The IR spectrum can also be saved to the lab book for later analysis.

IR List position (cm^{-1}) & functional group	4.
1.	5.
2.	6.
3.	7.

6. To collect a ^{1}H NMR spectrum of your product, click on the NMR magnet located to the right of the chalkboard and drag the NMR sample tube to the flask on the lab bench. A window containing the NMR spectrum for your product should now open. You can zoom into various portions of the NMR spectrum by clicking and dragging over the desired area. The *Zoom Out* button is used to zoom back out to view the full spectrum. Identify all of the peaks in the NMR spectrum and record the chemical shift, the splitting, and the number of hydrogens for each peak in the NMR table below. The NMR spectrum can also be saved to the lab book for later analysis.

^{1}H NMR Structure: OH 2-Hexanol	Peak	Chemical Shift (δ)	Multiplicity[†]	H[‡]	Peak	Chemical Shift (δ)	Multiplicity[†]	H[‡]
	1				7			
	2				8			
	3				9			
	4				10			
	5				11			
	6				12			

[†] Specify the multiplicity as a singlet (s), doublet (d), triplet (t), quartet (q), or multiplet (m).
[‡] Specify the number of hydrogens associated with each peak.

7. *Do the IR and NMR spectra you measured and recorded in the tables above confirm that you*

    synthesized the assigned target compound? Explain. _____

    _____

    _____

    _____

VCL 2-5: Alkene Hydration – 3

For this assignment, the target compound that you should synthesize is **1-methyl-cyclohexanol.** Again, this is an electrophilic alkene addition reaction. Examine the product to determine the location of the new functionality. Keep in mind that multiple starting materials may give the same product, but not with the same selectivity. Remember to form the more substituted carbocation intermediate.

Synthesis Procedures

1. Start *Virtual ChemLab* and select *Alkene Hydration – 3* from the list of assignments in the electronic workbook. After entering the organic laboratory, go to the stockroom by clicking inside the *Stockroom* window. Next, select a round bottom flask and place it on the cork ring on the stockroom counter. Using the available reagents on the stockroom shelf, identify the appropriate starting materials required to synthesize the target compound and add them to the round bottom flask. Now add water (H_2O) as a solvent and click on the green *Return to Lab* arrow to return to the laboratory.

2. The round bottom flask containing the starting materials should now be on the stir plate. Click on the handle located in the upper right corner of the laboratory to pull down the TV. The TV should already be in *Tutorial* mode and the starting materials and solvent should be listed. From the group of reagents found on the lab bench, select the correct reagent to synthesize the target compound and add it to the flask on the stir plate. Now attach the heater, condenser, and N_2 gas to the round bottom flask so the reaction mixture can be heated.

3. Start the reaction by clicking on the *Stir* button on the front of the stir plate. You should be able to observe the reaction mixture stirring in the flask. Monitor the progress of the reaction using TLC measurements as necessary until the product has formed and the starting materials have been consumed. You can advance the laboratory time using the clock on the wall. With the electronic lab book open (click on the lab book on the lab bench), you can also save your TLC plates by clicking *Save* on the TLC window.

4. When the reaction is complete, "work up" your reaction by first dragging and dropping the separatory funnel (located in a drawer) on the flask and then adding H_2O to the funnel. Extract the organic layer in the funnel by clicking on the top layer and dragging it to the cork ring on the lab bench. Your target compound should now be in this flask.

   List the starting materials, solvent, reagent, and products formed: _____

   _____

   How long did it take to finish the reaction? _____

   What are the TLC values (Rf) for (a) Starting Materials: _____ (b) Products: _____

   Write a mechanism for this reaction:

11

IR and NMR Spectra

After completing a reaction and working up the products, it is still necessary to confirm that the correct product was formed. The most common tools used for this analysis are Infrared (IR) and Nuclear Magnetic Resonance (NMR) spectroscopy. In the virtual laboratory, only ^{1}H NMR spectra are available. Details on interpreting IR and NMR spectra are found in your textbook. Your instructor may or may not ask you to perform this section depending on how your class is structured.

5.   To collect an IR spectrum of your product, click on the IR spectrometer located underneath the laboratory clock and drag the salt plate icon to the flask on the lab bench. A window containing the IR spectrum for your product should now open. Identify the relevant peaks in the IR spectrum and record the position and associated functional group for each in the IR table below. The IR spectrum can also be saved to the lab book for later analysis.

IR List position (cm^{-1}) & functional group	4.
1.	5.
2.	6.
3.	7.

6.   To collect a ^{1}H NMR spectrum of your product, click on the NMR magnet located to the right of the chalkboard and drag the NMR sample tube to the flask on the lab bench. A window containing the NMR spectrum for your product should now open. You can zoom into various portions of the NMR spectrum by clicking and dragging over the desired area. The *Zoom Out* button is used to zoom back out to view the full spectrum. Identify all of the peaks in the NMR spectrum and record the chemical shift, the splitting, and the number of hydrogens for each peak in the NMR table below. The NMR spectrum can also be saved to the lab book for later analysis.

^{1}H NMR Structure: 1-Methyl-cyclohexanol	Peak	Chemical Shift (δ)	Multiplicity†	H‡	Peak	Chemical Shift (δ)	Multiplicity†	H‡
	1				7			
	2				8			
	3				9			
	4				10			
	5				11			
	6				12			

† Specify the multiplicity as a singlet (s), doublet (d), triplet (t), quartet (q), or multiplet (m).
‡ Specify the number of hydrogens associated with each peak.

7.   *Do the IR and NMR spectra you measured and recorded in the tables above confirm that you synthesized the assigned target compound? Explain.* _____

_____

_____

_____

VCL 2-6: Etherfication – 1

For this assignment, the target compound that you should synthesize is **ethyl 2-hexyl ether.** Again, this is an electrophilic alkene addition reaction. Examine the product to determine the location of the new functionality. Keep in mind that different starting materials may give the same product, but not with the same selectivity. Remember to form the more substituted carbocation intermediate.

Synthesis Procedures

1. Start *Virtual ChemLab* and select *Etherfication – 1* from the list of assignments in the electronic workbook. After entering the organic laboratory, go to the stockroom by clicking inside the *Stockroom* window. Next, select a round bottom flask and place it on the cork ring on the stockroom counter. Using the available reagents on the stockroom shelf, identify the appropriate starting materials required to synthesize the target compound and add them to the round bottom flask. Now add ether (Et$_2$O) as a solvent and click on the green *Return to Lab* arrow to return to the laboratory.

2. The round bottom flask containing the starting materials should now be on the stir plate. Click on the handle located in the upper right corner of the laboratory to pull down the TV. The TV should already be in *Tutorial* mode and the starting materials and solvent should be listed. From the group of reagents found on the lab bench, select the correct reagent to synthesize the target compound and add it to the flask on the stir plate. Now attach the heater, condenser, and N$_2$ gas to the round bottom flask so the reaction mixture can be heated.

3. Start the reaction by clicking on the *Stir* button on the front of the stir plate. You should be able to observe the reaction mixture stirring in the flask. Monitor the progress of the reaction using TLC measurements as necessary until the product has formed and the starting materials have been consumed. You can advance the laboratory time using the clock on the wall. With the electronic lab book open (click on the lab book on the lab bench), you can also save your TLC plates by clicking *Save* on the TLC window.

4. When the reaction is complete, "work up" your reaction by first dragging and dropping the separatory funnel (located in a drawer) on the flask and then adding H$_2$O to the funnel. Extract the organic layer in the funnel by clicking on the top layer and dragging it to the cork ring on the lab bench. Your target compound should now be in this flask.

   List the starting materials, solvent, reagent, and products formed: _____

   _____

   How long did it take to finish the reaction? _____

   What are the TLC values (R$_f$) for (a) Starting Materials: _____ (b) Products: _____

   Write a mechanism for this reaction:

IR and NMR Spectra

After completing a reaction and working up the products, it is still necessary to confirm that the correct product was formed. The most common tools used for this analysis are Infrared (IR) and Nuclear Magnetic Resonance (NMR) spectroscopy. In the virtual laboratory, only ^{1}H NMR spectra are available. Details on interpreting IR and NMR spectra are found in your textbook. Your instructor may or may not ask you to perform this section depending on how your class is structured.

5. To collect an IR spectrum of your product, click on the IR spectrometer located underneath the laboratory clock and drag the salt plate icon to the flask on the lab bench. A window containing the IR spectrum for your product should now open. Identify the relevant peaks in the IR spectrum and record the position and associated functional group for each in the IR table below. The IR spectrum can also be saved to the lab book for later analysis.

IR List position (cm^{-1}) & functional group	4.
1.	5.
2.	6.
3.	7.

6. To collect a ^{1}H NMR spectrum of your product, click on the NMR magnet located to the right of the chalkboard and drag the NMR sample tube to the flask on the lab bench. A window containing the NMR spectrum for your product should now open. You can zoom into various portions of the NMR spectrum by clicking and dragging over the desired area. The *Zoom Out* button is used to zoom back out to view the full spectrum. Identify all of the peaks in the NMR spectrum and record the chemical shift, the splitting, and the number of hydrogens for each peak in the NMR table below. The NMR spectrum can also be saved to the lab book for later analysis.

^{1}H NMR	Peak	Chemical Shift (δ)	Multiplicity[†]	H[‡]	Peak	Chemical Shift (δ)	Multiplicity[†]	H[‡]
Structure:	1				7			
	2				8			
Ethyl 2-hexyl ether	3				9			
	4				10			
	5				11			
	6				12			

[†] Specify the multiplicity as a singlet (s), doublet (d), triplet (t), quartet (q), or multiplet (m).
[‡] Specify the number of hydrogens associated with each peak.

7. *Do the IR and NMR spectra you measured and recorded in the tables above confirm that you synthesized the assigned target compound? Explain.* _____

_____

_____

VCL 2-7: Alkene Hydration – 4

For this assignment, the target compound that you should synthesize is **2-methyl-2-pentanol.** This is another electrophilic alkene addition reaction. Examine the product to determine the location of the new functionality. Keep in mind that different starting materials may give the same product, but not with the same selectivity. Remember to form the more substituted carbocation intermediate.

Synthesis Procedures
1. Start *Virtual ChemLab* and select *Alkene Hydration – 4* from the list of assignments in the electronic workbook. After entering the organic laboratory, go to the stockroom by clicking inside the *Stockroom* window. Next, select a round bottom flask and place it on the cork ring on the stockroom counter. Using the available reagents on the stockroom shelf, identify the appropriate starting materials required to synthesize the target compound and add them to the round bottom flask. Now add water (H_2O) as a solvent and click on the green *Return to Lab* arrow to return to the laboratory.

2. The round bottom flask containing the starting materials should now be on the stir plate. Click on the handle located in the upper right corner of the laboratory to pull down the TV. The TV should already be in *Tutorial* mode and the starting materials and solvent should be listed. From the group of reagents found on the lab bench, select the correct reagent to synthesize the target compound and add it to the flask on the stir plate. Now attach the heater, condenser, and N_2 gas to the round bottom flask so the reaction mixture can be heated.

3. Start the reaction by clicking on the *Stir* button on the front of the stir plate. You should be able to observe the reaction mixture stirring in the flask. Monitor the progress of the reaction using TLC measurements as necessary until the product has formed and the starting materials have been consumed. You can advance the laboratory time using the clock on the wall. With the electronic lab book open (click on the lab book on the lab bench), you can also save your TLC plates by clicking *Save* on the TLC window.

4. When the reaction is complete, "work up" your reaction by first dragging and dropping the separatory funnel (located in a drawer) on the flask and then adding H_2O to the funnel. Extract the organic layer in the funnel by clicking on the top layer and dragging it to the cork ring on the lab bench. Your target compound should now be in this flask.

   List the starting materials, solvent, reagent, and products formed: _____

   _____

   How long did it take to finish the reaction? _____

   What are the TLC values (R_f) for (a) Starting Materials: _____ *(b) Products:* _____

   Write a mechanism for this reaction:

IR and NMR Spectra

After completing a reaction and working up the products, it is still necessary to confirm that the correct product was formed. The most common tools used for this analysis are Infrared (IR) and Nuclear Magnetic Resonance (NMR) spectroscopy. In the virtual laboratory, only ^{1}H NMR spectra are available. Details on interpreting IR and NMR spectra are found in your textbook. Your instructor may or may not ask you to perform this section depending on how your class is structured.

5. To collect an IR spectrum of your product, click on the IR spectrometer located underneath the laboratory clock and drag the salt plate icon to the flask on the lab bench. A window containing the IR spectrum for your product should now open. Identify the relevant peaks in the IR spectrum and record the position and associated functional group for each in the IR table below. The IR spectrum can also be saved to the lab book for later analysis.

IR List position (cm^{-1}) & functional group	4.
1.	5.
2.	6.
3.	7.

6. To collect a ^{1}H NMR spectrum of your product, click on the NMR magnet located to the right of the chalkboard and drag the NMR sample tube to the flask on the lab bench. A window containing the NMR spectrum for your product should now open. You can zoom into various portions of the NMR spectrum by clicking and dragging over the desired area. The *Zoom Out* button is used to zoom back out to view the full spectrum. Identify all of the peaks in the NMR spectrum and record the chemical shift, the splitting, and the number of hydrogens for each peak in the NMR table below. The NMR spectrum can also be saved to the lab book for later analysis.

^{1}H NMR Structure: 2-Methyl-2-pentanol	Peak	Chemical Shift (δ)	Multiplicity†	H‡	Peak	Chemical Shift (δ)	Multiplicity†	H‡
	1				7			
	2				8			
	3				9			
	4				10			
	5				11			
	6				12			

† Specify the multiplicity as a singlet (s), doublet (d), triplet (t), quartet (q), or multiplet (m).
‡ Specify the number of hydrogens associated with each peak.

7. *Do the IR and NMR spectra you measured and recorded in the tables above confirm that you synthesized the assigned target compound? Explain.* _____

_____

_____

_____

VCL 2-8: Alkene Halogenation – 3

For this assignment, the target compound that you should synthesize is **2-chloro-2,3-dimethylbutane.** Again, this is an electrophilic alkene addition reaction. Examine the product to determine the location of the new functionality. Keep in mind that different starting materials may give the same product, but not with the same selectivity. Remember to form the more substituted carbocation intermediate again.

Synthesis Procedures

1. Start *Virtual ChemLab* and select *Alkene Halogenation – 3* from the list of assignments in the electronic workbook. After entering the organic laboratory, go to the stockroom by clicking inside the *Stockroom* window. Next, select a round bottom flask and place it on the cork ring on the stockroom counter. Using the available reagents on the stockroom shelf, identify the appropriate starting materials required to synthesize the target compound and add them to the round bottom flask. Now add ether (Et_2O) as a solvent and click on the green *Return to Lab* arrow to return to the laboratory.

2. The round bottom flask containing the starting materials should now be on the stir plate. Click on the handle located in the upper right corner of the laboratory to pull down the TV. The TV should already be in *Tutorial* mode and the starting materials and solvent should be listed. From the group of reagents found on the lab bench, select the correct reagent to synthesize the target compound and add it to the flask on the stir plate. Now attach the heater, condenser, and N_2 gas to the round bottom flask so the reaction mixture can be heated.

3. Start the reaction by clicking on the *Stir* button on the front of the stir plate. You should be able to observe the reaction mixture stirring in the flask. Monitor the progress of the reaction using TLC measurements as necessary until the product has formed and the starting materials have been consumed. You can advance the laboratory time using the clock on the wall. With the electronic lab book open (click on the lab book on the lab bench), you can also save your TLC plates by clicking *Save* on the TLC window.

4. When the reaction is complete, "work up" your reaction by first dragging and dropping the separatory funnel (located in a drawer) on the flask and then adding H_2O to the funnel. Extract the organic layer in the funnel by clicking on the top layer and dragging it to the cork ring on the lab bench. Your target compound should now be in this flask.

    List the starting materials, solvent, reagent, and products formed: _____

    _____

    How long did it take to finish the reaction? _____

    What are the TLC values (R_f) for (a) Starting Materials: _____ *(b) Products:* _____

    Write a mechanism for this reaction:

IR and NMR Spectra

After completing a reaction and working up the products, it is still necessary to confirm that the correct product was formed. The most common tools used for this analysis are Infrared (IR) and Nuclear Magnetic Resonance (NMR) spectroscopy. In the virtual laboratory, only ^{1}H NMR spectra are available. Details on interpreting IR and NMR spectra are found in your textbook. Your instructor may or may not ask you to perform this section depending on how your class is structured.

5. To collect an IR spectrum of your product, click on the IR spectrometer located underneath the laboratory clock and drag the salt plate icon to the flask on the lab bench. A window containing the IR spectrum for your product should now open. Identify the relevant peaks in the IR spectrum and record the position and associated functional group for each in the IR table below. The IR spectrum can also be saved to the lab book for later analysis.

IR List position (cm^{-1}) & functional group	4.
1.	5.
2.	6.
3.	7.

6. To collect a ^{1}H NMR spectrum of your product, click on the NMR magnet located to the right of the chalkboard and drag the NMR sample tube to the flask on the lab bench. A window containing the NMR spectrum for your product should now open. You can zoom into various portions of the NMR spectrum by clicking and dragging over the desired area. The *Zoom Out* button is used to zoom back out to view the full spectrum. Identify all of the peaks in the NMR spectrum and record the chemical shift, the splitting, and the number of hydrogens for each peak in the NMR table below. The NMR spectrum can also be saved to the lab book for later analysis.

^{1}H NMR Structure: Cl 2-Chloro-2,3-dimethylbutane	Peak	Chemical Shift (δ)	Multiplicity†	H‡	Peak	Chemical Shift (δ)	Multiplicity†	H‡
	1				7			
	2				8			
	3				9			
	4				10			
	5				11			
	6				12			

† Specify the multiplicity as a singlet (s), doublet (d), triplet (t), quartet (q), or multiplet (m).
‡ Specify the number of hydrogens associated with each peak.

7. *Do the IR and NMR spectra you measured and recorded in the tables above confirm that you synthesized the assigned target compound? Explain.* _____

_____

_____

_____

VCL 2-9: Alkene Halogenation – 4

For this assignment, the target compound that you should synthesize is **1,2-dibromo-3,3-dimethyl butane.** Again, this is an electrophilic alkene addition reaction. Examine the product to determine the location of the new functionality. Keep in mind that different starting materials may give the same product, but not with the same selectivity. Keep in mind the bromonium ion intermediate.

Synthesis Procedures
1. Start *Virtual ChemLab* and select *Alkene Halogenation – 4* from the list of assignments in the electronic workbook. After entering the organic laboratory, go to the stockroom by clicking inside the *Stockroom* window. Next, select a round bottom flask and place it on the cork ring on the stockroom counter. Using the available reagents on the stockroom shelf, identify the appropriate starting materials required to synthesize the target compound and add them to the round bottom flask. Now add ether (Et_2O) as a solvent and click on the green *Return to Lab* arrow to return to the laboratory.

2. The round bottom flask containing the starting materials should now be on the stir plate. Click on the handle located in the upper right corner of the laboratory to pull down the TV. The TV should already be in *Tutorial* mode and the starting materials and solvent should be listed. From the group of reagents found on the lab bench, select the correct reagent to synthesize the target compound and add it to the flask on the stir plate. Now attach the heater, condenser, and N_2 gas to the round bottom flask so the reaction mixture can be heated.

3. Start the reaction by clicking on the *Stir* button on the front of the stir plate. You should be able to observe the reaction mixture stirring in the flask. Monitor the progress of the reaction using TLC measurements as necessary until the product has formed and the starting materials have been consumed. You can advance the laboratory time using the clock on the wall. With the electronic lab book open (click on the lab book on the lab bench), you can also save your TLC plates by clicking *Save* on the TLC window.

4. When the reaction is complete, "work up" your reaction by first dragging and dropping the separatory funnel (located in a drawer) on the flask and then adding H_2O to the funnel. Extract the organic layer in the funnel by clicking on the top layer and dragging it to the cork ring on the lab bench. Your target compound should now be in this flask.

List the starting materials, solvent, reagent, and products formed: _____

_____

How long did it take to finish the reaction? _____

What are the TLC values (R_f) for (a) Starting Materials: _____ *(b) Products:* _____

Write a mechanism for this reaction:

IR and NMR Spectra

After completing a reaction and working up the products, it is still necessary to confirm that the correct product was formed. The most common tools used for this analysis are Infrared (IR) and Nuclear Magnetic Resonance (NMR) spectroscopy. In the virtual laboratory, only ^{1}H NMR spectra are available. Details on interpreting IR and NMR spectra are found in your textbook. Your instructor may or may not ask you to perform this section depending on how your class is structured.

5. To collect an IR spectrum of your product, click on the IR spectrometer located underneath the laboratory clock and drag the salt plate icon to the flask on the lab bench. A window containing the IR spectrum for your product should now open. Identify the relevant peaks in the IR spectrum and record the position and associated functional group for each in the IR table below. The IR spectrum can also be saved to the lab book for later analysis.

IR List position (cm^{-1}) & functional group	4.
1.	5.
2.	6.
3.	7.

6. To collect a ^{1}H NMR spectrum of your product, click on the NMR magnet located to the right of the chalkboard and drag the NMR sample tube to the flask on the lab bench. A window containing the NMR spectrum for your product should now open. You can zoom into various portions of the NMR spectrum by clicking and dragging over the desired area. The *Zoom Out* button is used to zoom back out to view the full spectrum. Identify all of the peaks in the NMR spectrum and record the chemical shift, the splitting, and the number of hydrogens for each peak in the NMR table below. The NMR spectrum can also be saved to the lab book for later analysis.

^{1}H NMR Structure: Br —Br 1,2-Dibromo-3,3-dimethyl-butane	Peak	Chemical Shift (δ)	Multiplicity[†]	H[‡]	Peak	Chemical Shift (δ)	Multiplicity[†]	H[‡]
	1				7			
	2				8			
	3				9			
	4				10			
	5				11			
	6				12			

[†] Specify the multiplicity as a singlet (s), doublet (d), triplet (t), quartet (q), or multiplet (m).
[‡] Specify the number of hydrogens associated with each peak.

7. *Do the IR and NMR spectra you measured and recorded in the tables above confirm that you synthesized the assigned target compound? Explain.* _____

_____

_____

_____

VCL 2-10: Alkene Halogenation – 5

For this assignment, the target compound that you should synthesize is *trans*-**1,2-dibromo-1-methyl-cyclohexane.** Again, this is an electrophilic alkene addition reaction. Examine the product to determine the location of the new functionality. Keep in mind that different starting materials may give the same product, but not with the same selectivity. Keep in mind the bromonium ion intermediate and the consequences of its structure.

Synthesis Procedures

1. Start *Virtual ChemLab* and select *Alkene Halogenation – 5* from the list of assignments in the electronic workbook. After entering the organic laboratory, go to the stockroom by clicking inside the *Stockroom* window. Next, select a round bottom flask and place it on the cork ring on the stockroom counter. Using the available reagents on the stockroom shelf, identify the appropriate starting materials required to synthesize the target compound and add them to the round bottom flask. Now add ether (Et_2O) as a solvent and click on the green *Return to Lab* arrow to return to the laboratory.

2. The round bottom flask containing the starting materials should now be on the stir plate. Click on the handle located in the upper right corner of the laboratory to pull down the TV. The TV should already be in *Tutorial* mode and the starting materials and solvent should be listed. From the group of reagents found on the lab bench, select the correct reagent to synthesize the target compound and add it to the flask on the stir plate. Now attach the heater, condenser, and N_2 gas to the round bottom flask so the reaction mixture can be heated.

3. Start the reaction by clicking on the *Stir* button on the front of the stir plate. You should be able to observe the reaction mixture stirring in the flask. Monitor the progress of the reaction using TLC measurements as necessary until the product has formed and the starting materials have been consumed. You can advance the laboratory time using the clock on the wall. With the electronic lab book open (click on the lab book on the lab bench), you can also save your TLC plates by clicking *Save* on the TLC window.

4. When the reaction is complete, "work up" your reaction by first dragging and dropping the separatory funnel (located in a drawer) on the flask and then adding H_2O to the funnel. Extract the organic layer in the funnel by clicking on the top layer and dragging it to the cork ring on the lab bench. Your target compound should now be in this flask.

List the starting materials, solvent, reagent, and products formed: _____

_____

How long did it take to finish the reaction? _____

What are the TLC values (R_f) for (a) Starting Materials: _____ *(b) Products:* _____

Write a mechanism for this reaction:

IR and NMR Spectra

After completing a reaction and working up the products, it is still necessary to confirm that the correct product was formed. The most common tools used for this analysis are Infrared (IR) and Nuclear Magnetic Resonance (NMR) spectroscopy. In the virtual laboratory, only ^{1}H NMR spectra are available. Details on interpreting IR and NMR spectra are found in your textbook. Your instructor may or may not ask you to perform this section depending on how your class is structured.

5. To collect an IR spectrum of your product, click on the IR spectrometer located underneath the laboratory clock and drag the salt plate icon to the flask on the lab bench. A window containing the IR spectrum for your product should now open. Identify the relevant peaks in the IR spectrum and record the position and associated functional group for each in the IR table below. The IR spectrum can also be saved to the lab book for later analysis.

IR List position (cm^{-1}) & functional group	4.
1.	5.
2.	6.
3.	7.

6. To collect a ^{1}H NMR spectrum of your product, click on the NMR magnet located to the right of the chalkboard and drag the NMR sample tube to the flask on the lab bench. A window containing the NMR spectrum for your product should now open. You can zoom into various portions of the NMR spectrum by clicking and dragging over the desired area. The *Zoom Out* button is used to zoom back out to view the full spectrum. Identify all of the peaks in the NMR spectrum and record the chemical shift, the splitting, and the number of hydrogens for each peak in the NMR table below. The NMR spectrum can also be saved to the lab book for later analysis.

^{1}H NMR	Peak	Chemical Shift (δ)	Multiplicity[†]	H[‡]	Peak	Chemical Shift (δ)	Multiplicity[†]	H[‡]
	1				7			
Structure:	2				8			
	3				9			
	4				10			
trans-1,2-Dibromo-1-methyl-cyclohexane	5				11			
	6				12			

[†] Specify the multiplicity as a singlet (s), doublet (d), triplet (t), quartet (q), or multiplet (m).
[‡] Specify the number of hydrogens associated with each peak.

7. *Do the IR and NMR spectra you measured and recorded in the tables above confirm that you synthesized the assigned target compound? Explain.* _____

_____

_____

_____

VCL 2-11: Halohydrin Formation – 1

For this assignment, the target compound that you should synthesize is **1-bromo-2-hexanol.** Again, this is an electrophilic alkene addition reaction. Examine the product to determine the location of the new functionality. Keep in mind the bromonium ion intermediate and the consequences of its structure. The nucleophile again attacks at the more substituted position.

Synthesis Procedures

1. Start *Virtual ChemLab* and select *Halohydrin Formation – 1* from the list of assignments in the electronic workbook. After entering the organic laboratory, go to the stockroom by clicking inside the *Stockroom* window. Next, select a round bottom flask and place it on the cork ring on the stockroom counter. Using the available reagents on the stockroom shelf, identify the appropriate starting materials required to synthesize the target compound and add them to the round bottom flask. Now add water (H_2O) as a solvent and click on the green *Return to Lab* arrow to return to the laboratory.

2. The round bottom flask containing the starting materials should now be on the stir plate. Click on the handle located in the upper right corner of the laboratory to pull down the TV. The TV should already be in *Tutorial* mode and the starting materials and solvent should be listed. From the group of reagents found on the lab bench, select the correct reagent to synthesize the target compound and add it to the flask on the stir plate. Now attach the heater, condenser, and N_2 gas to the round bottom flask so the reaction mixture can be heated.

3. Start the reaction by clicking on the *Stir* button on the front of the stir plate. You should be able to observe the reaction mixture stirring in the flask. Monitor the progress of the reaction using TLC measurements as necessary until the product has formed and the starting materials have been consumed. You can advance the laboratory time using the clock on the wall. With the electronic lab book open (click on the lab book on the lab bench), you can also save your TLC plates by clicking *Save* on the TLC window.

4. When the reaction is complete, "work up" your reaction by first dragging and dropping the separatory funnel (located in a drawer) on the flask and then adding H_2O to the funnel. Extract the organic layer in the funnel by clicking on the top layer and dragging it to the cork ring on the lab bench. Your target compound should now be in this flask.

   List the starting materials, solvent, reagent, and products formed: _____

   _____

   How long did it take to finish the reaction? _____

   What are the TLC values (R_f) for (a) Starting Materials: _____ *(b) Products:* _____

   Write a mechanism for this reaction:

IR and NMR Spectra

After completing a reaction and working up the products, it is still necessary to confirm that the correct product was formed. The most common tools used for this analysis are Infrared (IR) and Nuclear Magnetic Resonance (NMR) spectroscopy. In the virtual laboratory, only ^{1}H NMR spectra are available. Details on interpreting IR and NMR spectra are found in your textbook. Your instructor may or may not ask you to perform this section depending on how your class is structured.

5. To collect an IR spectrum of your product, click on the IR spectrometer located underneath the laboratory clock and drag the salt plate icon to the flask on the lab bench. A window containing the IR spectrum for your product should now open. Identify the relevant peaks in the IR spectrum and record the position and associated functional group for each in the IR table below. The IR spectrum can also be saved to the lab book for later analysis.

IR List position (cm^{-1}) & functional group	4.
1.	5.
2.	6.
3.	7.

6. To collect a ^{1}H NMR spectrum of your product, click on the NMR magnet located to the right of the chalkboard and drag the NMR sample tube to the flask on the lab bench. A window containing the NMR spectrum for your product should now open. You can zoom into various portions of the NMR spectrum by clicking and dragging over the desired area. The *Zoom Out* button is used to zoom back out to view the full spectrum. Identify all of the peaks in the NMR spectrum and record the chemical shift, the splitting, and the number of hydrogens for each peak in the NMR table below. The NMR spectrum can also be saved to the lab book for later analysis.

^{1}H NMR Structure: OH /\/\/\Br 1-Bromo-2-hexanol	Peak	Chemical Shift (δ)	Multiplicity[†]	H[‡]	Peak	Chemical Shift (δ)	Multiplicity[†]	H[‡]
	1				7			
	2				8			
	3				9			
	4				10			
	5				11			
	6				12			

[†] Specify the multiplicity as a singlet (s), doublet (d), triplet (t), quartet (q), or multiplet (m).
[‡] Specify the number of hydrogens associated with each peak.

7. *Do the IR and NMR spectra you measured and recorded in the tables above confirm that you synthesized the assigned target compound? Explain.* _____

_____

_____

_____

VCL 2-12: Epoxidation – 1

For this assignment, the target compound that you should synthesize is **3,3-dimethyl-1,2-epoxybutane**. Again, this is an electrophilic alkene addition reaction. Examine the product to determine the location of the new functionality. The alkene is the electron-rich partner, and an electrophilic reagent is needed.

Synthesis Procedures

1. Start *Virtual ChemLab* and select *Epoxidation – 1* from the list of assignments in the electronic workbook. After entering the organic laboratory, go to the stockroom by clicking inside the *Stockroom* window. Next, select a round bottom flask and place it on the cork ring on the stockroom counter. Using the available reagents on the stockroom shelf, identify the appropriate starting materials required to synthesize the target compound and add them to the round bottom flask. Now add ether (Et_2O) as a solvent and click on the green *Return to Lab* arrow to return to the laboratory.

2. The round bottom flask containing the starting materials should now be on the stir plate. Click on the handle located in the upper right corner of the laboratory to pull down the TV. The TV should already be in *Tutorial* mode and the starting materials and solvent should be listed. From the group of reagents found on the lab bench, select the correct reagent to synthesize the target compound and add it to the flask on the stir plate. Now attach the heater, condenser, and N_2 gas to the round bottom flask so the reaction mixture can be heated.

3. Start the reaction by clicking on the *Stir* button on the front of the stir plate. You should be able to observe the reaction mixture stirring in the flask. Monitor the progress of the reaction using TLC measurements as necessary until the product has formed and the starting materials have been consumed. You can advance the laboratory time using the clock on the wall. With the electronic lab book open (click on the lab book on the lab bench), you can also save your TLC plates by clicking *Save* on the TLC window.

4. When the reaction is complete, "work up" your reaction by first dragging and dropping the separatory funnel (located in a drawer) on the flask and then adding NaOH to the funnel. Extract the organic layer in the funnel by clicking on the top layer and dragging it to the cork ring on the lab bench. Your target compound should now be in this flask.

    List the starting materials, solvent, reagent, and products formed: _____

    _____

    How long did it take to finish the reaction _____

    What are the TLC values (R_f) for (a) Starting Materials: _____ *(b) Products:* _____

    Write a mechanism for this reaction:

IR and NMR Spectra

After completing a reaction and working up the products, it is still necessary to confirm that the correct product was formed. The most common tools used for this analysis are Infrared (IR) and Nuclear Magnetic Resonance (NMR) spectroscopy. In the virtual laboratory, only ^{1}H NMR spectra are available. Details on interpreting IR and NMR spectra are found in your textbook. Your instructor may or may not ask you to perform this section depending on how your class is structured.

5. To collect an IR spectrum of your product, click on the IR spectrometer located underneath the laboratory clock and drag the salt plate icon to the flask on the lab bench. A window containing the IR spectrum for your product should now open. Identify the relevant peaks in the IR spectrum and record the position and associated functional group for each in the IR table below. The IR spectrum can also be saved to the lab book for later analysis.

IR List position (cm^{-1}) & functional group	4.
1.	5.
2.	6.
3.	7.

6. To collect a ^{1}H NMR spectrum of your product, click on the NMR magnet located to the right of the chalkboard and drag the NMR sample tube to the flask on the lab bench. A window containing the NMR spectrum for your product should now open. You can zoom into various portions of the NMR spectrum by clicking and dragging over the desired area. The *Zoom Out* button is used to zoom back out to view the full spectrum. Identify all of the peaks in the NMR spectrum and record the chemical shift, the splitting, and the number of hydrogens for each peak in the NMR table below. The NMR spectrum can also be saved to the lab book for later analysis.

^{1}H NMR	Peak	Chemical Shift (δ)	Multiplicity[†]	H[‡]	Peak	Chemical Shift (δ)	Multiplicity[†]	H[‡]
Structure:	1				7			
	2				8			
	3				9			
3,3-Dimethyl-1,2-epoxybutane	4				10			
	5				11			
	6				12			

[†] Specify the multiplicity as a singlet (s), doublet (d), triplet (t), quartet (q), or multiplet (m).
[‡] Specify the number of hydrogens associated with each peak.

7. *Do the IR and NMR spectra you measured and recorded in the tables above confirm that you synthesized the assigned target compound? Explain.* _____

_____

_____

_____

VCL 2-13: Hydroboration – 1

For this assignment, the target compound that you should synthesize is **2-methyl-1-butanol.** Again, this is an electrophilic alkene addition reaction. Examine the product to determine the location of the new functionality. You will now need an electrophile that is not a proton, H^+. The regioselectivity is still dictated by placement of the electrophile at the terminal position.

Synthesis Procedures

1. Start *Virtual ChemLab* and select *Hydroboration – 1* from the list of assignments in the electronic workbook. After entering the organic laboratory, go to the stockroom by clicking inside the *Stockroom* window. Next, select a round bottom flask and place it on the cork ring on the stockroom counter. Using the available reagents on the stockroom shelf, identify the appropriate starting materials required to synthesize the target compound and add them to the round bottom flask. Now add ether (Et_2O) as a solvent and click on the green *Return to Lab* arrow to return to the laboratory.

2. The round bottom flask containing the starting materials should now be on the stir plate. Click on the handle located in the upper right corner of the laboratory to pull down the TV. The TV should already be in *Tutorial* mode and the starting materials and solvent should be listed. From the group of reagents found on the lab bench, select the correct reagent to synthesize the target compound and add it to the flask on the stir plate. Now attach the heater, condenser, and N_2 gas to the round bottom flask so the reaction mixture can be heated.

3. Start the reaction by clicking on the *Stir* button on the front of the stir plate. You should be able to observe the reaction mixture stirring in the flask. Monitor the progress of the reaction using TLC measurements as necessary until the product has formed and the starting materials have been consumed. You can advance the laboratory time using the clock on the wall. With the electronic lab book open (click on the lab book on the lab bench), you can also save your TLC plates by clicking *Save* on the TLC window.

4. When the reaction is complete, "work up" your reaction by first dragging and dropping the separatory funnel (located in a drawer) on the flask and then adding H_2O to the funnel. Extract the organic layer in the funnel by clicking on the top layer and dragging it to the cork ring on the lab bench. Your target compound should now be in this flask.

   List the starting materials, solvent, reagent, and products formed: _____

   _____

   How long did it take to finish the reaction? _____

   What are the TLC values (R_f) for (a) Starting Materials: _____ (b) Products: _____

   Write a mechanism for this reaction:

27

Chapter 2

IR and NMR Spectra

After completing a reaction and working up the products, it is still necessary to confirm that the correct product was formed. The most common tools used for this analysis are Infrared (IR) and Nuclear Magnetic Resonance (NMR) spectroscopy. In the virtual laboratory, only ^{1}H NMR spectra are available. Details on interpreting IR and NMR spectra are found in your textbook. Your instructor may or may not ask you to perform this section depending on how your class is structured.

5. To collect an IR spectrum of your product, click on the IR spectrometer located underneath the laboratory clock and drag the salt plate icon to the flask on the lab bench. A window containing the IR spectrum for your product should now open. Identify the relevant peaks in the IR spectrum and record the position and associated functional group for each in the IR table below. The IR spectrum can also be saved to the lab book for later analysis.

IR List position (cm^{-1}) & functional group	4.
1.	5.
2.	6.
3.	7.

6. To collect a ^{1}H NMR spectrum of your product, click on the NMR magnet located to the right of the chalkboard and drag the NMR sample tube to the flask on the lab bench. A window containing the NMR spectrum for your product should now open. You can zoom into various portions of the NMR spectrum by clicking and dragging over the desired area. The *Zoom Out* button is used to zoom back out to view the full spectrum. Identify all of the peaks in the NMR spectrum and record the chemical shift, the splitting, and the number of hydrogens for each peak in the NMR table below. The NMR spectrum can also be saved to the lab book for later analysis.

^{1}H NMR	Peak	Chemical Shift (δ)	Multiplicity[†]	H[‡]	Peak	Chemical Shift (δ)	Multiplicity[†]	H[‡]
	1				7			
Structure:	2				8			
	3				9			
2-Methyl-1-butanol	4				10			
	5				11			
	6				12			

[†] Specify the multiplicity as a singlet (s), doublet (d), triplet (t), quartet (q), or multiplet (m).
[‡] Specify the number of hydrogens associated with each peak.

7. *Do the IR and NMR spectra you measured and recorded in the tables above confirm that you synthesized the assigned target compound? Explain.* _____

_____

_____

_____

VCL 2-14: Hydroboration – 2

For this assignment, the target compound that you should synthesize is ***trans*-2-methyl-cyclohexanol.** Again, this is an electrophilic alkene addition reaction. Examine the product to determine the location of the new functionality. You will now need an electrophile that is not a proton, H^+. The regioselectivity is still dictated by placement of the electrophile at the terminal position. Also, keep in mind the stereochemical consequences of the electrophilic addition step.

Synthesis Procedures

1. Start *Virtual ChemLab* and select *Hydroboration – 2* from the list of assignments in the electronic workbook. After entering the organic laboratory, go to the stockroom by clicking inside the *Stockroom* window. Next, select a round bottom flask and place it on the cork ring on the stockroom counter. Using the available reagents on the stockroom shelf, identify the appropriate starting materials required to synthesize the target compound and add them to the round bottom flask. Now add ether (Et$_2$O) as a solvent and click on the green *Return to Lab* arrow to return to the laboratory.

2. The round bottom flask containing the starting materials should now be on the stir plate. Click on the handle located in the upper right corner of the laboratory to pull down the TV. The TV should already be in *Tutorial* mode and the starting materials and solvent should be listed. From the group of reagents found on the lab bench, select the correct reagent to synthesize the target compound and add it to the flask on the stir plate. Now attach the heater, condenser, and N$_2$ gas to the round bottom flask so the reaction mixture can be heated.

3. Start the reaction by clicking on the *Stir* button on the front of the stir plate. You should be able to observe the reaction mixture stirring in the flask. Monitor the progress of the reaction using TLC measurements as necessary until the product has formed and the starting materials have been consumed. You can advance the laboratory time using the clock on the wall. With the electronic lab book open (click on the lab book on the lab bench), you can also save your TLC plates by clicking *Save* on the TLC window.

4. When the reaction is complete, "work up" your reaction by first dragging and dropping the separatory funnel (located in a drawer) on the flask and then adding H$_2$O to the funnel. Extract the organic layer in the funnel by clicking on the top layer and dragging it to the cork ring on the lab bench. Your target compound should now be in this flask.

    List the starting materials, solvent, reagent, and products formed: _____

    _____

    How long did it take to finish the reaction? _____

    What are the TLC values (R_f) for (a) Starting Materials: _____ *(b) Products:* _____

    Write a mechanism for this reaction:

IR and NMR Spectra

After completing a reaction and working up the products, it is still necessary to confirm that the correct product was formed. The most common tools used for this analysis are Infrared (IR) and Nuclear Magnetic Resonance (NMR) spectroscopy. In the virtual laboratory, only ^{1}H NMR spectra are available. Details on interpreting IR and NMR spectra are found in your textbook. Your instructor may or may not ask you to perform this section depending on how your class is structured.

5. To collect an IR spectrum of your product, click on the IR spectrometer located underneath the laboratory clock and drag the salt plate icon to the flask on the lab bench. A window containing the IR spectrum for your product should now open. Identify the relevant peaks in the IR spectrum and record the position and associated functional group for each in the IR table below. The IR spectrum can also be saved to the lab book for later analysis.

IR List position (cm^{-1}) & functional group	4.
1.	5.
2.	6.
3.	7.

6. To collect a ^{1}H NMR spectrum of your product, click on the NMR magnet located to the right of the chalkboard and drag the NMR sample tube to the flask on the lab bench. A window containing the NMR spectrum for your product should now open. You can zoom into various portions of the NMR spectrum by clicking and dragging over the desired area. The *Zoom Out* button is used to zoom back out to view the full spectrum. Identify all of the peaks in the NMR spectrum and record the chemical shift, the splitting, and the number of hydrogens for each peak in the NMR table below. The NMR spectrum can also be saved to the lab book for later analysis.

^{1}**H NMR**	Peak	Chemical Shift (δ)	Multiplicity†	H‡	Peak	Chemical Shift (δ)	Multiplicity†	H‡
	1				7			
Structure:	2				8			
	3				9			
trans-2-Methyl-cyclohexanol	4				10			
	5				11			
	6				12			

† Specify the multiplicity as a singlet (s), doublet (d), triplet (t), quartet (q), or multiplet (m).
‡ Specify the number of hydrogens associated with each peak.

7. *Do the IR and NMR spectra you measured and recorded in the tables above confirm that you synthesized the assigned target compound? Explain.* _____

_____

_____

VCL 2-15: Alkene Bromination – 1

For this assignment, the target compound that you should synthesize is ***anti*-2,3-dibromo-butane.** This is a stereospecific electrophilic alkene addition reaction. Examine the product to determine the location of the new functionality. Keep in mind the bromonium ion intermediate and the consequences of its structure. The nucleophile again attacks in a manner that controls the stereochemistry of the product.

Synthesis Procedures

1. Start *Virtual ChemLab* and select *Alkene Bromination – 1* from the list of assignments in the electronic workbook. After entering the organic laboratory, go to the stockroom by clicking inside the *Stockroom* window. Next, select a round bottom flask and place it on the cork ring on the stockroom counter. Using the available reagents on the stockroom shelf, identify the appropriate starting materials required to synthesize the target compound and add them to the round bottom flask. Now add ether (Et_2O) as a solvent and click on the green *Return to Lab* arrow to return to the laboratory.

2. The round bottom flask containing the starting materials should now be on the stir plate. Click on the handle located in the upper right corner of the laboratory to pull down the TV. The TV should already be in *Tutorial* mode and the starting materials and solvent should be listed. From the group of reagents found on the lab bench, select the correct reagent to synthesize the target compound and add it to the flask on the stir plate.

3. Start the reaction by clicking on the *Stir* button on the front of the stir plate. You should be able to observe the reaction mixture stirring in the flask. Monitor the progress of the reaction using TLC measurements as necessary until the product has formed and the starting materials have been consumed. You can advance the laboratory time using the clock on the wall. With the electronic lab book open (click on the lab book on the lab bench), you can also save your TLC plates by clicking *Save* on the TLC window.

4. When the reaction is complete, "work up" your reaction by first dragging and dropping the separatory funnel (located in a drawer) on the flask and then adding H_2O to the funnel. Extract the organic layer in the funnel by clicking on the top layer and dragging it to the cork ring on the lab bench. Your target compound should now be in this flask.

   List the starting materials, solvent, reagent, and products formed: _____

   _____

   How long did it take to finish the reaction? _____

   What are the TLC values (R_f) for (a) Starting Materials: _____ *(b) Products:* _____

   Write a mechanism for this reaction:

31

IR and NMR Spectra

After completing a reaction and working up the products, it is still necessary to confirm that the correct product was formed. The most common tools used for this analysis are Infrared (IR) and Nuclear Magnetic Resonance (NMR) spectroscopy. In the virtual laboratory, only ^{1}H NMR spectra are available. Details on interpreting IR and NMR spectra are found in your textbook. Your instructor may or may not ask you to perform this section depending on how your class is structured.

5. To collect an IR spectrum of your product, click on the IR spectrometer located underneath the laboratory clock and drag the salt plate icon to the flask on the lab bench. A window containing the IR spectrum for your product should now open. Identify the relevant peaks in the IR spectrum and record the position and associated functional group for each in the IR table below. The IR spectrum can also be saved to the lab book for later analysis.

IR List position (cm^{-1}) & functional group	4.
1.	5.
2.	6.
3.	7.

6. To collect a ^{1}H NMR spectrum of your product, click on the NMR magnet located to the right of the chalkboard and drag the NMR sample tube to the flask on the lab bench. A window containing the NMR spectrum for your product should now open. You can zoom into various portions of the NMR spectrum by clicking and dragging over the desired area. The *Zoom Out* button is used to zoom back out to view the full spectrum. Identify all of the peaks in the NMR spectrum and record the chemical shift, the splitting, and the number of hydrogens for each peak in the NMR table below. The NMR spectrum can also be saved to the lab book for later analysis.

^{1}H NMR	Peak	Chemical Shift (δ)	Multiplicity[†]	H[‡]	Peak	Chemical Shift (δ)	Multiplicity[†]	H[‡]
	1				7			
Structure:	2				8			
	3				9			
anti-2,3-Dibromo-butane	4				10			
	5				11			
	6				12			

[†] Specify the multiplicity as a singlet (s), doublet (d), triplet (t), quartet (q), or multiplet (m).
[‡] Specify the number of hydrogens associated with each peak.

7. *Do the IR and NMR spectra you measured and recorded in the tables above confirm that you synthesized the assigned target compound? Explain.* _____

_____

_____

VCL 2-16: Alkene Bromination – 2

For this assignment, the target compound that you should synthesize is **(1R)-*trans*-1,2-dibromo-cyclohexane.** This is a stereospecific electrophilic alkene addition reaction. Examine the product to determine the location of the new functionality. Keep in mind the bromonium ion intermediate and the consequences of its structure. The nucleophile again attacks in a manner that controls the stereochemistry of the product.

Synthesis Procedures

1. Start *Virtual ChemLab* and select *Alkene Bromination – 2* from the list of assignments in the electronic workbook. After entering the organic laboratory, go to the stockroom by clicking inside the *Stockroom* window. Next, select a round bottom flask and place it on the cork ring on the stockroom counter. Using the available reagents on the stockroom shelf, identify the appropriate starting materials required to synthesize the target compound and add them to the round bottom flask. Now add ether (Et_2O) as a solvent and click on the green *Return to Lab* arrow to return to the laboratory.

2. The round bottom flask containing the starting materials should now be on the stir plate. Click on the handle located in the upper right corner of the laboratory to pull down the TV. The TV should already be in *Tutorial* mode and the starting materials and solvent should be listed. From the group of reagents found on the lab bench, select the correct reagent to synthesize the target compound and add it to the flask on the stir plate.

3. Start the reaction by clicking on the *Stir* button on the front of the stir plate. You should be able to observe the reaction mixture stirring in the flask. Monitor the progress of the reaction using TLC measurements as necessary until the product has formed and the starting materials have been consumed. You can advance the laboratory time using the clock on the wall. With the electronic lab book open (click on the lab book on the lab bench), you can also save your TLC plates by clicking *Save* on the TLC window.

4. When the reaction is complete, "work up" your reaction by first dragging and dropping the separatory funnel (located in a drawer) on the flask and then adding H_2O to the funnel. Extract the organic layer in the funnel by clicking on the top layer and dragging it to the cork ring on the lab bench. Your target compound should now be in this flask.

List the starting materials, solvent, reagent, and products formed: _____

_____

How long did it take to finish the reaction? _____

What are the TLC values (R_f) for (a) Starting Materials: _____ *(b) Products:* _____

Write a mechanism for this reaction:

IR and NMR Spectra

After completing a reaction and working up the products, it is still necessary to confirm that the correct product was formed. The most common tools used for this analysis are Infrared (IR) and Nuclear Magnetic Resonance (NMR) spectroscopy. In the virtual laboratory, only ^{1}H NMR spectra are available. Details on interpreting IR and NMR spectra are found in your textbook. Your instructor may or may not ask you to perform this section depending on how your class is structured.

5. To collect an IR spectrum of your product, click on the IR spectrometer located underneath the laboratory clock and drag the salt plate icon to the flask on the lab bench. A window containing the IR spectrum for your product should now open. Identify the relevant peaks in the IR spectrum and record the position and associated functional group for each in the IR table below. The IR spectrum can also be saved to the lab book for later analysis.

IR List position (cm^{-1}) & functional group	4.
1.	5.
2.	6.
3.	7.

6. To collect a ^{1}H NMR spectrum of your product, click on the NMR magnet located to the right of the chalkboard and drag the NMR sample tube to the flask on the lab bench. A window containing the NMR spectrum for your product should now open. You can zoom into various portions of the NMR spectrum by clicking and dragging over the desired area. The *Zoom Out* button is used to zoom back out to view the full spectrum. Identify all of the peaks in the NMR spectrum and record the chemical shift, the splitting, and the number of hydrogens for each peak in the NMR table below. The NMR spectrum can also be saved to the lab book for later analysis.

^{1}**H NMR**	Peak	Chemical Shift (δ)	Multiplicity†	H‡	Peak	Chemical Shift (δ)	Multiplicity†	H‡
	1				7			
Structure:	2				8			
	3				9			
	4				10			
(1R)-*trans*-1,2-Dibromo-cyclohexane	5				11			
	6				12			

† Specify the multiplicity as a singlet (s), doublet (d), triplet (t), quartet (q), or multiplet (m).
‡ Specify the number of hydrogens associated with each peak.

7. *Do the IR and NMR spectra you measured and recorded in the tables above confirm that you synthesized the assigned target compound? Explain.* _____

_____

_____

VCL 2-17: Halohydrin Formation – 2

For this assignment, the target compound that you should synthesize is **anti-3-bromo-butan-2-ol.** This is a stereospecific electrophilic alkene addition reaction. Examine the product to determine the location of the new functionality. Keep in mind the bromonium ion intermediate and the consequences of its structure. The nucleophile again attacks in a manner that controls the stereochemistry of the product.

Synthesis Procedures
1. Start *Virtual ChemLab* and select *Halohydrin Formation – 2* from the list of assignments in the electronic workbook. After entering the organic laboratory, go to the stockroom by clicking inside the *Stockroom* window. Next, select a round bottom flask and place it on the cork ring on the stockroom counter. Using the available reagents on the stockroom shelf, identify the appropriate starting materials required to synthesize the target compound and add them to the round bottom flask. Now add water (H_2O) as a solvent and click on the green *Return to Lab* arrow to return to the laboratory.

2. The round bottom flask containing the starting materials should now be on the stir plate. Click on the handle located in the upper right corner of the laboratory to pull down the TV. The TV should already be in *Tutorial* mode and the starting materials and solvent should be listed. From the group of reagents found on the lab bench, select the correct reagent to synthesize the target compound and add it to the flask on the stir plate. Now put the round bottom flask in the ice bath so the reaction mixture can be cooled.

3. Start the reaction by clicking on the *Stir* button on the front of the stir plate. You should be able to observe the reaction mixture stirring in the flask. Monitor the progress of the reaction using TLC measurements as necessary until the product has formed and the starting materials have been consumed. You can advance the laboratory time using the clock on the wall. With the electronic lab book open (click on the lab book on the lab bench), you can also save your TLC plates by clicking *Save* on the TLC window.

4. When the reaction is complete, "work up" your reaction by first dragging and dropping the separatory funnel (located in a drawer) on the flask and then adding H_2O to the funnel. Extract the organic layer in the funnel by clicking on the top layer and dragging it to the cork ring on the lab bench. Your target compound should now be in this flask.

List the starting materials, solvent, reagent, and products formed: _____

_____

How long did it take to finish the reaction? _____

What are the TLC values (R_f) for (a) Starting Materials: _____ *(b) Products:* _____

Write a mechanism for this reaction:

35

Chapter 2

IR and NMR Spectra

After completing a reaction and working up the products, it is still necessary to confirm that the correct product was formed. The most common tools used for this analysis are Infrared (IR) and Nuclear Magnetic Resonance (NMR) spectroscopy. In the virtual laboratory, only ^{1}H NMR spectra are available. Details on interpreting IR and NMR spectra are found in your textbook. Your instructor may or may not ask you to perform this section depending on how your class is structured.

5. To collect an IR spectrum of your product, click on the IR spectrometer located underneath the laboratory clock and drag the salt plate icon to the flask on the lab bench. A window containing the IR spectrum for your product should now open. Identify the relevant peaks in the IR spectrum and record the position and associated functional group for each in the IR table below. The IR spectrum can also be saved to the lab book for later analysis.

IR List position (cm^{-1}) & functional group	4.
1.	5.
2.	6.
3.	7.

6. To collect a ^{1}H NMR spectrum of your product, click on the NMR magnet located to the right of the chalkboard and drag the NMR sample tube to the flask on the lab bench. A window containing the NMR spectrum for your product should now open. You can zoom into various portions of the NMR spectrum by clicking and dragging over the desired area. The *Zoom Out* button is used to zoom back out to view the full spectrum. Identify all of the peaks in the NMR spectrum and record the chemical shift, the splitting, and the number of hydrogens for each peak in the NMR table below. The NMR spectrum can also be saved to the lab book for later analysis.

^{1}H NMR	Peak	Chemical Shift (δ)	Multiplicity†	H‡	Peak	Chemical Shift (δ)	Multiplicity†	H‡
	1				7			
Structure:	2				8			
Br	3				9			
OH	4				10			
anti-3-Bromo-butan-2-ol	5				11			
	6				12			

† Specify the multiplicity as a singlet (s), doublet (d), triplet (t), quartet (q), or multiplet (m).
‡ Specify the number of hydrogens associated with each peak.

7. *Do the IR and NMR spectra you measured and recorded in the tables above confirm that you synthesized the assigned target compound? Explain.* _____

_____

_____

VCL 2-18: Epoxidation – 2

For this assignment, the target compound that you should synthesize is **2,3-epoxy-cyclohexanol.** Again, this is an electrophilic alkene addition reaction. Examine the product to determine the location of the new functionality. The alkene is the electron rich partner and an electrophilic reagent is needed. The epoxide is formed on the same face of the alkene located *cis* to the hydroxyl group. Invoke an interaction with the hydroxyl to direct the reagent to this face.

Synthesis Procedures

1. Start *Virtual ChemLab* and select *Epoxidation – 2* from the list of assignments in the electronic workbook. After entering the organic laboratory, go to the stockroom by clicking inside the *Stockroom* window. Next, select a round bottom flask and place it on the cork ring on the stockroom counter. Using the available reagents on the stockroom shelf, identify the appropriate starting materials required to synthesize the target compound and add them to the round bottom flask. Now add ether (Et_2O) as a solvent and click on the green *Return to Lab* arrow to return to the laboratory.

2. The round bottom flask containing the starting materials should now be on the stir plate. Click on the handle located in the upper right corner of the laboratory to pull down the TV. The TV should already be in *Tutorial* mode and the starting materials and solvent should be listed. From the group of reagents found on the lab bench, select the correct reagent to synthesize the target compound and add it to the flask on the stir plate. Now attach the heater, condenser, and N_2 gas to the round bottom flask so the reaction mixture can be heated.

3. Start the reaction by clicking on the *Stir* button on the front of the stir plate. You should be able to observe the reaction mixture stirring in the flask. Monitor the progress of the reaction using TLC measurements as necessary until the product has formed and the starting materials have been consumed. You can advance the laboratory time using the clock on the wall. With the electronic lab book open (click on the lab book on the lab bench), you can also save your TLC plates by clicking *Save* on the TLC window.

4. When the reaction is complete, "work up" your reaction by first dragging and dropping the separatory funnel (located in a drawer) on the flask and then adding NaOH to the funnel. Extract the organic layer in the funnel by clicking on the top layer and dragging it to the cork ring on the lab bench. Your target compound should now be in this flask.

   List the starting materials, solvent, reagent, and products formed: _____
   _____

   How long did it take to finish the reaction? _____

   What are the TLC values (R_f) for (a) Starting Materials: _____ (b) Products: _____

   Write a mechanism for this reaction:

IR and NMR Spectra

After completing a reaction and working up the products, it is still necessary to confirm that the correct product was formed. The most common tools used for this analysis are Infrared (IR) and Nuclear Magnetic Resonance (NMR) spectroscopy. In the virtual laboratory, only ^1H NMR spectra are available. Details on interpreting IR and NMR spectra are found in your textbook. Your instructor may or may not ask you to perform this section depending on how your class is structured.

5. To collect an IR spectrum of your product, click on the IR spectrometer located underneath the laboratory clock and drag the salt plate icon to the flask on the lab bench. A window containing the IR spectrum for your product should now open. Identify the relevant peaks in the IR spectrum and record the position and associated functional group for each in the IR table below. The IR spectrum can also be saved to the lab book for later analysis.

IR List position (cm^{-1}) & functional group	4.
1.	5.
2.	6.
3.	7.

6. To collect a ^1H NMR spectrum of your product, click on the NMR magnet located to the right of the chalkboard and drag the NMR sample tube to the flask on the lab bench. A window containing the NMR spectrum for your product should now open. You can zoom into various portions of the NMR spectrum by clicking and dragging over the desired area. The *Zoom Out* button is used to zoom back out to view the full spectrum. Identify all of the peaks in the NMR spectrum and record the chemical shift, the splitting, and the number of hydrogens for each peak in the NMR table below. The NMR spectrum can also be saved to the lab book for later analysis.

^{1}H NMR	Peak	Chemical Shift (δ)	Multiplicity[†]	H[‡]	Peak	Chemical Shift (δ)	Multiplicity[†]	H[‡]
	1				7			
Structure:	2				8			
OH	3				9			
	4				10			
2,3-Epoxy-cyclohexanol	5				11			
	6				12			

[†] Specify the multiplicity as a singlet (s), doublet (d), triplet (t), quartet (q), or multiplet (m).
[‡] Specify the number of hydrogens associated with each peak.

7. *Do the IR and NMR spectra you measured and recorded in the tables above confirm that you synthesized the assigned target compound? Explain.* _____

_____

_____

_____

VCL 3-1: Diene Halogenation – 1

For this assignment, the target compound that you should synthesize is **3-chloro-1-butene.** Again, this is an electrophilic alkene addition reaction. Examine the product to determine the location of the new functionality. Keep in mind the nature of the intermediate. The regioselectivity is controlled by the stability of this intermediate. Assume that only one equivalent of reagent is used.

Synthesis Procedures
1. Start *Virtual ChemLab* and select *Diene Halogenation – 1* from the list of assignments in the electronic workbook. After entering the organic laboratory, go to the stockroom by clicking inside the *Stockroom* window. Next, select a round bottom flask and place it on the cork ring on the stockroom counter. Using the available reagents on the stockroom shelf, identify the appropriate starting materials required to synthesize the target compound and add them to the round bottom flask. Now add ether (Et_2O) as a solvent and click on the green *Return to Lab* arrow to return to the laboratory.

2. The round bottom flask containing the starting materials should now be on the stir plate. Click on the handle located in the upper right corner of the laboratory to pull down the TV. The TV should already be in *Tutorial* mode and the starting materials and solvent should be listed. From the group of reagents found on the lab bench, select the correct reagent to synthesize the target compound and add it to the flask on the stir plate. Now put the round bottom flask in the ice bath so the reaction mixture can be cooled.

3. Start the reaction by clicking on the *Stir* button on the front of the stir plate. You should be able to observe the reaction mixture stirring in the flask. Monitor the progress of the reaction using TLC measurements as necessary until the product has formed and the starting materials have been consumed. You can advance the laboratory time using the clock on the wall. With the electronic lab book open (click on the lab book on the lab bench), you can also save your TLC plates by clicking *Save* on the TLC window.

4. When the reaction is complete, "work up" your reaction by first dragging and dropping the separatory funnel (located in a drawer) on the flask and then adding H_2O to the funnel. Extract the organic layer in the funnel by clicking on the top layer and dragging it to the cork ring on the lab bench. Your target compound should now be in this flask.

   List the starting materials, solvent, reagent, and products formed: _____

   _____

   How long did it take to finish the reaction? _____

   What are the TLC values (R_f) for (a) Starting Materials: _____ (b) Products: _____

   Write a mechanism for this reaction:

IR and NMR Spectra

After completing a reaction and working up the products, it is still necessary to confirm that the correct product was formed. The most common tools used for this analysis are Infrared (IR) and Nuclear Magnetic Resonance (NMR) spectroscopy. In the virtual laboratory, only ^{1}H NMR spectra are available. Details on interpreting IR and NMR spectra are found in your textbook. Your instructor may or may not ask you to perform this section depending on how your class is structured.

5. To collect an IR spectrum of your product, click on the IR spectrometer located underneath the laboratory clock and drag the salt plate icon to the flask on the lab bench. A window containing the IR spectrum for your product should now open. Identify the relevant peaks in the IR spectrum and record the position and associated functional group for each in the IR table below. The IR spectrum can also be saved to the lab book for later analysis.

IR List position (cm^{-1}) & functional group	4.
1.	5.
2.	6.
3.	7.

6. To collect a ^{1}H NMR spectrum of your product, click on the NMR magnet located to the right of the chalkboard and drag the NMR sample tube to the flask on the lab bench. A window containing the NMR spectrum for your product should now open. You can zoom into various portions of the NMR spectrum by clicking and dragging over the desired area. The *Zoom Out* button is used to zoom back out to view the full spectrum. Identify all of the peaks in the NMR spectrum and record the chemical shift, the splitting, and the number of hydrogens for each peak in the NMR table below. The NMR spectrum can also be saved to the lab book for later analysis.

^{1}**H NMR**	Peak	Chemical Shift (δ)	Multiplicity[†]	H[‡]	Peak	Chemical Shift (δ)	Multiplicity[†]	H[‡]
Structure: 3-Chloro-1-butene	1				7			
	2				8			
	3				9			
	4				10			
	5				11			
	6				12			

[†] Specify the multiplicity as a singlet (s), doublet (d), triplet (t), quartet (q), or multiplet (m).
[‡] Specify the number of hydrogens associated with each peak.

7. *Do the IR and NMR spectra you measured and recorded in the tables above confirm that you synthesized the assigned target compound? Explain.* _____

_____

_____

_____

VCL 3-2: Etherfication – 2

For this assignment, the target compound that you should synthesize is **cyclopent-2-enyl ethyl ether.** Again, this is an electrophilic alkene addition reaction. Examine the product to determine the location of the new functionality. Keep in mind the nature of the intermediate. The regioselectivity is controlled by the stability of this intermediate. Assume that only one equivalent of reagent is used.

Synthesis Procedures

1. Start *Virtual ChemLab* and select *Etherfication – 2* from the list of assignments in the electronic workbook. After entering the organic laboratory, go to the stockroom by clicking inside the *Stockroom* window. Next, select a round bottom flask and place it on the cork ring on the stockroom counter. Using the available reagents on the stockroom shelf, identify the appropriate starting materials required to synthesize the target compound and add them to the round bottom flask. Now add ether alcohol (EtOH) as a solvent and click on the green *Return to Lab* arrow to return to the laboratory.

2. The round bottom flask containing the starting materials should now be on the stir plate. Click on the handle located in the upper right corner of the laboratory to pull down the TV. The TV should already be in *Tutorial* mode and the starting materials and solvent should be listed. From the group of reagents found on the lab bench, select the correct reagent to synthesize the target compound and add it to the flask on the stir plate. Now attach the heater, condenser, and N_2 gas to the round bottom flask so the reaction mixture can be heated.

3. Start the reaction by clicking on the *Stir* button on the front of the stir plate. You should be able to observe the reaction mixture stirring in the flask. Monitor the progress of the reaction using TLC measurements as necessary until the product has formed and the starting materials have been consumed. You can advance the laboratory time using the clock on the wall. With the electronic lab book open (click on the lab book on the lab bench), you can also save your TLC plates by clicking *Save* on the TLC window.

4. When the reaction is complete, "work up" your reaction by first dragging and dropping the separatory funnel (located in a drawer) on the flask and then adding H_2O to the funnel. Extract the organic layer in the funnel by clicking on the top layer and dragging it to the cork ring on the lab bench. Your target compound should now be in this flask.

   List the starting materials, solvent, reagent, and products formed: _____

   _____

   How long did it take to finish the reaction? _____

   What are the TLC values (R_f) for (a) Starting Materials: _____ (b) Products: _____

   Write a mechanism for this reaction:

IR and NMR Spectra

After completing a reaction and working up the products, it is still necessary to confirm that the correct product was formed. The most common tools used for this analysis are Infrared (IR) and Nuclear Magnetic Resonance (NMR) spectroscopy. In the virtual laboratory, only ^{1}H NMR spectra are available. Details on interpreting IR and NMR spectra are found in your textbook. Your instructor may or may not ask you to perform this section depending on how your class is structured.

5. To collect an IR spectrum of your product, click on the IR spectrometer located underneath the laboratory clock and drag the salt plate icon to the flask on the lab bench. A window containing the IR spectrum for your product should now open. Identify the relevant peaks in the IR spectrum and record the position and associated functional group for each in the IR table below. The IR spectrum can also be saved to the lab book for later analysis.

IR List position (cm^{-1}) & functional group	4.
1.	5.
2.	6.
3.	7.

6. To collect a ^{1}H NMR spectrum of your product, click on the NMR magnet located to the right of the chalkboard and drag the NMR sample tube to the flask on the lab bench. A window containing the NMR spectrum for your product should now open. You can zoom into various portions of the NMR spectrum by clicking and dragging over the desired area. The *Zoom Out* button is used to zoom back out to view the full spectrum. Identify all of the peaks in the NMR spectrum and record the chemical shift, the splitting, and the number of hydrogens for each peak in the NMR table below. The NMR spectrum can also be saved to the lab book for later analysis.

^{1}H NMR	Peak	Chemical Shift (δ)	Multiplicity[†]	H[‡]	Peak	Chemical Shift (δ)	Multiplicity[†]	H[‡]
Structure:	1				7			
	2				8			
	3				9			
Cyclopent-2-enyl ethyl ether	4				10			
	5				11			
	6				12			

[†] Specify the multiplicity as a singlet (s), doublet (d), triplet (t), quartet (q), or multiplet (m).
[‡] Specify the number of hydrogens associated with each peak.

7. *Do the IR and NMR spectra you measured and recorded in the tables above confirm that you synthesized the assigned target compound? Explain.* _____

_____

_____

_____

VCL 3-3: Diene Halogenation – 2

For this assignment, the target compound that you should synthesize is **1-chloro-2-butene.** Again, this is an electrophilic alkene addition reaction. Examine the product to determine the location of the new functionality. Keep in mind the intermediate and the selectivity of the incoming nucleophile. A key here is the relative stabilities of the two potential products. The alkene is the electron-rich partner and an electrophilic reagent is needed.

Synthesis Procedures
1. Start *Virtual ChemLab* and select *Diene Halogenation – 1* from the list of assignments in the electronic workbook. After entering the organic laboratory, go to the stockroom by clicking inside the *Stockroom* window. Next, select a round bottom flask and place it on the cork ring on the stockroom counter. Using the available reagents on the stockroom shelf, identify the appropriate starting materials required to synthesize the target compound and add them to the round bottom flask. Now add ether (Et₂O) as a solvent and click on the green *Return to Lab* arrow to return to the laboratory.

2. The round bottom flask containing the starting materials should now be on the stir plate. Click on the handle located in the upper right corner of the laboratory to pull down the TV. The TV should already be in *Tutorial* mode and the starting materials and solvent should be listed. From the group of reagents found on the lab bench, select the correct reagent to synthesize the target compound and add it to the flask on the stir plate. Now attach the heater, condenser, and N₂ gas to the round bottom flask so the reaction mixture can be heated.

3. Start the reaction by clicking on the *Stir* button on the front of the stir plate. You should be able to observe the reaction mixture stirring in the flask. Monitor the progress of the reaction using TLC measurements as necessary until the product has formed and the starting materials have been consumed. You can advance the laboratory time using the clock on the wall. With the electronic lab book open (click on the lab book on the lab bench), you can also save your TLC plates by clicking *Save* on the TLC window.

4. When the reaction is complete, "work up" your reaction by first dragging and dropping the separatory funnel (located in a drawer) on the flask and then adding H₂O to the funnel. Extract the organic layer in the funnel by clicking on the top layer and dragging it to the cork ring on the lab bench. Your target compound should now be in this flask.

List the starting materials, solvent, reagent, and products formed: _____

_____

How long did it take to finish the reaction? _____

What are the TLC values (Rf) for (a) Starting Materials: _____ *(b) Products:* _____

Write a mechanism for this reaction:

Chapter 3

IR and NMR Spectra

After completing a reaction and working up the products, it is still necessary to confirm that the correct product was formed. The most common tools used for this analysis are Infrared (IR) and Nuclear Magnetic Resonance (NMR) spectroscopy. In the virtual laboratory, only ^{1}H NMR spectra are available. Details on interpreting IR and NMR spectra are found in your textbook. Your instructor may or may not ask you to perform this section depending on how your class is structured.

5. To collect an IR spectrum of your product, click on the IR spectrometer located underneath the laboratory clock and drag the salt plate icon to the flask on the lab bench. A window containing the IR spectrum for your product should now open. Identify the relevant peaks in the IR spectrum and record the position and associated functional group for each in the IR table below. The IR spectrum can also be saved to the lab book for later analysis.

IR List position (cm^{-1}) & functional group	4.
1.	5.
2.	6.
3.	7.

6. To collect a ^{1}H NMR spectrum of your product, click on the NMR magnet located to the right of the chalkboard and drag the NMR sample tube to the flask on the lab bench. A window containing the NMR spectrum for your product should now open. You can zoom into various portions of the NMR spectrum by clicking and dragging over the desired area. The *Zoom Out* button is used to zoom back out to view the full spectrum. Identify all of the peaks in the NMR spectrum and record the chemical shift, the splitting, and the number of hydrogens for each peak in the NMR table below. The NMR spectrum can also be saved to the lab book for later analysis.

^{1}H NMR Structure: Cl⌒⌒ 1-Chloro-2-butene	Peak	Chemical Shift (δ)	Multiplicity†	H‡	Peak	Chemical Shift (δ)	Multiplicity†	H‡
	1				7			
	2				8			
	3				9			
	4				10			
	5				11			
	6				12			

† Specify the multiplicity as a singlet (s), doublet (d), triplet (t), quartet (q), or multiplet (m).
‡ Specify the number of hydrogens associated with each peak.

7. *Do the IR and NMR spectra you measured and recorded in the tables above confirm that you synthesized the assigned target compound? Explain.* _____

_____

_____

VCL 3-4: Diels Alder – 1

For this assignment, the target compound that you should synthesize is **cyclohex-3-ene carboxylic acid methyl ester.** This is a cycloaddition reaction. Examine the product to determine the reactive partners. Keep in mind the position of the alkene in the product. Try pushing the electrons backwards to reveal the needed substrates.

Synthesis Procedures

1. Start *Virtual ChemLab* and select *Diels Alder – 1* from the list of assignments in the electronic workbook. After entering the organic laboratory, go to the stockroom by clicking inside the *Stockroom* window. Next, select a round bottom flask and place it on the cork ring on the stockroom counter. Using the available reagents on the stockroom shelf, identify the appropriate starting materials required to synthesize the target compound and add them to the round bottom flask. Now add ether (Et_2O) as a solvent and click on the green *Return to Lab* arrow to return to the laboratory.

2. The round bottom flask containing the starting materials should now be on the stir plate. Click on the handle located in the upper right corner of the laboratory to pull down the TV. The TV should already be in *Tutorial* mode and the starting materials and solvent should be listed. From the group of reagents found on the lab bench, select the correct reagent to synthesize the target compound and add it to the flask on the stir plate. Now attach the heater, condenser, and N_2 gas to the round bottom flask so the reaction mixture can be heated.

3. Start the reaction by clicking on the *Stir* button on the front of the stir plate. You should be able to observe the reaction mixture stirring in the flask. Monitor the progress of the reaction using TLC measurements as necessary until the product has formed and the starting materials have been consumed. You can advance the laboratory time using the clock on the wall. With the electronic lab book open (click on the lab book on the lab bench), you can also save your TLC plates by clicking *Save* on the TLC window.

4. When the reaction is complete, "work up" your reaction by first dragging and dropping the separatory funnel (located in a drawer) on the flask and then adding H_2O to the funnel. Extract the organic layer in the funnel by clicking on the top layer and dragging it to the cork ring on the lab bench. Your target compound should now be in this flask.

   List the starting materials, solvent, reagent, and products formed: _____

   _____

   How long did it take to finish the reaction? _____

   What are the TLC values (R_f) for (a) Starting Materials: _____ (b) Products: _____

   Write a mechanism for this reaction:

IR and NMR Spectra

After completing a reaction and working up the products, it is still necessary to confirm that the correct product was formed. The most common tools used for this analysis are Infrared (IR) and Nuclear Magnetic Resonance (NMR) spectroscopy. In the virtual laboratory, only ^{1}H NMR spectra are available. Details on interpreting IR and NMR spectra are found in your textbook. Your instructor may or may not ask you to perform this section depending on how your class is structured.

5. To collect an IR spectrum of your product, click on the IR spectrometer located underneath the laboratory clock and drag the salt plate icon to the flask on the lab bench. A window containing the IR spectrum for your product should now open. Identify the relevant peaks in the IR spectrum and record the position and associated functional group for each in the IR table below. The IR spectrum can also be saved to the lab book for later analysis.

IR List position (cm^{-1}) & functional group	4.
1.	5.
2.	6.
3.	7.

6. To collect a ^{1}H NMR spectrum of your product, click on the NMR magnet located to the right of the chalkboard and drag the NMR sample tube to the flask on the lab bench. A window containing the NMR spectrum for your product should now open. You can zoom into various portions of the NMR spectrum by clicking and dragging over the desired area. The *Zoom Out* button is used to zoom back out to view the full spectrum. Identify all of the peaks in the NMR spectrum and record the chemical shift, the splitting, and the number of hydrogens for each peak in the NMR table below. The NMR spectrum can also be saved to the lab book for later analysis.

^{1}H NMR Structure: Cyclohex-3-ene carboxylic acid methyl ester	Peak	Chemical Shift (δ)	Multiplicity[†]	H[‡]	Peak	Chemical Shift (δ)	Multiplicity[†]	H[‡]
	1				7			
	2				8			
	3				9			
	4				10			
	5				11			
	6				12			

[†] Specify the multiplicity as a singlet (s), doublet (d), triplet (t), quartet (q), or multiplet (m).
[‡] Specify the number of hydrogens associated with each peak.

7. *Do the IR and NMR spectra you measured and recorded in the tables above confirm that you synthesized the assigned target compound? Explain.* _____

_____

_____

_____

VCL 3-5: Diels Alder – 2

For this assignment, the target compound that you should synthesize is **bicyclo[2.2.1]hept-5-ene-2-carboxylic acid methyl ester.** This is a cycloaddition reaction. Examine the product to determine the reactive partners. Keep in mind the position of the alkene in the product. Try pushing the electrons backwards to reveal the needed substrates. Keep in mind the stereochemistry of the process.

Synthesis Procedures

1. Start *Virtual ChemLab* and select *Diels Alder – 2* from the list of assignments in the electronic workbook. After entering the organic laboratory, go to the stockroom by clicking inside the *Stockroom* window. Next, select a round bottom flask and place it on the cork ring on the stockroom counter. Using the available reagents on the stockroom shelf, identify the appropriate starting materials required to synthesize the target compound and add them to the round bottom flask. Now add ether (Et_2O) as a solvent and click on the green *Return to Lab* arrow to return to the laboratory.

2. The round bottom flask containing the starting materials should now be on the stir plate. Click on the handle located in the upper right corner of the laboratory to pull down the TV. The TV should already be in *Tutorial* mode and the starting materials and solvent should be listed. From the group of reagents found on the lab bench, select the correct reagent to synthesize the target compound and add it to the flask on the stir plate. Now attach the heater, condenser, and N_2 gas to the round bottom flask so the reaction mixture can be heated.

3. Start the reaction by clicking on the *Stir* button on the front of the stir plate. You should be able to observe the reaction mixture stirring in the flask. Monitor the progress of the reaction using TLC measurements as necessary until the product has formed and the starting materials have been consumed. You can advance the laboratory time using the clock on the wall. With the electronic lab book open (click on the lab book on the lab bench), you can also save your TLC plates by clicking *Save* on the TLC window.

4. When the reaction is complete, "work up" your reaction by first dragging and dropping the separatory funnel (located in a drawer) on the flask and then adding H_2O to the funnel. Extract the organic layer in the funnel by clicking on the top layer and dragging it to the cork ring on the lab bench. Your target compound should now be in this flask.

List the starting materials, solvent, reagent, and products formed: _____

_____

How long did it take to finish the reaction? _____

What are the TLC values (R_f) for (a) Starting Materials: _____ (b) Products: _____

Write a mechanism for this reaction:

IR and NMR Spectra

After completing a reaction and working up the products, it is still necessary to confirm that the correct product was formed. The most common tools used for this analysis are Infrared (IR) and Nuclear Magnetic Resonance (NMR) spectroscopy. In the virtual laboratory, only ^{1}H NMR spectra are available. Details on interpreting IR and NMR spectra are found in your textbook. Your instructor may or may not ask you to perform this section depending on how your class is structured.

5. To collect an IR spectrum of your product, click on the IR spectrometer located underneath the laboratory clock and drag the salt plate icon to the flask on the lab bench. A window containing the IR spectrum for your product should now open. Identify the relevant peaks in the IR spectrum and record the position and associated functional group for each in the IR table below. The IR spectrum can also be saved to the lab book for later analysis.

IR List position (cm^{-1}) & functional group	4.
1.	5.
2.	6.
3.	7.

6. To collect a ^{1}H NMR spectrum of your product, click on the NMR magnet located to the right of the chalkboard and drag the NMR sample tube to the flask on the lab bench. A window containing the NMR spectrum for your product should now open. You can zoom into various portions of the NMR spectrum by clicking and dragging over the desired area. The *Zoom Out* button is used to zoom back out to view the full spectrum. Identify all of the peaks in the NMR spectrum and record the chemical shift, the splitting, and the number of hydrogens for each peak in the NMR table below. The NMR spectrum can also be saved to the lab book for later analysis.

^{1}**H NMR** Structure: Bicyclo[2.2.1]hept-5-ene-2-carboxylic acid methyl ester	Peak	Chemical Shift (δ)	Multiplicity[†]	H[‡]	Peak	Chemical Shift (δ)	Multiplicity[†]	H[‡]
	1				7			
	2				8			
	3				9			
	4				10			
	5				11			
	6				12			

[†] Specify the multiplicity as a singlet (s), doublet (d), triplet (t), quartet (q), or multiplet (m).
[‡] Specify the number of hydrogens associated with each peak.

7. *Do the IR and NMR spectra you measured and recorded in the tables above confirm that you synthesized the assigned target compound? Explain.* _____

_____

_____

_____

VCL 3-6: Diels Alder – 3

For this assignment, the target compound that you should synthesize is **cyclohexa-1,4-diene-1,2-dicarboxylic acid dimethyl ester.** This is a cycloaddition reaction. Examine the product to determine the reactive partners. Keep in mind the position of the alkenes in the product. Try pushing the electrons backwards to reveal the needed substrates.

Synthesis Procedures

1. Start *Virtual ChemLab* and select *Diels Alder – 3* from the list of assignments in the electronic workbook. After entering the organic laboratory, go to the stockroom by clicking inside the *Stockroom* window. Next, select a round bottom flask and place it on the cork ring on the stockroom counter. Using the available reagents on the stockroom shelf, identify the appropriate starting materials required to synthesize the target compound and add them to the round bottom flask. Now add ether (Et_2O) as a solvent and click on the green *Return to Lab* arrow to return to the laboratory.

2. The round bottom flask containing the starting materials should now be on the stir plate. Click on the handle located in the upper right corner of the laboratory to pull down the TV. The TV should already be in *Tutorial* mode and the starting materials and solvent should be listed. From the group of reagents found on the lab bench, select the correct reagent to synthesize the target compound and add it to the flask on the stir plate. Now attach the heater, condenser, and N_2 gas to the round bottom flask so the reaction mixture can be heated.

3. Start the reaction by clicking on the *Stir* button on the front of the stir plate. You should be able to observe the reaction mixture stirring in the flask. Monitor the progress of the reaction using TLC measurements as necessary until the product has formed and the starting materials have been consumed. You can advance the laboratory time using the clock on the wall. With the electronic lab book open (click on the lab book on the lab bench), you can also save your TLC plates by clicking *Save* on the TLC window.

4. When the reaction is complete, "work up" your reaction by first dragging and dropping the separatory funnel (located in a drawer) on the flask and then adding H_2O to the funnel. Extract the organic layer in the funnel by clicking on the top layer and dragging it to the cork ring on the lab bench. Your target compound should now be in this flask.

   List the starting materials, solvent, reagent, and products formed: _____

   _____

   How long did it take to finish the reaction? _____

   What are the TLC values (R_f) for (a) Starting Materials: _____ (b) Products: _____

   Write a mechanism for this reaction:

Chapter 3

IR and NMR Spectra

After completing a reaction and working up the products, it is still necessary to confirm that the correct product was formed. The most common tools used for this analysis are Infrared (IR) and Nuclear Magnetic Resonance (NMR) spectroscopy. In the virtual laboratory, only ^{1}H NMR spectra are available. Details on interpreting IR and NMR spectra are found in your textbook. Your instructor may or may not ask you to perform this section depending on how your class is structured.

5. To collect an IR spectrum of your product, click on the IR spectrometer located underneath the laboratory clock and drag the salt plate icon to the flask on the lab bench. A window containing the IR spectrum for your product should now open. Identify the relevant peaks in the IR spectrum and record the position and associated functional group for each in the IR table below. The IR spectrum can also be saved to the lab book for later analysis.

IR List position (cm^{-1}) & functional group	4.
1.	5.
2.	6.
3.	7.

6. To collect a ^{1}H NMR spectrum of your product, click on the NMR magnet located to the right of the chalkboard and drag the NMR sample tube to the flask on the lab bench. A window containing the NMR spectrum for your product should now open. You can zoom into various portions of the NMR spectrum by clicking and dragging over the desired area. The *Zoom Out* button is used to zoom back out to view the full spectrum. Identify all of the peaks in the NMR spectrum and record the chemical shift, the splitting, and the number of hydrogens for each peak in the NMR table below. The NMR spectrum can also be saved to the lab book for later analysis.

^{1}H NMR	Peak	Chemical Shift (δ)	Multiplicity[†]	H[‡]	Peak	Chemical Shift (δ)	Multiplicity[†]	H[‡]
Structure:	1				7			
	2				8			
	3				9			
	4				10			
Cyclohexa-1,4-diene-1,2-dicarboxylic acid dimethyl ester	5				11			
	6				12			

[†] Specify the multiplicity as a singlet (s), doublet (d), triplet (t), quartet (q), or multiplet (m).
[‡] Specify the number of hydrogens associated with each peak.

7. *Do the IR and NMR spectra you measured and recorded in the tables above confirm that you synthesized the assigned target compound? Explain.* _____

_____

_____

VCL 3-7: Diels Alder – 4

For this assignment, the target compound that you should synthesize is **bicyclo[2.2.1]hepta-2,5-diene-2,3-dicarboxylic acid dimethyl ester.** This is a cycloaddition reaction. Examine the product to determine the reactive partners. Keep in mind the position of the alkenes in the product. Try pushing the electrons backwards to reveal the needed substrates.

Synthesis Procedures

1. Start *Virtual ChemLab* and select *Diels Alder –4* from the list of assignments in the electronic workbook. After entering the organic laboratory, go to the stockroom by clicking inside the *Stockroom* window. Next, select a round bottom flask and place it on the cork ring on the stockroom counter. Using the available reagents on the stockroom shelf, identify the appropriate starting materials required to synthesize the target compound and add them to the round bottom flask. Now add ether (Et_2O) as a solvent and click on the green *Return to Lab* arrow to return to the laboratory.

2. The round bottom flask containing the starting materials should now be on the stir plate. Click on the handle located in the upper right corner of the laboratory to pull down the TV. The TV should already be in *Tutorial* mode and the starting materials and solvent should be listed. From the group of reagents found on the lab bench, select the correct reagent to synthesize the target compound and add it to the flask on the stir plate. Now attach the heater, condenser, and N_2 gas to the round bottom flask so the reaction mixture can be heated.

3. Start the reaction by clicking on the *Stir* button on the front of the stir plate. You should be able to observe the reaction mixture stirring in the flask. Monitor the progress of the reaction using TLC measurements as necessary until the product has formed and the starting materials have been consumed. You can advance the laboratory time using the clock on the wall. With the electronic lab book open (click on the lab book on the lab bench), you can also save your TLC plates by clicking *Save* on the TLC window.

4. When the reaction is complete, "work up" your reaction by first dragging and dropping the separatory funnel (located in a drawer) on the flask and then adding H_2O to the funnel. Extract the organic layer in the funnel by clicking on the top layer and dragging it to the cork ring on the lab bench. Your target compound should now be in this flask.

List the starting materials, solvent, reagent, and products formed: _____

_____

_____

How long did it take to finish the reaction? _____

What are the TLC values (R_f) for (a) Starting Materials: _____ *(b) Products:* _____

Write a mechanism for this reaction:

IR and NMR Spectra

After completing a reaction and working up the products, it is still necessary to confirm that the correct product was formed. The most common tools used for this analysis are Infrared (IR) and Nuclear Magnetic Resonance (NMR) spectroscopy. In the virtual laboratory, only ^{1}H NMR spectra are available. Details on interpreting IR and NMR spectra are found in your textbook. Your instructor may or may not ask you to perform this section depending on how your class is structured.

5. To collect an IR spectrum of your product, click on the IR spectrometer located underneath the laboratory clock and drag the salt plate icon to the flask on the lab bench. A window containing the IR spectrum for your product should now open. Identify the relevant peaks in the IR spectrum and record the position and associated functional group for each in the IR table below. The IR spectrum can also be saved to the lab book for later analysis.

IR List position (cm^{-1}) & functional group	4.
1.	5.
2.	6.
3.	7.

6. To collect a ^{1}H NMR spectrum of your product, click on the NMR magnet located to the right of the chalkboard and drag the NMR sample tube to the flask on the lab bench. A window containing the NMR spectrum for your product should now open. You can zoom into various portions of the NMR spectrum by clicking and dragging over the desired area. The *Zoom Out* button is used to zoom back out to view the full spectrum. Identify all of the peaks in the NMR spectrum and record the chemical shift, the splitting, and the number of hydrogens for each peak in the NMR table below. The NMR spectrum can also be saved to the lab book for later analysis.

^{1}H NMR	Peak	Chemical Shift (δ)	Multiplicity[†]	H[‡]	Peak	Chemical Shift (δ)	Multiplicity[†]	H[‡]
Structure:	1				7			
	2				8			
	3				9			
	4				10			
Bicyclo[2.2.1]hepta-2,5-diene-2,3-dicarboxylic acid dimethyl ester	5				11			
	6				12			

[†] Specify the multiplicity as a singlet (s), doublet (d), triplet (t), quartet (q), or multiplet (m).
[‡] Specify the number of hydrogens associated with each peak.

7. *Do the IR and NMR spectra you measured and recorded in the tables above confirm that you synthesized the assigned target compound? Explain.* _____

_____

_____

_____

VCL 3-8: Diels Alder – 5

For this assignment, the target compound that you should synthesize is **4-hydroxy-phthalic acid dimethyl ester.** This is a challenging cycloaddition reaction. Examine the product to determine the reactive partners. Keep in mind that the product of the cycloaddition may be further transformed to form the benzene functionality. The relative positions of the esters and the hydroxyl are maintained.

Synthesis Procedures

1. Start *Virtual ChemLab* and select *Diels Alder –5* from the list of assignments in the electronic workbook. After entering the organic laboratory, go to the stockroom by clicking inside the *Stockroom* window. Next, select a round bottom flask and place it on the cork ring on the stockroom counter. Using the available reagents on the stockroom shelf, identify the appropriate starting materials required to synthesize the target compound and add them to the round bottom flask. Now add ether (Et_2O) as a solvent and click on the green *Return to Lab* arrow to return to the laboratory.

2. The round bottom flask containing the starting materials should now be on the stir plate. Click on the handle located in the upper right corner of the laboratory to pull down the TV. The TV should already be in *Tutorial* mode and the starting materials and solvent should be listed. From the group of reagents found on the lab bench, select the correct reagent to synthesize the target compound and add it to the flask on the stir plate. Now attach the heater, condenser, and N_2 gas to the round bottom flask so the reaction mixture can be heated.

3. Start the reaction by clicking on the *Stir* button on the front of the stir plate. You should be able to observe the reaction mixture stirring in the flask. Monitor the progress of the reaction using TLC measurements as necessary until the product has formed and the starting materials have been consumed. You can advance the laboratory time using the clock on the wall. With the electronic lab book open (click on the lab book on the lab bench), you can also save your TLC plates by clicking *Save* on the TLC window.

4. When the reaction is complete, "work up" your reaction by first dragging and dropping the separatory funnel (located in a drawer) on the flask and then adding H_2O to the funnel. Extract the organic layer in the funnel by clicking on the top layer and dragging it to the cork ring on the lab bench. Your target compound should now be in this flask.

   List the starting materials, solvent, reagent, and products formed: _____

   _____

   _____

   How long did it take to finish the reaction? _____

   What are the TLC values (R_f) for (a) Starting Materials: _____ *(b) Products:* _____

   Write a mechanism for this reaction:

IR and NMR Spectra

After completing a reaction and working up the products, it is still necessary to confirm that the correct product was formed. The most common tools used for this analysis are Infrared (IR) and Nuclear Magnetic Resonance (NMR) spectroscopy. In the virtual laboratory, only ^{1}H NMR spectra are available. Details on interpreting IR and NMR spectra are found in your textbook. Your instructor may or may not ask you to perform this section depending on how your class is structured.

5. To collect an IR spectrum of your product, click on the IR spectrometer located underneath the laboratory clock and drag the salt plate icon to the flask on the lab bench. A window containing the IR spectrum for your product should now open. Identify the relevant peaks in the IR spectrum and record the position and associated functional group for each in the IR table below. The IR spectrum can also be saved to the lab book for later analysis.

IR List position (cm^{-1}) & functional group	4.
1.	5.
2.	6.
3.	7.

6. To collect a ^{1}H NMR spectrum of your product, click on the NMR magnet located to the right of the chalkboard and drag the NMR sample tube to the flask on the lab bench. A window containing the NMR spectrum for your product should now open. You can zoom into various portions of the NMR spectrum by clicking and dragging over the desired area. The *Zoom Out* button is used to zoom back out to view the full spectrum. Identify all of the peaks in the NMR spectrum and record the chemical shift, the splitting, and the number of hydrogens for each peak in the NMR table below. The NMR spectrum can also be saved to the lab book for later analysis.

^{1}H NMR Structure: 4-Hydroxy-phthalic acid dimethyl ester	Peak	Chemical Shift (δ)	Multiplicity†	H‡	Peak	Chemical Shift (δ)	Multiplicity†	H‡
	1				7			
	2				8			
	3				9			
	4				10			
	5				11			
	6				12			

† Specify the multiplicity as a singlet (s), doublet (d), triplet (t), quartet (q), or multiplet (m).
‡ Specify the number of hydrogens associated with each peak.

7. *Do the IR and NMR spectra you measured and recorded in the tables above confirm that you synthesized the assigned target compound? Explain.* _____

_____

_____

_____

VCL 4-1: Alkyl Halide Solvolysis

For this assignment, the target compound that you should synthesize is **2-methyl-2-propanol**. This is a substitution reaction. Keep in mind the substitution pattern of the product and the nature of the intermediate dictated by this arrangement.

Synthesis Procedures

1. Start *Virtual ChemLab* and select *Alkyl Halide Solvolysis* from the list of assignments in the electronic workbook. After entering the organic laboratory, go to the stockroom by clicking inside the *Stockroom* window. Next, select a round bottom flask and place it on the cork ring on the stockroom counter. Using the available reagents on the stockroom shelf, identify the appropriate starting materials required to synthesize the target compound and add them to the round bottom flask. Now add water (H_2O) as a solvent and click on the green *Return to Lab* arrow to return to the laboratory.

2. The round bottom flask containing the starting materials should now be on the stir plate. Click on the handle located in the upper right corner of the laboratory to pull down the TV. The TV should already be in *Tutorial* mode and the starting materials and solvent should be listed. From the group of reagents found on the lab bench, select the correct reagent to synthesize the target compound and add it to the flask on the stir plate.

3. Start the reaction by clicking on the *Stir* button on the front of the stir plate. You should be able to observe the reaction mixture stirring in the flask. Monitor the progress of the reaction using TLC measurements as necessary until the product has formed and the starting materials have been consumed. You can advance the laboratory time using the clock on the wall. With the electronic lab book open (click on the lab book on the lab bench), you can also save your TLC plates by clicking *Save* on the TLC window.

4. When the reaction is complete, "work up" your reaction by first dragging and dropping the separatory funnel (located in a drawer) on the flask and then adding H_2O to the funnel. Extract the organic layer in the funnel by clicking on the top layer and dragging it to the cork ring on the lab bench. Your target compound should now be in this flask.

List the starting materials, solvent, reagent, and products formed: _____

_____

How long did it take to finish the reaction? _____

What are the TLC values (R_f) for (a) Starting Materials: _____ *(b) Products:* _____

Write a mechanism for this reaction:

IR and NMR Spectra

After completing a reaction and working up the products, it is still necessary to confirm that the correct product was formed. The most common tools used for this analysis are Infrared (IR) and Nuclear Magnetic Resonance (NMR) spectroscopy. In the virtual laboratory, only ^{1}H NMR spectra are available. Details on interpreting IR and NMR spectra are found in your textbook. Your instructor may or may not ask you to perform this section depending on how your class is structured.

5. To collect an IR spectrum of your product, click on the IR spectrometer located underneath the laboratory clock and drag the salt plate icon to the flask on the lab bench. A window containing the IR spectrum for your product should now open. Identify the relevant peaks in the IR spectrum and record the position and associated functional group for each in the IR table below. The IR spectrum can also be saved to the lab book for later analysis.

IR List position (cm^{-1}) & functional group	4.
1.	5.
2.	6.
3.	7.

6. To collect a ^{1}H NMR spectrum of your product, click on the NMR magnet located to the right of the chalkboard and drag the NMR sample tube to the flask on the lab bench. A window containing the NMR spectrum for your product should now open. You can zoom into various portions of the NMR spectrum by clicking and dragging over the desired area. The *Zoom Out* button is used to zoom back out to view the full spectrum. Identify all of the peaks in the NMR spectrum and record the chemical shift, the splitting, and the number of hydrogens for each peak in the NMR table below. The NMR spectrum can also be saved to the lab book for later analysis.

^{1}H NMR	Peak	Chemical Shift (δ)	Multiplicity[†]	H[‡]	Peak	Chemical Shift (δ)	Multiplicity[†]	H[‡]
Structure:	1				7			
	2				8			
⊣—OH	3				9			
2-Methyl-2-propanol	4				10			
	5				11			
	6				12			

[†] Specify the multiplicity as a singlet (s), doublet (d), triplet (t), quartet (q), or multiplet (m).
[‡] Specify the number of hydrogens associated with each peak.

7. *Do the IR and NMR spectra you measured and recorded in the tables above confirm that you synthesized the assigned target compound? Explain.* _____

_____

_____

VCL 4-2: Nucleophilic Substitution – 1

For this assignment, the target compound that you should synthesize is **butanol.** This is a substitution reaction. Keep in mind the substitution pattern of the product and the mechanism accommodated by this arrangement.

Synthesis Procedures

1. Start *Virtual ChemLab* and select *Nucleophilic Substitution – 1* from the list of assignments in the electronic workbook. After entering the organic laboratory, go to the stockroom by clicking inside the *Stockroom* window. Next, select a round bottom flask and place it on the cork ring on the stockroom counter. Using the available reagents on the stockroom shelf, identify the appropriate starting materials required to synthesize the target compound and add them to the round bottom flask. Now add ether (Et_2O) as a solvent and click on the green *Return to Lab* arrow to return to the laboratory.

2. The round bottom flask containing the starting materials should now be on the stir plate. Click on the handle located in the upper right corner of the laboratory to pull down the TV. The TV should already be in *Tutorial* mode and the starting materials and solvent should be listed. From the group of reagents found on the lab bench, select the correct reagent to synthesize the target compound and add it to the flask on the stir plate. Now attach the heater, condenser, and N_2 gas to the round bottom flask so the reaction mixture can be heated.

3. Start the reaction by clicking on the *Stir* button on the front of the stir plate. You should be able to observe the reaction mixture stirring in the flask. Monitor the progress of the reaction using TLC measurements as necessary until the product has formed and the starting materials have been consumed. You can advance the laboratory time using the clock on the wall. With the electronic lab book open (click on the lab book on the lab bench), you can also save your TLC plates by clicking *Save* on the TLC window.

4. When the reaction is complete, "work up" your reaction by first dragging and dropping the separatory funnel (located in a drawer) on the flask and then adding H_2O to the funnel. Extract the organic layer in the funnel by clicking on the top layer and dragging it to the cork ring on the lab bench. Your target compound should now be in this flask.

    List the starting materials, solvent, reagent, and products formed: _____

    _____

    How long did it take to finish the reaction? _____

    What are the TLC values (R_f) for (a) Starting Materials: _____ *(b) Products:* _____

    Write a mechanism for this reaction:

IR and NMR Spectra

After completing a reaction and working up the products, it is still necessary to confirm that the correct product was formed. The most common tools used for this analysis are Infrared (IR) and Nuclear Magnetic Resonance (NMR) spectroscopy. In the virtual laboratory, only ^{1}H NMR spectra are available. Details on interpreting IR and NMR spectra are found in your textbook. Your instructor may or may not ask you to perform this section depending on how your class is structured.

5. To collect an IR spectrum of your product, click on the IR spectrometer located underneath the laboratory clock and drag the salt plate icon to the flask on the lab bench. A window containing the IR spectrum for your product should now open. Identify the relevant peaks in the IR spectrum and record the position and associated functional group for each in the IR table below. The IR spectrum can also be saved to the lab book for later analysis.

IR List position (cm^{-1}) & functional group	4.
1.	5.
2.	6.
3.	7.

6. To collect a ^{1}H NMR spectrum of your product, click on the NMR magnet located to the right of the chalkboard and drag the NMR sample tube to the flask on the lab bench. A window containing the NMR spectrum for your product should now open. You can zoom into various portions of the NMR spectrum by clicking and dragging over the desired area. The *Zoom Out* button is used to zoom back out to view the full spectrum. Identify all of the peaks in the NMR spectrum and record the chemical shift, the splitting, and the number of hydrogens for each peak in the NMR table below. The NMR spectrum can also be saved to the lab book for later analysis.

^{1}H NMR Structure: ∿∿OH Butanol	Peak	Chemical Shift (δ)	Multiplicity†	H‡	Peak	Chemical Shift (δ)	Multiplicity†	H‡
	1				7			
	2				8			
	3				9			
	4				10			
	5				11			
	6				12			

† Specify the multiplicity as a singlet (s), doublet (d), triplet (t), quartet (q), or multiplet (m).
‡ Specify the number of hydrogens associated with each peak.

7. *Do the IR and NMR spectra you measured and recorded in the tables above confirm that you*

synthesized the assigned target compound? Explain. _____

_____

_____

_____

VCL 4-3: Williamson Ether Synthesis – 1

For this assignment, the target compound that you should synthesize is **benzyl methyl ether.** This is a substitution reaction. Examine the product and determine which bonds may be formed. Keep in mind the substitution pattern of the product and the nature of the mechanism accommodated by this arrangement.

Synthesis Procedures
1. Start *Virtual ChemLab* and select *Williamson Ether Synthesis –1* from the list of assignments in the electronic workbook. After entering the organic laboratory, go to the stockroom by clicking inside the *Stockroom* window. Next, select a round bottom flask and place it on the cork ring on the stockroom counter. Using the available reagents on the stockroom shelf, identify the appropriate starting materials required to synthesize the target compound and add them to the round bottom flask. Now add ether (Et$_2$O) as a solvent and click on the green *Return to Lab* arrow to return to the laboratory.

2. The round bottom flask containing the starting materials should now be on the stir plate. Click on the handle located in the upper right corner of the laboratory to pull down the TV. The TV should already be in *Tutorial* mode and the starting materials and solvent should be listed. From the group of reagents found on the lab bench, select the correct reagent to synthesize the target compound and add it to the flask on the stir plate.

3. Start the reaction by clicking on the *Stir* button on the front of the stir plate. You should be able to observe the reaction mixture stirring in the flask. Monitor the progress of the reaction using TLC measurements as necessary until the product has formed and the starting materials have been consumed. You can advance the laboratory time using the clock on the wall. With the electronic lab book open (click on the lab book on the lab bench), you can also save your TLC plates by clicking *Save* on the TLC window.

4. When the reaction is complete, "work up" your reaction by first dragging and dropping the separatory funnel (located in a drawer) on the flask and then adding H$_2$O to the funnel. Extract the organic layer in the funnel by clicking on the top layer and dragging it to the cork ring on the lab bench. Your target compound should now be in this flask.

   List the starting materials, solvent, reagent, and products formed: _____

   _____

   How long did it take to finish the reaction? _____

   What are the TLC values (R_f) for (a) Starting Materials: _____ (b) Products: _____

   Write a mechanism for this reaction:

IR and NMR Spectra

After completing a reaction and working up the products, it is still necessary to confirm that the correct product was formed. The most common tools used for this analysis are Infrared (IR) and Nuclear Magnetic Resonance (NMR) spectroscopy. In the virtual laboratory, only ^{1}H NMR spectra are available. Details on interpreting IR and NMR spectra are found in your textbook. Your instructor may or may not ask you to perform this section depending on how your class is structured.

5. To collect an IR spectrum of your product, click on the IR spectrometer located underneath the laboratory clock and drag the salt plate icon to the flask on the lab bench. A window containing the IR spectrum for your product should now open. Identify the relevant peaks in the IR spectrum and record the position and associated functional group for each in the IR table below. The IR spectrum can also be saved to the lab book for later analysis.

IR List position (cm^{-1}) & functional group	4.
1.	5.
2.	6.
	7.

6. To collect a ^{1}H NMR spectrum of your product, click on the NMR magnet located to the right of the chalkboard and drag the NMR sample tube to the flask on the lab bench. A window containing the NMR spectrum for your product should now open. You can zoom into various portions of the NMR spectrum by clicking and dragging over the desired area. The *Zoom Out* button is used to zoom back out to view the full spectrum. Identify all of the peaks in the NMR spectrum and record the chemical shift, the splitting, and the number of hydrogens for each peak in the NMR table below. The NMR spectrum can also be saved to the lab book for later analysis.

^{1}**H NMR** Structure: Benzyl methyl ether	Peak	Chemical Shift (δ)	Multiplicity†	H‡	Peak	Chemical Shift (δ)	Multiplicity†	H‡
	1				7			
	2				8			
	3				9			
	4				10			
	5				11			
	6				12			

† Specify the multiplicity as a singlet (s), doublet (d), triplet (t), quartet (q), or multiplet (m).
‡ Specify the number of hydrogens associated with each peak.

7. *Do the IR and NMR spectra you measured and recorded in the tables above confirm that you*

    synthesized the assigned target compound? Explain. _____

    _____

    _____

    _____

VCL 4-4: Alkene Formation

For this assignment, the target compound that you should synthesize is **bicyclo[2.2.1]hept-2-ene.** This is an elimination reaction. Examine the product and determine the positions within the substrate where functionality may be lost. Keep in mind the substitution pattern of the product and the nature of the mechanism accommodated by this arrangement.

Synthesis Procedures

1. Start *Virtual ChemLab* and select *Alkene Formation* from the list of assignments in the electronic workbook. After entering the organic laboratory, go to the stockroom by clicking inside the *Stockroom* window. Next, select a round bottom flask and place it on the cork ring on the stockroom counter. Using the available reagents on the stockroom shelf, identify the appropriate starting materials required to synthesize the target compound and add them to the round bottom flask. Now add ether (Et_2O) as a solvent and click on the green *Return to Lab* arrow to return to the laboratory.

2. The round bottom flask containing the starting materials should now be on the stir plate. Click on the handle located in the upper right corner of the laboratory to pull down the TV. The TV should already be in *Tutorial* mode and the starting materials and solvent should be listed. From the group of reagents found on the lab bench, select the correct reagent to synthesize the target compound and add it to the flask on the stir plate. Now attach the heater, condenser, and N_2 gas to the round bottom flask so the reaction mixture can be heated.

3. Start the reaction by clicking on the *Stir* button on the front of the stir plate. You should be able to observe the reaction mixture stirring in the flask. Monitor the progress of the reaction using TLC measurements as necessary until the product has formed and the starting materials have been consumed. You can advance the laboratory time using the clock on the wall. With the electronic lab book open (click on the lab book on the lab bench), you can also save your TLC plates by clicking *Save* on the TLC window.

4. When the reaction is complete, "work up" your reaction by first dragging and dropping the separatory funnel (located in a drawer) on the flask and then adding H_2O to the funnel. Extract the organic layer in the funnel by clicking on the top layer and dragging it to the cork ring on the lab bench. Your target compound should now be in this flask.

    List the starting materials, solvent, reagent, and products formed: _____

    _____

    How long did it take to finish the reaction? _____

    What are the TLC values (R_f) for (a) Starting Materials: _____ *(b) Products:* _____

    Write a mechanism for this reaction:

IR and NMR Spectra

After completing a reaction and working up the products, it is still necessary to confirm that the correct product was formed. The most common tools used for this analysis are Infrared (IR) and Nuclear Magnetic Resonance (NMR) spectroscopy. In the virtual laboratory, only ^{1}H NMR spectra are available. Details on interpreting IR and NMR spectra are found in your textbook. Your instructor may or may not ask you to perform this section depending on how your class is structured.

5. To collect an IR spectrum of your product, click on the IR spectrometer located underneath the laboratory clock and drag the salt plate icon to the flask on the lab bench. A window containing the IR spectrum for your product should now open. Identify the relevant peaks in the IR spectrum and record the position and associated functional group for each in the IR table below. The IR spectrum can also be saved to the lab book for later analysis.

IR List position (cm^{-1}) & functional group	4.
1.	5.
2.	6.
3.	7.

6. To collect a ^{1}H NMR spectrum of your product, click on the NMR magnet located to the right of the chalkboard and drag the NMR sample tube to the flask on the lab bench. A window containing the NMR spectrum for your product should now open. You can zoom into various portions of the NMR spectrum by clicking and dragging over the desired area. The *Zoom Out* button is used to zoom back out to view the full spectrum. Identify all of the peaks in the NMR spectrum and record the chemical shift, the splitting, and the number of hydrogens for each peak in the NMR table below. The NMR spectrum can also be saved to the lab book for later analysis.

^{1}H NMR Structure: Bicyclo[2.2.1] hept-2-ene	Peak	Chemical Shift (δ)	Multiplicity†	H‡	Peak	Chemical Shift (δ)	Multiplicity†	H‡
	1				7			
	2				8			
	3				9			
	4				10			
	5				11			
	6				12			

† Specify the multiplicity as a singlet (s), doublet (d), triplet (t), quartet (q), or multiplet (m).
‡ Specify the number of hydrogens associated with each peak.

7. *Do the IR and NMR spectra you measured and recorded in the tables above confirm that you*

   synthesized the assigned target compound? Explain. _____

   _____

   _____

VCL 4-5: Nucleophilic Substitution – 2

For this assignment, the target compound that you should synthesize is **benzyl alcohol.** This is a substitution reaction. Keep in mind the substitution pattern of the product and the mechanism accommodated by this arrangement.

Synthesis Procedures

1. Start *Virtual ChemLab* and select *Nucleophilic Substitution – 2* from the list of assignments in the electronic workbook. After entering the organic laboratory, go to the stockroom by clicking inside the *Stockroom* window. Next, select a round bottom flask and place it on the cork ring on the stockroom counter. Using the available reagents on the stockroom shelf, identify the appropriate starting materials required to synthesize the target compound and add them to the round bottom flask. Now add ether (Et_2O) as a solvent and click on the green *Return to Lab* arrow to return to the laboratory.

2. The round bottom flask containing the starting materials should now be on the stir plate. Click on the handle located in the upper right corner of the laboratory to pull down the TV. The TV should already be in *Tutorial* mode and the starting materials and solvent should be listed. From the group of reagents found on the lab bench, select the correct reagent to synthesize the target compound and add it to the flask on the stir plate. Now attach the heater, condenser, and N_2 gas to the round bottom flask so the reaction mixture can be heated.

3. Start the reaction by clicking on the *Stir* button on the front of the stir plate. You should be able to observe the reaction mixture stirring in the flask. Monitor the progress of the reaction using TLC measurements as necessary until the product has formed and the starting materials have been consumed. You can advance the laboratory time using the clock on the wall. With the electronic lab book open (click on the lab book on the lab bench), you can also save your TLC plates by clicking *Save* on the TLC window.

4. When the reaction is complete, "work up" your reaction by first dragging and dropping the separatory funnel (located in a drawer) on the flask and then adding H_2O to the funnel. Extract the organic layer in the funnel by clicking on the top layer and dragging it to the cork ring on the lab bench. Your target compound should now be in this flask.

    List the starting materials, solvent, reagent, and products formed: _____

    _____

    How long did it take to finish the reaction? _____

    What are the TLC values (R_f) for (a) Starting Materials: _____ *(b) Products:* _____

    Write a mechanism for this reaction:

IR and NMR Spectra

After completing a reaction and working up the products, it is still necessary to confirm that the correct product was formed. The most common tools used for this analysis are Infrared (IR) and Nuclear Magnetic Resonance (NMR) spectroscopy. In the virtual laboratory, only ^{1}H NMR spectra are available. Details on interpreting IR and NMR spectra are found in your textbook. Your instructor may or may not ask you to perform this section depending on how your class is structured.

5. To collect an IR spectrum of your product, click on the IR spectrometer located underneath the laboratory clock and drag the salt plate icon to the flask on the lab bench. A window containing the IR spectrum for your product should now open. Identify the relevant peaks in the IR spectrum and record the position and associated functional group for each in the IR table below. The IR spectrum can also be saved to the lab book for later analysis.

IR List position (cm^{-1}) & functional group	4.
1.	5.
2.	6.
3.	7.

6. To collect a ^{1}H NMR spectrum of your product, click on the NMR magnet located to the right of the chalkboard and drag the NMR sample tube to the flask on the lab bench. A window containing the NMR spectrum for your product should now open. You can zoom into various portions of the NMR spectrum by clicking and dragging over the desired area. The *Zoom Out* button is used to zoom back out to view the full spectrum. Identify all of the peaks in the NMR spectrum and record the chemical shift, the splitting, and the number of hydrogens for each peak in the NMR table below. The NMR spectrum can also be saved to the lab book for later analysis.

^{1}H NMR	Peak	Chemical Shift (δ)	Multiplicity†	H‡	Peak	Chemical Shift (δ)	Multiplicity†	H‡
	1				7			
Structure:	2				8			
	3				9			
Benzyl alcohol	4				10			
	5				11			
	6				12			

† Specify the multiplicity as a singlet (s), doublet (d), triplet (t), quartet (q), or multiplet (m).
‡ Specify the number of hydrogens associated with each peak.

7. *Do the IR and NMR spectra you measured and recorded in the tables above confirm that you synthesized the assigned target compound? Explain.* _____

_____

_____

_____

VCL 4-6: Williamson Ether Synthesis – 2

For this assignment, the target compound that you should synthesize is **1-methoxy butane.** This is a substitution reaction. Examine the product and determine which bonds may be formed. Keep in mind the substitution pattern of the product and the nature of the mechanism accommodated by this arrangement.

Synthesis Procedures

1. Start *Virtual ChemLab* and select *Williamson Ether Synthesis – 2* from the list of assignments in the electronic workbook. After entering the organic laboratory, go to the stockroom by clicking inside the *Stockroom* window. Next, select a round bottom flask and place it on the cork ring on the stockroom counter. Using the available reagents on the stockroom shelf, identify the appropriate starting materials required to synthesize the target compound and add them to the round bottom flask. Now add ether (Et$_2$O) as a solvent and click on the green *Return to Lab* arrow to return to the laboratory.

2. The round bottom flask containing the starting materials should now be on the stir plate. Click on the handle located in the upper right corner of the laboratory to pull down the TV. The TV should already be in *Tutorial* mode and the starting materials and solvent should be listed. From the group of reagents found on the lab bench, select the correct reagent to synthesize the target compound and add it to the flask on the stir plate.

3. Start the reaction by clicking on the *Stir* button on the front of the stir plate. You should be able to observe the reaction mixture stirring in the flask. Monitor the progress of the reaction using TLC measurements as necessary until the product has formed and the starting materials have been consumed. You can advance the laboratory time using the clock on the wall. With the electronic lab book open (click on the lab book on the lab bench), you can also save your TLC plates by clicking *Save* on the TLC window.

4. When the reaction is complete, "work up" your reaction by first dragging and dropping the separatory funnel (located in a drawer) on the flask and then adding H$_2$O to the funnel. Extract the organic layer in the funnel by clicking on the top layer and dragging it to the cork ring on the lab bench. Your target compound should now be in this flask.

List the starting materials, solvent, reagent, and products formed: _____

_____

How long did it take to finish the reaction? _____

What are the TLC values (R$_f$) for (a) Starting Materials: _____ *(b) Products:* _____

Write a mechanism for this reaction:

IR and NMR Spectra

After completing a reaction and working up the products, it is still necessary to confirm that the correct product was formed. The most common tools used for this analysis are Infrared (IR) and Nuclear Magnetic Resonance (NMR) spectroscopy. In the virtual laboratory, only ^{1}H NMR spectra are available. Details on interpreting IR and NMR spectra are found in your textbook. Your instructor may or may not ask you to perform this section depending on how your class is structured.

5. To collect an IR spectrum of your product, click on the IR spectrometer located underneath the laboratory clock and drag the salt plate icon to the flask on the lab bench. A window containing the IR spectrum for your product should now open. Identify the relevant peaks in the IR spectrum and record the position and associated functional group for each in the IR table below. The IR spectrum can also be saved to the lab book for later analysis.

IR List position (cm^{-1}) & functional group	4.
1.	5.
2.	6.
	7.

6. To collect a ^{1}H NMR spectrum of your product, click on the NMR magnet located to the right of the chalkboard and drag the NMR sample tube to the flask on the lab bench. A window containing the NMR spectrum for your product should now open. You can zoom into various portions of the NMR spectrum by clicking and dragging over the desired area. The *Zoom Out* button is used to zoom back out to view the full spectrum. Identify all of the peaks in the NMR spectrum and record the chemical shift, the splitting, and the number of hydrogens for each peak in the NMR table below. The NMR spectrum can also be saved to the lab book for later analysis.

^{1}H NMR	Peak	Chemical Shift (δ)	Multiplicity†	H‡	Peak	Chemical Shift (δ)	Multiplicity†	H‡
Structure: OMe 1-Methoxy butane	1				7			
	2				8			
	3				9			
	4				10			
	5				11			
	6				12			

† Specify the multiplicity as a singlet (s), doublet (d), triplet (t), quartet (q), or multiplet (m).
‡ Specify the number of hydrogens associated with each peak.

7. *Do the IR and NMR spectra you measured and recorded in the tables above confirm that you synthesized the assigned target compound? Explain.* _____

_____

_____

_____

VCL 4-7: Amine Formation

For this assignment, the target compound that you should synthesize is **benzyl-diisopropylamine.** This is a substitution reaction. Examine the product and determine which bonds may be formed in the process. Select the location of potential leaving groups.

Synthesis Procedures

1. Start *Virtual ChemLab* and select *Amine Formation* from the list of assignments in the electronic workbook. After entering the organic laboratory, go to the stockroom by clicking inside the *Stockroom* window. Next, select a round bottom flask and place it on the cork ring on the stockroom counter. Using the available reagents on the stockroom shelf, identify the appropriate starting materials required to synthesize the target compound and add them to the round bottom flask. Select the appropriate solvent and click on the green *Return to Lab* arrow to return to the laboratory.

2. The round bottom flask containing the starting materials should now be on the stir plate. Click on the handle located in the upper right corner of the laboratory to pull down the TV. The TV should already be in *Tutorial* mode and the starting materials and solvent should be listed. From the group of reagents found on the lab bench, select the correct reagent to synthesize the target compound and add it to the flask on the stir plate.

3. Start the reaction by clicking on the *Stir* button on the front of the stir plate. You should be able to observe the reaction mixture stirring in the flask. Monitor the progress of the reaction using TLC measurements as necessary until the product has formed and the starting materials have been consumed. You can advance the laboratory time using the clock on the wall. With the electronic lab book open (click on the lab book on the lab bench), you can also save your TLC plates by clicking *Save* on the TLC window.

4. When the reaction is complete, "work up" your reaction by first dragging and dropping the separatory funnel (located in a drawer) on the flask and then adding H_2O the funnel. Extract the organic layer in the funnel by clicking on the top layer and dragging it to the cork ring on the lab bench. Your target compound should now be in this flask.

List the starting materials, solvent, reagent, and products formed: _____

_____

How long did it take to finish the reaction? _____

What are the TLC values (R_f) for (a) Starting Materials: _____ *(b) Products:* _____

Write a mechanism for this reaction:

IR and NMR Spectra

After completing a reaction and working up the products, it is still necessary to confirm that the correct product was formed. The most common tools used for this analysis are Infrared (IR) and Nuclear Magnetic Resonance (NMR) spectroscopy. In the virtual laboratory, only ^{1}H NMR spectra are available. Details on interpreting IR and NMR spectra are found in your textbook. Your instructor may or may not ask you to perform this section depending on how your class is structured.

5. To collect an IR spectrum of your product, click on the IR spectrometer located underneath the laboratory clock and drag the salt plate icon to the flask on the lab bench. A window containing the IR spectrum for your product should now open. Identify the relevant peaks in the IR spectrum and record the position and associated functional group for each in the IR table below. The IR spectrum can also be saved to the lab book for later analysis.

IR List position (cm^{-1}) & functional group	4.
1.	5.
2.	6.
3.	7.

6. To collect a ^{1}H NMR spectrum of your product, click on the NMR magnet located to the right of the chalkboard and drag the NMR sample tube to the flask on the lab bench. A window containing the NMR spectrum for your product should now open. You can zoom into various portions of the NMR spectrum by clicking and dragging over the desired area. The *Zoom Out* button is used to zoom back out to view the full spectrum. Identify all of the peaks in the NMR spectrum and record the chemical shift, the splitting, and the number of hydrogens for each peak in the NMR table below. The NMR spectrum can also be saved to the lab book for later analysis.

^{1}H NMR	Peak	Chemical Shift (δ)	Multiplicity†	H‡	Peak	Chemical Shift (δ)	Multiplicity†	H‡
	1				7			
Structure:	2				8			
	3				9			
	4				10			
Benzyl-diisopropylamine	5				11			
	6				12			

† Specify the multiplicity as a singlet (s), doublet (d), triplet (t), quartet (q), or multiplet (m).
‡ Specify the number of hydrogens associated with each peak.

7. *Do the IR and NMR spectra you measured and recorded in the tables above confirm that you*

    synthesized the assigned target compound? Explain. _____

    _____

    _____

    _____

VCL 5-1: Alcohol Halogenation – 1

For this assignment, the target compound that you should synthesize is **chloro-cyclohexane**. This is a substitution reaction. Keep in mind the substitution pattern of the product and the mechanism accommodated by this arrangement when selecting the reagent.

Synthesis Procedures

1. Start *Virtual ChemLab* and select *Alcohol Halogenation – 1* from the list of assignments in the electronic workbook. After entering the organic laboratory, go to the stockroom by clicking inside the *Stockroom* window. Next, select a round bottom flask and place it on the cork ring on the stockroom counter. Using the available reagents on the stockroom shelf, identify the appropriate starting materials required to synthesize the target compound and add them to the round bottom flask. Select the appropriate solvent and click on the green *Return to Lab* arrow to return to the laboratory.

2. The round bottom flask containing the starting materials should now be on the stir plate. Click on the handle located in the upper right corner of the laboratory to pull down the TV. The TV should already be in *Tutorial* mode and the starting materials and solvent should be listed. From the group of reagents found on the lab bench, select the correct reagent to synthesize the target compound and add it to the flask on the stir plate. Now attach the heater, condenser, and N_2 gas to the round bottom flask so the reaction mixture can be heated.

3. Start the reaction by clicking on the *Stir* button on the front of the stir plate. You should be able to observe the reaction mixture stirring in the flask. Monitor the progress of the reaction using TLC measurements as necessary until the product has formed and the starting materials have been consumed. You can advance the laboratory time using the clock on the wall. With the electronic lab book open (click on the lab book on the lab bench), you can also save your TLC plates by clicking *Save* on the TLC window.

4. When the reaction is complete, "work up" your reaction by first dragging and dropping the separatory funnel (located in a drawer) on the flask and then adding H_2O to the funnel. Extract the organic layer in the funnel by clicking on the top layer and dragging it to the cork ring on the lab bench. Your target compound should now be in this flask.

List the starting materials, solvent, reagent, and products formed: _____

_____

How long did it take to finish the reaction? _____

What are the TLC values (R_f) for (a) Starting Materials: _____ *(b) Products:* _____

Write a mechanism for this reaction:

IR and NMR Spectra

After completing a reaction and working up the products, it is still necessary to confirm that the correct product was formed. The most common tools used for this analysis are Infrared (IR) and Nuclear Magnetic Resonance (NMR) spectroscopy. In the virtual laboratory, only ^{1}H NMR spectra are available. Details on interpreting IR and NMR spectra are found in your textbook. Your instructor may or may not ask you to perform this section depending on how your class is structured.

5. To collect an IR spectrum of your product, click on the IR spectrometer located underneath the laboratory clock and drag the salt plate icon to the flask on the lab bench. A window containing the IR spectrum for your product should now open. Identify the relevant peaks in the IR spectrum and record the position and associated functional group for each in the IR table below. The IR spectrum can also be saved to the lab book for later analysis.

IR List position (cm^{-1}) & functional group	4.
1.	5.
2.	6.
3.	7.

6. To collect a ^{1}H NMR spectrum of your product, click on the NMR magnet located to the right of the chalkboard and drag the NMR sample tube to the flask on the lab bench. A window containing the NMR spectrum for your product should now open. You can zoom into various portions of the NMR spectrum by clicking and dragging over the desired area. The *Zoom Out* button is used to zoom back out to view the full spectrum. Identify all of the peaks in the NMR spectrum and record the chemical shift, the splitting, and the number of hydrogens for each peak in the NMR table below. The NMR spectrum can also be saved to the lab book for later analysis.

^{1}H NMR	Peak	Chemical Shift (δ)	Multiplicity†	H‡	Peak	Chemical Shift (δ)	Multiplicity†	H‡
Structure:	1				7			
	2				8			
Chloro-cyclohexane	3				9			
	4				10			
	5				11			
	6				12			

† Specify the multiplicity as a singlet (s), doublet (d), triplet (t), quartet (q), or multiplet (m).
‡ Specify the number of hydrogens associated with each peak.

7. *Do the IR and NMR spectra you measured and recorded in the tables above confirm that you synthesized the assigned target compound? Explain.* _____

_____

_____

_____

VCL 5-2: Alcohol Halogenation – 2

For this assignment, the target compound that you should synthesize is **2-chloro-2-methyl propane.** This is a substitution reaction. Keep in mind the substitution pattern of the product and the mechanism accommodated by this arrangement when selecting the reagent.

Synthesis Procedures
1. Start *Virtual ChemLab* and select *Alcohol Halogenation – 2* from the list of assignments in the electronic workbook. After entering the organic laboratory, go to the stockroom by clicking inside the *Stockroom* window. Next, select a round bottom flask and place it on the cork ring on the stockroom counter. Using the available reagents on the stockroom shelf, identify the appropriate starting materials required to synthesize the target compound and add them to the round bottom flask. Select the appropriate solvent and click on the green *Return to Lab* arrow to return to the laboratory.

2. The round bottom flask containing the starting materials should now be on the stir plate. Click on the handle located in the upper right corner of the laboratory to pull down the TV. The TV should already be in *Tutorial* mode and the starting materials and solvent should be listed. From the group of reagents found on the lab bench, select the correct reagent to synthesize the target compound and add it to the flask on the stir plate. Now attach the heater, condenser, and N_2 gas to the round bottom flask so the reaction mixture can be heated.

3. Start the reaction by clicking on the *Stir* button on the front of the stir plate. You should be able to observe the reaction mixture stirring in the flask. Monitor the progress of the reaction using TLC measurements as necessary until the product has formed and the starting materials have been consumed. You can advance the laboratory time using the clock on the wall. With the electronic lab book open (click on the lab book on the lab bench), you can also save your TLC plates by clicking *Save* on the TLC window.

4. When the reaction is complete, "work up" your reaction by first dragging and dropping the separatory funnel (located in a drawer) on the flask and then adding H_2O to the funnel. Extract the organic layer in the funnel by clicking on the top layer and dragging it to the cork ring on the lab bench. Your target compound should now be in this flask.

List the starting materials, solvent, reagent, and products formed: _____

_____

How long did it take to finish the reaction? _____

What are the TLC values (R_f) for (a) Starting Materials: _____ *(b) Products:* _____

Write a mechanism for this reaction:

IR and NMR Spectra

After completing a reaction and working up the products, it is still necessary to confirm that the correct product was formed. The most common tools used for this analysis are Infrared (IR) and Nuclear Magnetic Resonance (NMR) spectroscopy. In the virtual laboratory, only ^{1}H NMR spectra are available. Details on interpreting IR and NMR spectra are found in your textbook. Your instructor may or may not ask you to perform this section depending on how your class is structured.

5. To collect an IR spectrum of your product, click on the IR spectrometer located underneath the laboratory clock and drag the salt plate icon to the flask on the lab bench. A window containing the IR spectrum for your product should now open. Identify the relevant peaks in the IR spectrum and record the position and associated functional group for each in the IR table below. The IR spectrum can also be saved to the lab book for later analysis.

IR List position (cm^{-1}) & functional group	4.
1.	5.
2.	6.
3.	7.

6. To collect a ^{1}H NMR spectrum of your product, click on the NMR magnet located to the right of the chalkboard and drag the NMR sample tube to the flask on the lab bench. A window containing the NMR spectrum for your product should now open. You can zoom into various portions of the NMR spectrum by clicking and dragging over the desired area. The *Zoom Out* button is used to zoom back out to view the full spectrum. Identify all of the peaks in the NMR spectrum and record the chemical shift, the splitting, and the number of hydrogens for each peak in the NMR table below. The NMR spectrum can also be saved to the lab book for later analysis.

^{1}H NMR Structure: $\longmapsto$Cl 2-Chloro-2-methyl propane	Peak	Chemical Shift (δ)	Multiplicity[†]	H[‡]	Peak	Chemical Shift (δ)	Multiplicity[†]	H[‡]
	1				7			
	2				8			
	3				9			
	4				10			
	5				11			
	6				12			

[†] Specify the multiplicity as a singlet (s), doublet (d), triplet (t), quartet (q), or multiplet (m).
[‡] Specify the number of hydrogens associated with each peak.

7. *Do the IR and NMR spectra you measured and recorded in the tables above confirm that you synthesized the assigned target compound? Explain.* _____

_____

_____

_____

VCL 5-3: Alcohol Halogenation – 3

For this assignment, the target compound that you should synthesize is **1-chloro-3-methylbutane.** This is a substitution reaction. Keep in mind the substitution pattern of the product and the mechanism accommodated by this arrangement when selecting the reagent.

Synthesis Procedures

1. Start *Virtual ChemLab* and select *Alcohol Halogenation – 3* from the list of assignments in the electronic workbook. After entering the organic laboratory, go to the stockroom by clicking inside the *Stockroom* window. Next, select a round bottom flask and place it on the cork ring on the stockroom counter. Using the available reagents on the stockroom shelf, identify the appropriate starting materials required to synthesize the target compound and add them to the round bottom flask. Select the appropriate solvent and click on the green *Return to Lab* arrow to return to the laboratory.

2. The round bottom flask containing the starting materials should now be on the stir plate. Click on the handle located in the upper right corner of the laboratory to pull down the TV. The TV should already be in *Tutorial* mode and the starting materials and solvent should be listed. From the group of reagents found on the lab bench, select the correct reagent to synthesize the target compound and add it to the flask on the stir plate. Now attach the heater, condenser, and N_2 gas to the round bottom flask so the reaction mixture can be heated.

3. Start the reaction by clicking on the *Stir* button on the front of the stir plate. You should be able to observe the reaction mixture stirring in the flask. Monitor the progress of the reaction using TLC measurements as necessary until the product has formed and the starting materials have been consumed. You can advance the laboratory time using the clock on the wall. With the electronic lab book open (click on the lab book on the lab bench), you can also save your TLC plates by clicking *Save* on the TLC window.

4. When the reaction is complete, "work up" your reaction by first dragging and dropping the separatory funnel (located in a drawer) on the flask and then adding H_2O to the funnel. Extract the organic layer in the funnel by clicking on the top layer and dragging it to the cork ring on the lab bench. Your target compound should now be in this flask.

   *List the starting materials, solvent, reagent, and products formed:*_____

   _____

   How long did it take to finish the reaction? _____

   What are the TLC values (R_f) for (a) Starting Materials: _____ *(b) Products:* _____

   Write a mechanism for this reaction:

Chapter 5

IR and NMR Spectra

After completing a reaction and working up the products, it is still necessary to confirm that the correct product was formed. The most common tools used for this analysis are Infrared (IR) and Nuclear Magnetic Resonance (NMR) spectroscopy. In the virtual laboratory, only ^{1}H NMR spectra are available. Details on interpreting IR and NMR spectra are found in your textbook. Your instructor may or may not ask you to perform this section depending on how your class is structured.

5. To collect an IR spectrum of your product, click on the IR spectrometer located underneath the laboratory clock and drag the salt plate icon to the flask on the lab bench. A window containing the IR spectrum for your product should now open. Identify the relevant peaks in the IR spectrum and record the position and associated functional group for each in the IR table below. The IR spectrum can also be saved to the lab book for later analysis.

IR List position (cm^{-1}) & functional group	4.
1.	5.
2.	6.
3.	7.

6. To collect a ^{1}H NMR spectrum of your product, click on the NMR magnet located to the right of the chalkboard and drag the NMR sample tube to the flask on the lab bench. A window containing the NMR spectrum for your product should now open. You can zoom into various portions of the NMR spectrum by clicking and dragging over the desired area. The *Zoom Out* button is used to zoom back out to view the full spectrum. Identify all of the peaks in the NMR spectrum and record the chemical shift, the splitting, and the number of hydrogens for each peak in the NMR table below. The NMR spectrum can also be saved to the lab book for later analysis.

^{1}H NMR	Peak	Chemical Shift (δ)	Multiplicity[†]	H[‡]	Peak	Chemical Shift (δ)	Multiplicity[†]	H[‡]
	1				7			
Structure:	2				8			
	3				9			
1-Chloro-3-methylbutane	4				10			
	5				11			
	6				12			

[†] Specify the multiplicity as a singlet (s), doublet (d), triplet (t), quartet (q), or multiplet (m).
[‡] Specify the number of hydrogens associated with each peak.

7. *Do the IR and NMR spectra you measured and recorded in the tables above confirm that you synthesized the assigned target compound? Explain.* _____

_____

_____

_____

74

VCL 5-4: Alcohol Dehydration

For this assignment, the target compound that you should synthesize is **cyclohexene.** This is an elimination react. Assess the potential of the possible leaving groups. Keep in mind the mechanism and how that controls the outcome of the process.

Synthesis Procedures

1. Start *Virtual ChemLab* and select *Alcohol Dehydration* from the list of assignments in the electronic workbook. After entering the organic laboratory, go to the stockroom by clicking inside the *Stockroom* window. Next, select a round bottom flask and place it on the cork ring on the stockroom counter. Using the available reagents on the stockroom shelf, identify the appropriate starting materials required to synthesize the target compound and add them to the round bottom flask. Select the appropriate solvent and click on the green *Return to Lab* arrow to return to the laboratory.

2. The round bottom flask containing the starting materials should now be on the stir plate. Click on the handle located in the upper right corner of the laboratory to pull down the TV. The TV should already be in *Tutorial* mode and the starting materials and solvent should be listed. From the group of reagents found on the lab bench, select the correct reagent to synthesize the target compound and add it to the flask on the stir plate. Now attach the heater, condenser, and N_2 gas to the round bottom flask so the reaction mixture can be heated.

3. Start the reaction by clicking on the *Stir* button on the front of the stir plate. You should be able to observe the reaction mixture stirring in the flask. Monitor the progress of the reaction using TLC measurements as necessary until the product has formed and the starting materials have been consumed. You can advance the laboratory time using the clock on the wall. With the electronic lab book open (click on the lab book on the lab bench), you can also save your TLC plates by clicking *Save* on the TLC window.

4. When the reaction is complete, "work up" your reaction by first dragging and dropping the separatory funnel (located in a drawer) on the flask and then adding H_2O to the funnel. Extract the organic layer in the funnel by clicking on the top layer and dragging it to the cork ring on the lab bench. Your target compound should now be in this flask.

   *List the starting materials, solvent, reagent, and products formed:*_____

   _____

   How long did it take to finish the reaction? _____

   What are the TLC values (R_f) for (a) Starting Materials: _____ *(b) Products:* _____

   Write a mechanism for this reaction:

IR and NMR Spectra

After completing a reaction and working up the products, it is still necessary to confirm that the correct product was formed. The most common tools used for this analysis are Infrared (IR) and Nuclear Magnetic Resonance (NMR) spectroscopy. In the virtual laboratory, only ^{1}H NMR spectra are available. Details on interpreting IR and NMR spectra are found in your textbook. Your instructor may or may not ask you to perform this section depending on how your class is structured.

5. To collect an IR spectrum of your product, click on the IR spectrometer located underneath the laboratory clock and drag the salt plate icon to the flask on the lab bench. A window containing the IR spectrum for your product should now open. Identify the relevant peaks in the IR spectrum and record the position and associated functional group for each in the IR table below. The IR spectrum can also be saved to the lab book for later analysis.

IR List position (cm⁻¹) & functional group	4.
1.	5.
2.	6.
3.	7.

6. To collect a ^{1}H NMR spectrum of your product, click on the NMR magnet located to the right of the chalkboard and drag the NMR sample tube to the flask on the lab bench. A window containing the NMR spectrum for your product should now open. You can zoom into various portions of the NMR spectrum by clicking and dragging over the desired area. The *Zoom Out* button is used to zoom back out to view the full spectrum. Identify all of the peaks in the NMR spectrum and record the chemical shift, the splitting, and the number of hydrogens for each peak in the NMR table below. The NMR spectrum can also be saved to the lab book for later analysis.

^{1}H NMR	Peak	Chemical Shift (δ)	Multiplicity[†]	H[‡]	Peak	Chemical Shift (δ)	Multiplicity[†]	H[‡]
Structure:	1				7			
	2				8			
	3				9			
Cyclohexene	4				10			
	5				11			
	6				12			

[†] Specify the multiplicity as a singlet (s), doublet (d), triplet (t), quartet (q), or multiplet (m).
[‡] Specify the number of hydrogens associated with each peak.

7. *Do the IR and NMR spectra you measured and recorded in the tables above confirm that you synthesized the assigned target compound? Explain.* _____

_____

_____

_____

VCL 6-1: Interpreting IR Spectra

Interpreting IR spectra is a skill that often requires some amount of practice, which, in turn, necessitates access to a collection of IR spectra. *Virtual ChemLab* has a spectra library containing more than 700 IR spectra. In this assignment, you will take advantage of this by interpreting the IR spectra of four similar compounds with different functional groups. After completing this assignment, you may wish to select other compounds for additional practice.

1. *Write the IUPAC names for the following four structures:*

2. To obtain the IR spectra of these compounds, start *Virtual ChemLab* and select *Interpreting IR Spectra* from the list of assignments in the electronic workbook or click on the *Organic Chemistry* door. After entering the organic laboratory, pull down the TV by clicking on the TV handle in the upper right-hand corner of the laboratory and then click on the *Spectra* button at the bottom of the TV. It may take up to a minute to load the spectra library. After the spectra library is loaded, you should see a list of all the compounds in the spectra library in alphabetical order by IUPAC name. Mousing over a name in the list will show the structure on the chalkboard. The two buttons on top of the TV are used to select whether the IR or NMR spectra are shown when a compound is selected. Make sure the IR button has been selected.

3. By using the *Up* or *Down* arrows on the TV or dragging the *Scroll Bar*, find the names for the four compounds you have been given and click on the name to display the IR spectrum for each. *Identify the relevant peaks for each of the IR spectra and record the position and associated functional group for each in the IR tables on the next page.*

IR Tables

List position (cm⁻¹) & functional group	4.
1.	5.
2.	6.
3.	7.

List position (cm⁻¹) & functional group	4.
1.	5.
2.	6.
3.	7.

List position (cm⁻¹) & functional group	4.
1.	5.
2.	6.
3.	7.

List position (cm⁻¹) & functional group	4. 900 OH dimer
1.	5.
2.	6.
3.	7.

VCL 6-2: Interpreting NMR Spectra – 1

Interpreting NMR spectra is a skill that often requires some amount of practice, which, in turn, necessitates access to a collection of NMR spectra. *Virtual ChemLab* has a spectra library containing over 700 ^{1}H NMR spectra. In this assignment, you will take advantage of this by first predicting the NMR spectra for two closely related compounds and then checking your predictions by looking up the actual spectra in the spectra library. After completing this assignment, you may wish to select other compounds for additional practice.

1. *Write the IUPAC names for the following two structures:*

    _____

    _____

2. *Predict the NMR spectra for each of these two compounds by listing, in the NMR tables below, the chemical shift, the splitting, and the number of hydrogens associated with each predicted peak. Sort the peaks from largest chemical shift to lowest.*

^{1}H NMR Structure:	Peak	Chemical Shift (δ)	Multiplicity[†]	H[‡]	Peak	Chemical Shift (δ)	Multiplicity[†]	H[‡]
	1				7			
	2				8			
	3				9			
	4				10			
	5				11			
	6				12			

^{1}H NMR Structure:	Peak	Chemical Shift (δ)	Multiplicity[†]	H[‡]	Peak	Chemical Shift (δ)	Multiplicity[†]	H[‡]
	1				7			
	2				8			
	3				9			
	4				10			
	5				11			
	6				12			

[†] Specify the multiplicity as a singlet (s), doublet (d), triplet (t), quartet (q), or multiplet (m).
[‡] Specify the number of hydrogens associated with each peak.

3. To check your predictions, start *Virtual ChemLab* and select *Interpreting NMR Spectra – 1* from the list of assignments in the electronic workbook or click on the *Organic Chemistry* door. After entering the organic laboratory, pull down the TV by clicking on the TV handle in the upper right-hand corner of the laboratory and then click on the *Spectra* button at the bottom of the TV. It may take up to a minute to load the spectra library. After the spectra library is loaded, you should see a list of all the compounds in the spectra library in alphabetical order by IUPAC name. Mousing over a name in the list will show the structure on the chalkboard. The two buttons on top of the TV are used to select whether the IR or NMR spectra are shown when a compound is selected. Click on the NMR button to display the NMR spectra.

4. By using the *Up* or *Down* arrows on the TV or dragging the *Scroll Bar*, find the names for the two compounds you have been given and click on the name to display the NMR spectrum for each. *In the NMR tables below, list the chemical shift, the splitting, and the number of hydrogens associated with each peak for each compound. Compare your answers to your predictions.*

^{1}H NMR Structure:	Peak	Chemical Shift (δ)	Multiplicity[†]	H[‡]	Peak	Chemical Shift (δ)	Multiplicity[†]	H[‡]
	1				7			
	2				8			
	3				9			
	4				10			
	5				11			
	6				12			

^{1}H NMR Structure:	Peak	Chemical Shift (δ)	Multiplicity[†]	H[‡]	Peak	Chemical Shift (δ)	Multiplicity[†]	H[‡]
	1				7			
	2				8			
	3				9			
	4				10			
	5				11			
	6				12			

5. *Using the peak information you listed in the tables for both structures, assign each peak to that portion of the structure that produces the peak in the NMR spectrum.*

VCL 6-3: Interpreting NMR Spectra – 2

Interpreting NMR spectra is a skill that often requires some amount of practice, which, in turn, necessitates access to a collection of NMR spectra. *Virtual ChemLab* has a spectra library containing more than 700 ^{1}H NMR spectra. In this assignment, you will take advantage of this by first predicting the NMR spectra for two closely related compounds and then checking your predictions by looking up the actual spectra in the spectra library. After completing this assignment, you may wish to select other compounds for additional practice.

1. *Write the IUPAC names for the following two structures:*

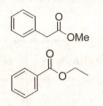

       _____

       _____

2. *Predict the NMR spectra for each of these two compounds by listing, in the NMR tables below, the chemical shift, the splitting, and the number of hydrogens associated with each predicted peak. Sort the peaks from largest chemical shift to lowest.*

^{1}H NMR Structure: (PhCH₂COOMe)	Peak	Chemical Shift (δ)	Multiplicity†	H‡	Peak	Chemical Shift (δ)	Multiplicity†	H‡
	1				7			
	2				8			
	3				9			
	4				10			
	5				11			
	6				12			

^{1}H NMR Structure: (PhCOOEt)	Peak	Chemical Shift (δ)	Multiplicity†	H‡	Peak	Chemical Shift (δ)	Multiplicity†	H‡
	1				7			
	2				8			
	3				9			
	4				10			
	5				11			
	6				12			

† Specify the multiplicity as a singlet (s), doublet (d), triplet (t), quartet (q), or multiplet (m).
‡ Specify the number of hydrogens associated with each peak.

3. To check your predictions, start *Virtual ChemLab* and select *Interpreting NMR Spectra – 2* from the list of assignments in the electronic workbook or click on the *Organic Chemistry* door. After entering the organic laboratory, pull down the TV by clicking on the TV handle in the upper right-hand corner of the laboratory and then click on the *Spectra* button at the bottom of the TV. It may take up to a minute to load the spectra library. After the spectra library is loaded, you should see a list of all the compounds in the spectra library in alphabetical order by IUPAC name. Mousing over a name in the list will show the structure on the chalkboard. The two buttons on top of the TV are used to select whether the IR or NMR spectra are shown when a compound is selected. Click on the NMR button to display the NMR spectra.

4. By using the *Up* or *Down* arrows on the TV or dragging the *Scroll Bar*, find the names for the two compounds you have been given and click on the name to display the NMR spectrum for each. *In the NMR tables below, list the chemical shift, the splitting, and the number of hydrogens associated with each peak for each compound. Compare your answers to your predictions.*

¹H NMR Structure:	Peak	Chemical Shift (δ)	Multiplicity†	H‡	Peak	Chemical Shift (δ)	Multiplicity†	H‡
	1				7			
	2				8			
	3				9			
	4				10			
	5				11			
	6				12			

¹H NMR Structure:	Peak	Chemical Shift (δ)	Multiplicity†	H‡	Peak	Chemical Shift (δ)	Multiplicity†	H‡
	1				7			
	2				8			
	3				9			
	4				10			
	5				11			
	6				12			

5. *Using the peak information you listed in the tables for both structures, assign each peak to that portion of the structure that produces the peak in the NMR spectrum.*

VCL 6-4: Interpreting NMR Spectra – 3

Interpreting NMR spectra is a skill that often requires some amount of practice, which, in turn, necessitates access to a collection of NMR spectra. *Virtual ChemLab* has a spectra library containing more than 700 ^{1}H NMR spectra. In this assignment, you will take advantage of this by first predicting the NMR spectra for two closely related compounds and then checking your predictions by looking up the actual spectra in the spectra library. After completing this assignment, you may wish to select other compounds for additional practice.

1. *Write the IUPAC names for the following two structures:*

    _____

    _____

2. *Predict the NMR spectra for each of these two compounds by listing, in the NMR tables below, the chemical shift, the splitting, and the number of hydrogens associated with each predicted peak. Sort the peaks from largest chemical shift to lowest.*

^{1}H NMR	Peak	Chemical Shift (δ)	Multiplicity†	H‡	Peak	Chemical Shift (δ)	Multiplicity†	H‡
Structure:	1				7			
	2				8			
	3				9			
	4				10			
	5				11			
	6				12			

^{1}H NMR	Peak	Chemical Shift (δ)	Multiplicity†	H‡	Peak	Chemical Shift (δ)	Multiplicity†	H‡
Structure:	1				7			
	2				8			
	3				9			
	4				10			
	5				11			
	6				12			

† Specify the multiplicity as a singlet (s), doublet (d), triplet (t), quartet (q), or multiplet (m).
‡ Specify the number of hydrogens associated with each peak.

3. To check your predictions, start *Virtual ChemLab* and select *Interpreting NMR Spectra – 3* from the list of assignments in the electronic workbook or click on the *Organic Chemistry* door. After entering the organic laboratory, pull down the TV by clicking on the TV handle in the upper right-hand corner of the laboratory and then click on the *Spectra* button at the bottom of the TV. It may take up to a minute to load the spectra library. After the spectra library is loaded, you should see a list of all the compounds in the spectra library in alphabetical order by IUPAC name. Mousing over a name in the list will show the structure on the chalkboard. The two buttons on top of the TV are used to select whether the IR or NMR spectra are shown when a compound is selected. Click on the NMR button to display the NMR spectra.

4. By using the *Up* or *Down* arrows on the TV or dragging the *Scroll Bar*, find the names for the two compounds you have been given and click on the name to display the NMR spectrum for each. *In the NMR tables below, list the chemical shift, the splitting, and the number of hydrogens associated with each peak for each compound. Compare your answers to your predictions.*

¹H NMR Structure:	Peak	Chemical Shift (δ)	Multiplicity†	H‡	Peak	Chemical Shift (δ)	Multiplicity†	H‡
	1				7			
	2				8			
	3				9			
	4				10			
	5				11			
	6				12			

¹H NMR Structure:	Peak	Chemical Shift (δ)	Multiplicity†	H‡	Peak	Chemical Shift (δ)	Multiplicity†	H‡
	1				7			
	2				8			
	3				9			
	4				10			
	5				11			
	6				12			

5. *Using the peak information you listed in the tables for both structures, assign each peak to that portion of the structure that produces the peak in the NMR spectrum.*

VCL 6-5: Interpreting NMR Spectra – 4

Interpreting NMR spectra is a skill that often requires some amount of practice, which, in turn, necessitates access to a collection of NMR spectra. *Virtual ChemLab* has a spectra library containing more than 700 ^{1}H NMR spectra. In this assignment, you will take advantage of this by first predicting the NMR spectra for two closely related compounds and then checking your predictions by looking up the actual spectra in the spectra library. After completing this assignment, you may wish to select other compounds for additional practice.

1. *Write the IUPAC names for the following two structures:*

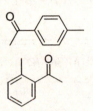

_____

_____

2. *Predict the NMR spectra for each of these two compounds by listing, in the NMR tables below, the chemical shift, the splitting, and the number of hydrogens associated with each predicted peak. Sort the peaks from largest chemical shift to lowest.*

^{1}**H NMR** Structure:	Peak	Chemical Shift (δ)	Multiplicity[†]	H[‡]	Peak	Chemical Shift (δ)	Multiplicity[†]	H[‡]
	1				7			
	2				8			
	3				9			
	4				10			
	5				11			
	6				12			

^{1}**H NMR** Structure:	Peak	Chemical Shift (δ)	Multiplicity[†]	H[‡]	Peak	Chemical Shift (δ)	Multiplicity[†]	H[‡]
	1				7			
	2				8			
	3				9			
	4				10			
	5				11			
	6				12			

[†] Specify the multiplicity as a singlet (s), doublet (d), triplet (t), quartet (q), or multiplet (m).
[‡] Specify the number of hydrogens associated with each peak.

3. To check your predictions, start *Virtual ChemLab* and select *Interpreting NMR Spectra – 4* from the list of assignments in the electronic workbook or click on the *Organic Chemistry* door. After entering the organic laboratory, pull down the TV by clicking on the TV handle in the upper right-hand corner of the laboratory and then click on the *Spectra* button at the bottom of the TV. It may take up to a minute to load the spectra library. After the spectra library is loaded, you should see a list of all the compounds in the spectra library in alphabetical order by IUPAC name. Mousing over a name in the list will show the structure on the chalkboard. The two buttons on top of the TV are used to select whether the IR or NMR spectra are shown when a compound is selected. Click on the NMR button to display the NMR spectra.

4. By using the *Up* or *Down* arrows on the TV or dragging the *Scroll Bar*, find the names for the two compounds you have been given and click on the name to display the NMR spectrum for each. *In the NMR tables below, list the chemical shift, the splitting, and the number of hydrogens associated with each peak for each compound. Compare your answers to your predictions.*

^{1}H NMR	Peak	Chemical Shift (δ)	Multiplicity†	H‡	Peak	Chemical Shift (δ)	Multiplicity†	H‡
Structure:	1				7			
	2				8			
	3				9			
	4				10			
	5				11			
	6				12			

^{1}H NMR	Peak	Chemical Shift (δ)	Multiplicity†	H‡	Peak	Chemical Shift (δ)	Multiplicity†	H‡
Structure:	1				7			
	2				8			
	3				9			
	4				10			
	5				11			
	6				12			

5. *Using the peak information you listed in the tables for both structures, assign each peak to that portion of the structure that produces the peak in the NMR spectrum.*

VCL 7-1: Qualitative Analysis – Alkenes

In this assignment, you will be given an unknown compound for which you will need to determine the chemical structure. This unknown will contain an alkene functional group but may also contain other functional groups as well. The tools you will have available to perform this analysis include 15 functional group tests, IR and NMR spectroscopy, plus other useful data.

1. Start *Virtual ChemLab* and select *Qualitative Analysis – Alkenes* from the list of assignments in the electronic workbook. After entering the organic laboratory, go to the stockroom by clicking inside the *Stockroom* window. Next, select a round bottom flask and place it on the cork ring on the stockroom counter. On the reagent shelf you will find two or more compounds that serve as practice unknowns and another bottle that is your assigned unknown. The practice unknowns can be used to gain proficiency with the functional group tests and IR and NMR spectra interpretation. When you are ready to analyze your unknown, click on the unknown bottle and add it to the round bottom flask. Click on the green *Return to Lab* arrow to return to the laboratory.

2. The round bottom flask containing the unknown should now be on the cork ring on the lab bench. The boiling point and C-H analysis for the unknown are listed on the chalkboard. If the unknown is a solid, the melting point can be measured by clicking on the melting point apparatus by the reagent shelf and dragging the melting point tube to the unknown in the flask. The melting point will be displayed on the red LED, which can be enlarged by mousing over the apparatus. It will also be useful to know the polarity of the unknown by performing a TLC measurement. Record all of this information in the data table below.

Data Table

C-H Analysis	Melting Point (°C)	Boiling Point (°C)	TLC (R_f)

3. To collect an IR spectrum of your unknown, click on the IR spectrometer located underneath the laboratory clock and drag the salt plate icon to the flask on the lab bench. A window containing the IR spectrum for your product should now open. Identify the relevant peaks in the IR spectrum and record the position and associated functional group for each in the IR table below. The IR spectrum can also be saved to the lab book for later analysis.

IR List position (cm^{-1}) & functional group	4.
1.	5.
2.	6.
3.	7.

4. To collect a ^{1}H NMR spectrum of your unknown, click on the NMR magnet located to the right of the chalkboard and drag the NMR sample tube to the flask on the lab bench. A window containing the NMR spectrum for your unknown should now open. You can zoom into various portions of the NMR spectrum by clicking and dragging over the desired area. The *Zoom Out* button is used to zoom back out to view the full spectrum. Identify all of the peaks in the NMR spectrum and record the chemical shift, the splitting, and the number of hydrogens for each peak in the NMR table on the reverse side. The NMR spectrum can also be saved to the lab book for later analysis.

^{1}H NMR	Peak	Chemical Shift (δ)	Multiplicity†	H‡	Peak	Chemical Shift (δ)	Multiplicity†	H‡
	1				7			
	2				8			
	3				9			
	4				10			
	5				11			
	6				12			

† Specify the multiplicity as a singlet (s), doublet (d), triplet (t), quartet (q), or multiplet (m).
‡ Specify the number of hydrogens associated with each peak.

5. To perform the functional group tests, pull down the TV by clicking on the handle located in the upper right-hand corner of the screen. Make sure the TV is in *Tutorial* mode. Next, click on the unknown and drag a test tube containing the unknown to the clamp over the stir plate. You should see a picture of your unknown in the TV. Now perform the bromine test by clicking on the reagent bottle labeled Br$_2$ and drag the pipet to the test tube. The results of the test are shown in the TV with either a picture or a short video clip. Record the results of the test as either positive or negative in the table below. (See your textbook for a description of the functional group tests.) Discard the test tube by dragging it to the red disposal bucket and repeat the procedure for the other functional group tests. Make sure to record all of your results in the table below.

Results for Functional Group Tests

Functional Group Test	+/–	Functional Group Test	+/–
Bromine Test		Iodoform Test	
Permanganate Test		Sodium Hydroxide	
Jones Oxidation Test		Hydroxamate Test	
Lucas Test		Hinsberg Test	
Periodic Acid		Hydrochloric Acid	
Tollens Test		Sodium Iodide/Acetone	
2,4-Dinitrophenylhydrazine		Sodium Iodide/Acetone + Heat	
Sodium Bisulfite Addition			

6. Using the data you have now collected, determine the structure of your unknown compound and report the name and structure below. Be sure to include your unknown number, which is shown on the chalkboard.

Unknown # _____   Name: _____

Structure:

VCL 7-2: Qualitative Analysis – Alcohols

In this assignment, you will be given an unknown compound for which you will need to determine its chemical structure. This unknown will contain an alcohol functional group but may also contain other functional groups as well. The tools you will have available to perform this analysis include 15 functional group tests, IR and NMR spectroscopy, plus other useful data.

1. Start *Virtual ChemLab* and select *Qualitative Analysis – Alcohols* from the list of assignments in the electronic workbook. After entering the organic laboratory, go to the stockroom by clicking inside the *Stockroom* window. Next, select a round bottom flask and place it on the cork ring on the stockroom counter. On the reagent shelf you will find two or more compounds that serve as practice unknowns and another bottle that is your assigned unknown. The practice unknowns can be used to gain proficiency with the functional group tests and IR and NMR spectra interpretation. When you are ready to analyze your unknown, click on the unknown bottle and add it to the round bottom flask. Click on the green *Return to Lab* arrow to return to the laboratory.

2. The round bottom flask containing the unknown should now be on the cork ring on the lab bench. The boiling point and C-H analysis for the unknown are listed on the chalkboard. If the unknown is a solid, the melting point can be measured by clicking on the melting point apparatus by the reagent shelf and dragging the melting point tube to the unknown in the flask. The melting point will be displayed on the red LED, which can be enlarged by mousing over the apparatus. It will also be useful to know the polarity of the unknown by performing a TLC measurement. Record all of this information in the data table below.

Data Table

C-H Analysis	Melting Point (°C)	Boiling Point (°C)	TLC (R_f)

3. To collect an IR spectrum of your unknown, click on the IR spectrometer located underneath the laboratory clock and drag the salt plate icon to the flask on the lab bench. A window containing the IR spectrum for your product should now open. Identify the relevant peaks in the IR spectrum and record the position and associated functional group for each in the IR table below. The IR spectrum can also be saved to the lab book for later analysis.

IR List position (cm^{-1}) & functional group	4.
1.	5.
2.	6.
3.	7.

4. To collect a ^{1}H NMR spectrum of your unknown, click on the NMR magnet located to the right of the chalkboard and drag the NMR sample tube to the flask on the lab bench. A window containing the NMR spectrum for your unknown should now open. You can zoom into various portions of the NMR spectrum by clicking and dragging over the desired area. The *Zoom Out* button is used to zoom back out to view the full spectrum. Identify all of the peaks in the NMR spectrum and record the chemical shift, the splitting, and the number of hydrogens for each peak in the NMR table on the reverse side. The NMR spectrum can also be saved to the lab book for later analysis.

^{1}H NMR	Peak	Chemical Shift (δ)	Multiplicity†	H‡	Peak	Chemical Shift (δ)	Multiplicity†	H‡
	1				7			
	2				8			
	3				9			
	4				10			
	5				11			
	6				12			

† Specify the multiplicity as a singlet (s), doublet (d), triplet (t), quartet (q), or multiplet (m).
‡ Specify the number of hydrogens associated with each peak.

5. To perform the functional group tests, pull down the TV by clicking on the handle located in the upper right-hand corner of the screen. Make sure the TV is in *Tutorial* mode. Next, click on the unknown and drag a test tube containing the unknown to the clamp over the stir plate. You should see a picture of your unknown in the TV. Now perform the bromine test by clicking on the reagent bottle labeled Br$_2$ and drag the pipet to the test tube. The results of the test are shown in the TV with either a picture or a short video clip. Record the results of the test as either positive or negative in the table below. (See your textbook for a description of the functional group tests.) Discard the test tube by dragging it to the red disposal bucket and repeat the procedure for the other functional group tests. Make sure to record all of your results in the table below.

Results for Functional Group Tests

Functional Group Test	+/–	Functional Group Test	+/–
Bromine Test		Iodoform Test	
Permanganate Test		Sodium Hydroxide	
Jones Oxidation Test		Hydroxamate Test	
Lucas Test		Hinsberg Test	
Periodic Acid		Hydrochloric Acid	
Tollens Test		Sodium Iodide/Acetone	
2,4-Dinitrophenylhydrazine		Sodium Iodide/Acetone + Heat	
Sodium Bisulfite Addition			

6. Using the data you have now collected, determine the structure of your unknown compound and report the name and structure below. Be sure to include your unknown number, which is shown on the chalkboard.

Unknown # _____ Name: _____

Structure:

VCL 7-3: Qualitative Analysis – Aldehydes

In this assignment, you will be given an unknown compound for which you will need to determine its chemical structure. This unknown will contain an aldehyde functional group but may also contain other functional groups as well. The tools you will have available to perform this analysis include 15 functional group tests, IR and NMR spectroscopy, plus other useful data.

1. Start *Virtual ChemLab* and select *Qualitative Analysis – Aldehydes* from the list of assignments in the electronic workbook. After entering the organic laboratory, go to the stockroom by clicking inside the *Stockroom* window. Next, select a round bottom flask and place it on the cork ring on the stockroom counter. On the reagent shelf you will find two or more compounds that serve as practice unknowns and another bottle that is your assigned unknown. The practice unknowns can be used to gain proficiency with the functional group tests and IR and NMR spectra interpretation. When you are ready to analyze your unknown, click on the unknown bottle and add it to the round bottom flask. Click on the green *Return to Lab* arrow to return to the laboratory.

2. The round bottom flask containing the unknown should now be on the cork ring on the lab bench. The boiling point and C-H analysis for the unknown are listed on the chalkboard. If the unknown is a solid, the melting point can be measured by clicking on the melting point apparatus by the reagent shelf and dragging the melting point tube to the unknown in the flask. The melting point will be displayed on the red LED, which can be enlarged by mousing over the apparatus. It will also be useful to know the polarity of the unknown by performing a TLC measurement. Record all of this information in the data table below.

Data Table

C-H Analysis	Melting Point (°C)	Boiling Point (°C)	TLC (R_f)

3. To collect an IR spectrum of your unknown, click on the IR spectrometer located underneath the laboratory clock and drag the salt plate icon to the flask on the lab bench. A window containing the IR spectrum for your product should now open. Identify the relevant peaks in the IR spectrum and record the position and associated functional group for each in the IR table below. The IR spectrum can also be saved to the lab book for later analysis.

IR List position (cm^{-1}) & functional group	4.
1.	5.
2.	6.
3.	7.

4. To collect a ^{1}H NMR spectrum of your unknown, click on the NMR magnet located to the right of the chalkboard and drag the NMR sample tube to the flask on the lab bench. A window containing the NMR spectrum for your unknown should now open. You can zoom into various portions of the NMR spectrum by clicking and dragging over the desired area. The *Zoom Out* button is used to zoom back out to view the full spectrum. Identify all of the peaks in the NMR spectrum and record the chemical shift, the splitting, and the number of hydrogens for each peak in the NMR table on the reverse side. The NMR spectrum can also be saved to the lab book for later analysis.

^{1}H NMR	Peak	Chemical Shift (δ)	Multiplicity†	H‡	Peak	Chemical Shift (δ)	Multiplicity†	H‡
	1				7			
	2				8			
	3				9			
	4				10			
	5				11			
	6				12			

† Specify the multiplicity as a singlet (s), doublet (d), triplet (t), quartet (q), or multiplet (m).
‡ Specify the number of hydrogens associated with each peak.

5. To perform the functional group tests, pull down the TV by clicking on the handle located in the upper right-hand corner of the screen. Make sure the TV is in *Tutorial* mode. Next, click on the unknown and drag a test tube containing the unknown to the clamp over the stir plate. You should see a picture of your unknown in the TV. Now perform the bromine test by clicking on the reagent bottle labeled Br$_2$ and drag the pipet to the test tube. The results of the test are shown in the TV with either a picture or a short video clip. Record the results of the test as either positive or negative in the table below. (See your textbook for a description of the functional group tests.) Discard the test tube by dragging it to the red disposal bucket and repeat the procedure for the other functional group tests. Make sure to record all of your results in the table below.

Results for Functional Group Tests

Functional Group Test	+/–	Functional Group Test	+/–
Bromine Test		Iodoform Test	
Permanganate Test		Sodium Hydroxide	
Jones Oxidation Test		Hydroxamate Test	
Lucas Test		Hinsberg Test	
Periodic Acid		Hydrochloric Acid	
Tollens Test		Sodium Iodide/Acetone	
2,4-Dinitrophenylhydrazine		Sodium Iodide/Acetone + Heat	
Sodium Bisulfite Addition			

6. Using the data you have now collected, determine the structure of your unknown compound and report the name and structure below. Be sure to include your unknown number, which is shown on the chalkboard.

Unknown # _____   Name: _____

Structure:

VCL 7-4: Qualitative Analysis – Ketones

In this assignment, you will be given an unknown compound for which you will need to determine the chemical structure. This unknown will contain a ketone functional group but may also contain other functional groups as well. The tools you will have available to perform this analysis include 15 functional group tests, IR and NMR spectroscopy, plus other useful data.

1. Start *Virtual ChemLab* and select *Qualitative Analysis – Ketones* from the list of assignments in the electronic workbook. After entering the organic laboratory, go to the stockroom by clicking inside the *Stockroom* window. Next, select a round bottom flask and place it on the cork ring on the stockroom counter. On the reagent shelf you will find two or more compounds that serve as practice unknowns and another bottle that is your assigned unknown. The practice unknowns can be used to gain proficiency with the functional group tests and IR and NMR spectra interpretation. When you are ready to analyze your unknown, click on the unknown bottle and add it to the round bottom flask. Click on the green *Return to Lab* arrow to return to the laboratory.

2. The round bottom flask containing the unknown should now be on the cork ring on the lab bench. The boiling point and C-H analysis for the unknown are listed on the chalkboard. If the unknown is a solid, the melting point can be measured by clicking on the melting point apparatus by the reagent shelf and dragging the melting point tube to the unknown in the flask. The melting point will be displayed on the red LED, which can be enlarged by mousing over the apparatus. It will also be useful to know the polarity of the unknown by performing a TLC measurement. Record all of this information in the data table below.

Data Table

C-H Analysis	Melting Point (°C)	Boiling Point (°C)	TLC (R_f)

3. To collect an IR spectrum of your unknown, click on the IR spectrometer located underneath the laboratory clock and drag the salt plate icon to the flask on the lab bench. A window containing the IR spectrum for your product should now open. Identify the relevant peaks in the IR spectrum and record the position and associated functional group for each in the IR table below. The IR spectrum can also be saved to the lab book for later analysis.

IR List position (cm^{-1}) & functional group	4.
1.	5.
2.	6.
3.	7.

4. To collect a ^{1}H NMR spectrum of your unknown, click on the NMR magnet located to the right of the chalkboard and drag the NMR sample tube to the flask on the lab bench. A window containing the NMR spectrum for your unknown should now open. You can zoom into various portions of the NMR spectrum by clicking and dragging over the desired area. The *Zoom Out* button is used to zoom back out to view the full spectrum. Identify all of the peaks in the NMR spectrum and record the chemical shift, the splitting, and the number of hydrogens for each peak in the NMR table on the reverse side. The NMR spectrum can also be saved to the lab book for later analysis.

¹H NMR	Peak	Chemical Shift (δ)	Multiplicity†	H‡	Peak	Chemical Shift (δ)	Multiplicity†	H‡
	1				7			
	2				8			
	3				9			
	4				10			
	5				11			
	6				12			

† Specify the multiplicity as a singlet (s), doublet (d), triplet (t), quartet (q), or multiplet (m).
‡ Specify the number of hydrogens associated with each peak.

5. To perform the functional group tests, pull down the TV by clicking on the handle located in the upper right-hand corner of the screen. Make sure the TV is in *Tutorial* mode. Next, click on the unknown and drag a test tube containing the unknown to the clamp over the stir plate. You should see a picture of your unknown in the TV. Now perform the bromine test by clicking on the reagent bottle labeled Br_2 and drag the pipet to the test tube. The results of the test are shown in the TV with either a picture or a short video clip. Record the results of the test as either positive or negative in the table below. (See your textbook for a description of the functional group tests.) Discard the test tube by dragging it to the red disposal bucket and repeat the procedure for the other functional group tests. Make sure to record all of your results in the table below.

Results for Functional Group Tests

Functional Group Test	+/−	Functional Group Test	+/−
Bromine Test		Iodoform Test	
Permanganate Test		Sodium Hydroxide	
Jones Oxidation Test		Hydroxamate Test	
Lucas Test		Hinsberg Test	
Periodic Acid		Hydrochloric Acid	
Tollens Test		Sodium Iodide/Acetone	
2,4-Dinitrophenylhydrazine		Sodium Iodide/Acetone + Heat	
Sodium Bisulfite Addition			

6. Using the data you have now collected, determine the structure of your unknown compound and report the name and structure below. Be sure to include your unknown number, which is shown on the chalkboard.

Unknown # _____   Name: _____

Structure:

VCL 7-5: Qualitative Analysis – Acids

In this assignment, you will be given an unknown compound for which you will need to determine the chemical structure. This unknown will contain an acid functional group but may also contain other functional groups as well. The tools you will have available to perform this analysis include 15 functional group tests, IR and NMR spectroscopy, plus other useful data.

1. Start *Virtual ChemLab* and select *Qualitative Analysis – Acids* from the list of assignments in the electronic workbook. After entering the organic laboratory, go to the stockroom by clicking inside the *Stockroom* window. Next, select a round bottom flask and place it on the cork ring on the stockroom counter. On the reagent shelf you will find two or more compounds that serve as practice unknowns and another bottle that is your assigned unknown. The practice unknowns can be used to gain proficiency with the functional group tests and IR and NMR spectra interpretation. When you are ready to analyze your unknown, click on the unknown bottle and add it to the round bottom flask. Click on the green *Return to Lab* arrow to return to the laboratory.

2. The round bottom flask containing the unknown should now be on the cork ring on the lab bench. The boiling point and C-H analysis for the unknown are listed on the chalkboard. If the unknown is a solid, the melting point can be measured by clicking on the melting point apparatus by the reagent shelf and dragging the melting point tube to the unknown in the flask. The melting point will be displayed on the red LED, which can be enlarged by mousing over the apparatus. It will also be useful to know the polarity of the unknown by performing a TLC measurement. Record all of this information in the data table below.

Data Table

C-H Analysis	Melting Point (°C)	Boiling Point (°C)	TLC (R_f)

3. To collect an IR spectrum of your unknown, click on the IR spectrometer located underneath the laboratory clock and drag the salt plate icon to the flask on the lab bench. A window containing the IR spectrum for your product should now open. Identify the relevant peaks in the IR spectrum and record the position and associated functional group for each in the IR table below. The IR spectrum can also be saved to the lab book for later analysis.

IR List position (cm^{-1}) & functional group	4.
1.	5.
2.	6.
3.	7.

4. To collect a ^{1}H NMR spectrum of your unknown, click on the NMR magnet located to the right of the chalkboard and drag the NMR sample tube to the flask on the lab bench. A window containing the NMR spectrum for your unknown should now open. You can zoom into various portions of the NMR spectrum by clicking and dragging over the desired area. The *Zoom Out* button is used to zoom back out to view the full spectrum. Identify all of the peaks in the NMR spectrum and record the chemical shift, the splitting, and the number of hydrogens for each peak in the NMR table on the reverse side. The NMR spectrum can also be saved to the lab book for later analysis.

^{1}H NMR	Peak	Chemical Shift (δ)	Multiplicity†	H‡	Peak	Chemical Shift (δ)	Multiplicity†	H‡
	1				7			
	2				8			
	3				9			
	4				10			
	5				11			
	6				12			

† Specify the multiplicity as a singlet (s), doublet (d), triplet (t), quartet (q), or multiplet (m).
‡ Specify the number of hydrogens associated with each peak.

5. To perform the functional group tests, pull down the TV by clicking on the handle located in the upper right-hand corner of the screen. Make sure the TV is in *Tutorial* mode. Next, click on the unknown and drag a test tube containing the unknown to the clamp over the stir plate. You should see a picture of your unknown in the TV. Now perform the bromine test by clicking on the reagent bottle labeled Br$_2$ and drag the pipet to the test tube. The results of the test are shown in the TV with either a picture or a short video clip. Record the results of the test as either positive or negative in the table below. (See your textbook for a description of the functional group tests.) Discard the test tube by dragging it to the red disposal bucket and repeat the procedure for the other functional group tests. Make sure to record all of your results in the table below.

Results for Functional Group Tests

Functional Group Test	+/−	Functional Group Test	+/−
Bromine Test		Iodoform Test	
Permanganate Test		Sodium Hydroxide	
Jones Oxidation Test		Hydroxamate Test	
Lucas Test		Hinsberg Test	
Periodic Acid		Hydrochloric Acid	
Tollens Test		Sodium Iodide/Acetone	
2,4-Dinitrophenylhydrazine		Sodium Iodide/Acetone + Heat	
Sodium Bisulfite Addition			

6. Using the data you have now collected, determine the structure of your unknown compound and report the name and structure below. Be sure to include your unknown number, which is shown on the chalkboard.

Unknown # _____   Name: _____

Structure:

VCL 7-6: Qualitative Analysis – Esters

In this assignment, you will be given an unknown compound for which you will need to determine the chemical structure. This unknown will contain an ester functional group but may also contain other functional groups as well. The tools you will have available to perform this analysis include 15 functional group tests, IR and NMR spectroscopy, plus other useful data.

1. Start *Virtual ChemLab* and select *Qualitative Analysis – Esters* from the list of assignments in the electronic workbook. After entering the organic laboratory, go to the stockroom by clicking inside the *Stockroom* window. Next, select a round bottom flask and place it on the cork ring on the stockroom counter. On the reagent shelf you will find two or more compounds that serve as practice unknowns and another bottle that is your assigned unknown. The practice unknowns can be used to gain proficiency with the functional group tests and IR and NMR spectra interpretation. When you are ready to analyze your unknown, click on the unknown bottle and add it to the round bottom flask. Click on the green *Return to Lab* arrow to return to the laboratory.

2. The round bottom flask containing the unknown should now be on the cork ring on the lab bench. The boiling point and C-H analysis for the unknown are listed on the chalkboard. If the unknown is a solid, the melting point can be measured by clicking on the melting point apparatus by the reagent shelf and dragging the melting point tube to the unknown in the flask. The melting point will be displayed on the red LED, which can be enlarged by mousing over the apparatus. It will also be useful to know the polarity of the unknown by performing a TLC measurement. Record all of this information in the data table below.

Data Table

C-H Analysis	Melting Point (°C)	Boiling Point (°C)	TLC (R_f)

3. To collect an IR spectrum of your unknown, click on the IR spectrometer located underneath the laboratory clock and drag the salt plate icon to the flask on the lab bench. A window containing the IR spectrum for your product should now open. Identify the relevant peaks in the IR spectrum and record the position and associated functional group for each in the IR table below. The IR spectrum can also be saved to the lab book for later analysis.

IR List position (cm⁻¹) & functional group	4.
1.	5.
2.	6.
3.	7.

4. To collect a ^{1}H NMR spectrum of your unknown, click on the NMR magnet located to the right of the chalkboard and drag the NMR sample tube to the flask on the lab bench. A window containing the NMR spectrum for your unknown should now open. You can zoom into various portions of the NMR spectrum by clicking and dragging over the desired area. The *Zoom Out* button is used to zoom back out to view the full spectrum. Identify all of the peaks in the NMR spectrum and record the chemical shift, the splitting, and the number of hydrogens for each peak in the NMR table on the reverse side. The NMR spectrum can also be saved to the lab book for later analysis.

^{1}H NMR	Peak	Chemical Shift (δ)	Multiplicity†	H‡	Peak	Chemical Shift (δ)	Multiplicity†	H‡
	1				7			
	2				8			
	3				9			
	4				10			
	5				11			
	6				12			

† Specify the multiplicity as a singlet (s), doublet (d), triplet (t), quartet (q), or multiplet (m).
‡ Specify the number of hydrogens associated with each peak.

5. To perform the functional group tests, pull down the TV by clicking on the handle located in the upper right-hand corner of the screen. Make sure the TV is in *Tutorial* mode. Next, click on the unknown and drag a test tube containing the unknown to the clamp over the stir plate. You should see a picture of your unknown in the TV. Now perform the bromine test by clicking on the reagent bottle labeled Br$_2$ and drag the pipet to the test tube. The results of the test are shown in the TV with either a picture or a short video clip. Record the results of the test as either positive or negative in the table below. (See your textbook for a description of the functional group tests.) Discard the test tube by dragging it to the red disposal bucket and repeat the procedure for the other functional group tests. Make sure to record all of your results in the table below.

Results for Functional Group Tests

Functional Group Test	+/–	Functional Group Test	+/–
Bromine Test		Iodoform Test	
Permanganate Test		Sodium Hydroxide	
Jones Oxidation Test		Hydroxamate Test	
Lucas Test		Hinsberg Test	
Periodic Acid		Hydrochloric Acid	
Tollens Test		Sodium Iodide/Acetone	
2,4-Dinitrophenylhydrazine		Sodium Iodide/Acetone + Heat	
Sodium Bisulfite Addition			

6. Using the data you have now collected, determine the structure of your unknown compound and report the name and structure below. Be sure to include your unknown number, which is shown on the chalkboard.

Unknown # _____   Name: _____

Structure:

VCL 7-7: Qualitative Analysis – Amines

In this assignment, you will be given an unknown compound for which you will need to determine the chemical structure. This unknown will contain an amine functional group but may also contain other functional groups as well. The tools you will have available to perform this analysis include 15 functional group tests, IR and NMR spectroscopy, plus other useful data.

1. Start *Virtual ChemLab* and select *Qualitative Analysis – Amines* from the list of assignments in the electronic workbook. After entering the organic laboratory, go to the stockroom by clicking inside the *Stockroom* window. Next, select a round bottom flask and place it on the cork ring on the stockroom counter. On the reagent shelf you will find two or more compounds that serve as practice unknowns and another bottle that is your assigned unknown. The practice unknowns can be used to gain proficiency with the functional group tests and IR and NMR spectra interpretation. When you are ready to analyze your unknown, click on the unknown bottle and add it to the round bottom flask. Click on the green *Return to Lab* arrow to return to the laboratory.

2. The round bottom flask containing the unknown should now be on the cork ring on the lab bench. The boiling point and C-H analysis for the unknown are listed on the chalkboard. If the unknown is a solid, the melting point can be measured by clicking on the melting point apparatus by the reagent shelf and dragging the melting point tube to the unknown in the flask. The melting point will be displayed on the red LED, which can be enlarged by mousing over the apparatus. It will also be useful to know the polarity of the unknown by performing a TLC measurement. Record all of this information in the data table below.

Data Table

C-H Analysis	Melting Point (°C)	Boiling Point (°C)	TLC (R_f)

3. To collect an IR spectrum of your unknown, click on the IR spectrometer located underneath the laboratory clock and drag the salt plate icon to the flask on the lab bench. A window containing the IR spectrum for your product should now open. Identify the relevant peaks in the IR spectrum and record the position and associated functional group for each in the IR table below. The IR spectrum can also be saved to the lab book for later analysis.

IR List position (cm^{-1}) & functional group	4.
1.	5.
2.	6.
3.	7.

4. To collect a ^{1}H NMR spectrum of your unknown, click on the NMR magnet located to the right of the chalkboard and drag the NMR sample tube to the flask on the lab bench. A window containing the NMR spectrum for your unknown should now open. You can zoom into various portions of the NMR spectrum by clicking and dragging over the desired area. The *Zoom Out* button is used to zoom back out to view the full spectrum. Identify all of the peaks in the NMR spectrum and record the chemical shift, the splitting, and the number of hydrogens for each peak in the NMR table on the reverse side. The NMR spectrum can also be saved to the lab book for later analysis.

¹H NMR	Peak	Chemical Shift (δ)	Multiplicity†	H‡	Peak	Chemical Shift (δ)	Multiplicity†	H‡
	1				7			
	2				8			
	3				9			
	4				10			
	5				11			
	6				12			

† Specify the multiplicity as a singlet (s), doublet (d), triplet (t), quartet (q), or multiplet (m).
‡ Specify the number of hydrogens associated with each peak.

5. To perform the functional group tests, pull down the TV by clicking on the handle located in the upper right-hand corner of the screen. Make sure the TV is in *Tutorial* mode. Next, click on the unknown and drag a test tube containing the unknown to the clamp over the stir plate. You should see a picture of your unknown in the TV. Now perform the bromine test by clicking on the reagent bottle labeled Br_2 and drag the pipet to the test tube. The results of the test are shown in the TV with either a picture or a short video clip. Record the results of the test as either positive or negative in the table below. (See your textbook for a description of the functional group tests.) Discard the test tube by dragging it to the red disposal bucket and repeat the procedure for the other functional group tests. Make sure to record all of your results in the table below.

Results for Functional Group Tests

Functional Group Test	+/–	Functional Group Test	+/–
Bromine Test		Iodoform Test	
Permanganate Test		Sodium Hydroxide	
Jones Oxidation Test		Hydroxamate Test	
Lucas Test		Hinsberg Test	
Periodic Acid		Hydrochloric Acid	
Tollens Test		Sodium Iodide/Acetone	
2,4-Dinitrophenylhydrazine		Sodium Iodide/Acetone + Heat	
Sodium Bisulfite Addition			

6. Using the data you have now collected, determine the structure of your unknown compound and report the name and structure below. Be sure to include your unknown number, which is shown on the chalkboard.

Unknown # _____   Name: _____

Structure:

VCL 7-8: Qualitative Analysis – Amides

In this assignment, you will be given an unknown compound for which you will need to determine the chemical structure. This unknown will contain an amide functional group but may also contain other functional groups as well. The tools you will have available to perform this analysis include 15 functional group tests, IR and NMR spectroscopy, plus other useful data.

1. Start *Virtual ChemLab* and select *Qualitative Analysis – Amides* from the list of assignments in the electronic workbook. After entering the organic laboratory, go to the stockroom by clicking inside the *Stockroom* window. Next, select a round bottom flask and place it on the cork ring on the stockroom counter. On the reagent shelf you will find two or more compounds that serve as practice unknowns and another bottle that is your assigned unknown. The practice unknowns can be used to gain proficiency with the functional group tests and IR and NMR spectra interpretation. When you are ready to analyze your unknown, click on the unknown bottle and add it to the round bottom flask. Click on the green *Return to Lab* arrow to return to the laboratory.

2. The round bottom flask containing the unknown should now be on the cork ring on the lab bench. The boiling point and C-H analysis for the unknown are listed on the chalkboard. If the unknown is a solid, the melting point can be measured by clicking on the melting point apparatus by the reagent shelf and dragging the melting point tube to the unknown in the flask. The melting point will be displayed on the red LED, which can be enlarged by mousing over the apparatus. It will also be useful to know the polarity of the unknown by performing a TLC measurement. Record all of this information in the data table below.

Data Table

C-H Analysis	Melting Point (°C)	Boiling Point (°C)	TLC (R_f)

3. To collect an IR spectrum of your unknown, click on the IR spectrometer located underneath the laboratory clock and drag the salt plate icon to the flask on the lab bench. A window containing the IR spectrum for your product should now open. Identify the relevant peaks in the IR spectrum and record the position and associated functional group for each in the IR table below. The IR spectrum can also be saved to the lab book for later analysis.

IR List position (cm^{-1}) & functional group	4.
1.	5.
2.	6.
3.	7.

4. To collect a ^{1}H NMR spectrum of your unknown, click on the NMR magnet located to the right of the chalkboard and drag the NMR sample tube to the flask on the lab bench. A window containing the NMR spectrum for your unknown should now open. You can zoom into various portions of the NMR spectrum by clicking and dragging over the desired area. The *Zoom Out* button is used to zoom back out to view the full spectrum. Identify all of the peaks in the NMR spectrum and record the chemical shift, the splitting, and the number of hydrogens for each peak in the NMR table on the reverse side. The NMR spectrum can also be saved to the lab book for later analysis.

¹H NMR	Peak	Chemical Shift (δ)	Multiplicity†	H‡	Peak	Chemical Shift (δ)	Multiplicity†	H‡
	1				7			
	2				8			
	3				9			
	4				10			
	5				11			
	6				12			

† Specify the multiplicity as a singlet (s), doublet (d), triplet (t), quartet (q), or multiplet (m).
‡ Specify the number of hydrogens associated with each peak.

5. To perform the functional group tests, pull down the TV by clicking on the handle located in the upper right-hand corner of the screen. Make sure the TV is in *Tutorial* mode. Next, click on the unknown and drag a test tube containing the unknown to the clamp over the stir plate. You should see a picture of your unknown in the TV. Now perform the bromine test by clicking on the reagent bottle labeled Br_2 and drag the pipet to the test tube. The results of the test are shown in the TV with either a picture or a short video clip. Record the results of the test as either positive or negative in the table below. (See your textbook for a description of the functional group tests.) Discard the test tube by dragging it to the red disposal bucket and repeat the procedure for the other functional group tests. Make sure to record all of your results in the table below.

Results for Functional Group Tests

Functional Group Test	+/–	Functional Group Test	+/–
Bromine Test		Iodoform Test	
Permanganate Test		Sodium Hydroxide	
Jones Oxidation Test		Hydroxamate Test	
Lucas Test		Hinsberg Test	
Periodic Acid		Hydrochloric Acid	
Tollens Test		Sodium Iodide/Acetone	
2,4-Dinitrophenylhydrazine		Sodium Iodide/Acetone + Heat	
Sodium Bisulfite Addition			

6. Using the data you have now collected, determine the structure of your unknown compound and report the name and structure below. Be sure to include your unknown number, which is shown on the chalkboard.

Unknown # _____   Name: _____

Structure:

VCL 7-9: Qualitative Analysis – Halides

In this assignment, you will be given an unknown compound for which you will need to determine the chemical structure. This unknown will contain a halide functional group but may also contain other functional groups as well. The tools you will have available to perform this analysis include 15 functional group tests, IR and NMR spectroscopy, plus other useful data.

1. Start *Virtual ChemLab* and select *Qualitative Analysis – Halides* from the list of assignments in the electronic workbook. After entering the organic laboratory, go to the stockroom by clicking inside the *Stockroom* window. Next, select a round bottom flask and place it on the cork ring on the stockroom counter. On the reagent shelf you will find two or more compounds that serve as practice unknowns and another bottle that is your assigned unknown. The practice unknowns can be used to gain proficiency with the functional group tests and IR and NMR spectra interpretation. When you are ready to analyze your unknown, click on the unknown bottle and add it to the round bottom flask. Click on the green *Return to Lab* arrow to return to the laboratory.

2. The round bottom flask containing the unknown should now be on the cork ring on the lab bench. The boiling point and C-H analysis for the unknown are listed on the chalkboard. If the unknown is a solid, the melting point can be measured by clicking on the melting point apparatus by the reagent shelf and dragging the melting point tube to the unknown in the flask. The melting point will be displayed on the red LED, which can be enlarged by mousing over the apparatus. It will also be useful to know the polarity of the unknown by performing a TLC measurement. Record all of this information in the data table below.

Data Table

C-H Analysis	Melting Point (°C)	Boiling Point (°C)	TLC (R_f)

3. To collect an IR spectrum of your unknown, click on the IR spectrometer located underneath the laboratory clock and drag the salt plate icon to the flask on the lab bench. A window containing the IR spectrum for your product should now open. Identify the relevant peaks in the IR spectrum and record the position and associated functional group for each in the IR table below. The IR spectrum can also be saved to the lab book for later analysis.

IR List position (cm^{-1}) & functional group	4.
1.	5.
2.	6.
3.	7.

4. To collect a ^{1}H NMR spectrum of your unknown, click on the NMR magnet located to the right of the chalkboard and drag the NMR sample tube to the flask on the lab bench. A window containing the NMR spectrum for your unknown should now open. You can zoom into various portions of the NMR spectrum by clicking and dragging over the desired area. The *Zoom Out* button is used to zoom back out to view the full spectrum. Identify all of the peaks in the NMR spectrum and record the chemical shift, the splitting, and the number of hydrogens for each peak in the NMR table on the reverse side. The NMR spectrum can also be saved to the lab book for later analysis.

^{1}H NMR	Peak	Chemical Shift (δ)	Multiplicity†	H‡	Peak	Chemical Shift (δ)	Multiplicity†	H‡
	1				7			
	2				8			
	3				9			
	4				10			
	5				11			
	6				12			

† Specify the multiplicity as a singlet (s), doublet (d), triplet (t), quartet (q), or multiplet (m).
‡ Specify the number of hydrogens associated with each peak.

5. To perform the functional group tests, pull down the TV by clicking on the handle located in the upper right-hand corner of the screen. Make sure the TV is in *Tutorial* mode. Next, click on the unknown and drag a test tube containing the unknown to the clamp over the stir plate. You should see a picture of your unknown in the TV. Now perform the bromine test by clicking on the reagent bottle labeled Br$_2$ and drag the pipet to the test tube. The results of the test are shown in the TV with either a picture or a short video clip. Record the results of the test as either positive or negative in the table below. (See your textbook for a description of the functional group tests.) Discard the test tube by dragging it to the red disposal bucket and repeat the procedure for the other functional group tests. Make sure to record all of your results in the table below.

Results for Functional Group Tests

Functional Group Test	+/−	Functional Group Test	+/−
Bromine Test		Iodoform Test	
Permanganate Test		Sodium Hydroxide	
Jones Oxidation Test		Hydroxamate Test	
Lucas Test		Hinsberg Test	
Periodic Acid		Hydrochloric Acid	
Tollens Test		Sodium Iodide/Acetone	
2,4-Dinitrophenylhydrazine		Sodium Iodide/Acetone + Heat	
Sodium Bisulfite Addition			

6. Using the data you have now collected, determine the structure of your unknown compound and report the name and structure below. Be sure to include your unknown number, which is shown on the chalkboard.

Unknown # _____   Name: _____

    Structure:

VCL 7-10: Qualitative Analysis – Ethers

In this assignment, you will be given an unknown compound for which you will need to determine the chemical structure. This unknown will contain an ether functional group but may also contain other functional groups as well. The tools you will have available to perform this analysis include 15 functional group tests, IR and NMR spectroscopy, plus other useful data.

1. Start *Virtual ChemLab* and select *Qualitative Analysis – Ethers* from the list of assignments in the electronic workbook. After entering the organic laboratory, go to the stockroom by clicking inside the *Stockroom* window. Next, select a round bottom flask and place it on the cork ring on the stockroom counter. On the reagent shelf you will find two or more compounds that serve as practice unknowns and another bottle that is your assigned unknown. The practice unknowns can be used to gain proficiency with the functional group tests and IR and NMR spectra interpretation. When you are ready to analyze your unknown, click on the unknown bottle and add it to the round bottom flask. Click on the green *Return to Lab* arrow to return to the laboratory.

2. The round bottom flask containing the unknown should now be on the cork ring on the lab bench. The boiling point and C-H analysis for the unknown are listed on the chalkboard. If the unknown is a solid, the melting point can be measured by clicking on the melting point apparatus by the reagent shelf and dragging the melting point tube to the unknown in the flask. The melting point will be displayed on the red LED, which can be enlarged by mousing over the apparatus. It will also be useful to know the polarity of the unknown by performing a TLC measurement. Record all of this information in the data table below.

Data Table

C-H Analysis	Melting Point (°C)	Boiling Point (°C)	TLC (R_f)

3. To collect an IR spectrum of your unknown, click on the IR spectrometer located underneath the laboratory clock and drag the salt plate icon to the flask on the lab bench. A window containing the IR spectrum for your product should now open. Identify the relevant peaks in the IR spectrum and record the position and associated functional group for each in the IR table below. The IR spectrum can also be saved to the lab book for later analysis.

IR List position (cm^{-1}) & functional group	4.
1.	5.
2.	6.
3.	7.

4. To collect a ^{1}H NMR spectrum of your unknown, click on the NMR magnet located to the right of the chalkboard and drag the NMR sample tube to the flask on the lab bench. A window containing the NMR spectrum for your unknown should now open. You can zoom into various portions of the NMR spectrum by clicking and dragging over the desired area. The *Zoom Out* button is used to zoom back out to view the full spectrum. Identify all of the peaks in the NMR spectrum and record the chemical shift, the splitting, and the number of hydrogens for each peak in the NMR table on the reverse side. The NMR spectrum can also be saved to the lab book for later analysis.

^{1}H NMR	Peak	Chemical Shift (δ)	Multiplicity[†]	H[‡]	Peak	Chemical Shift (δ)	Multiplicity[†]	H[‡]
	1				7			
	2				8			
	3				9			
	4				10			
	5				11			
	6				12			

[†] Specify the multiplicity as a singlet (s), doublet (d), triplet (t), quartet (q), or multiplet (m).
[‡] Specify the number of hydrogens associated with each peak.

5. To perform the functional group tests, pull down the TV by clicking on the handle located in the upper right-hand corner of the screen. Make sure the TV is in *Tutorial* mode. Next, click on the unknown and drag a test tube containing the unknown to the clamp over the stir plate. You should see a picture of your unknown in the TV. Now perform the bromine test by clicking on the reagent bottle labeled Br_2 and drag the pipet to the test tube. The results of the test are shown in the TV with either a picture or a short video clip. Record the results of the test as either positive or negative in the table below. (See your textbook for a description of the functional group tests.) Discard the test tube by dragging it to the red disposal bucket and repeat the procedure for the other functional group tests. Make sure to record all of your results in the table below.

Results for Functional Group Tests

Functional Group Test	+/–	Functional Group Test	+/–
Bromine Test		Iodoform Test	
Permanganate Test		Sodium Hydroxide	
Jones Oxidation Test		Hydroxamate Test	
Lucas Test		Hinsberg Test	
Periodic Acid		Hydrochloric Acid	
Tollens Test		Sodium Iodide/Acetone	
2,4-Dinitrophenylhydrazine		Sodium Iodide/Acetone + Heat	
Sodium Bisulfite Addition			

6. Using the data you have now collected, determine the structure of your unknown compound and report the name and structure below. Be sure to include your unknown number, which is shown on the chalkboard.

Unknown # _____   Name: _____

Structure:

VCL 7-11: Qualitative Analysis – General

In this assignment, you will be given an unknown compound for which you will need to determine the chemical structure. This unknown is a general unknown and can contain a single functional group or a combination of several functional groups. The tools you will have available to perform this analysis include 15 functional group tests, IR and NMR spectroscopy, plus other useful data.

1. Start *Virtual ChemLab* and select *Qualitative Analysis – General* from the list of assignments in the electronic workbook. After entering the organic laboratory, go to the stockroom by clicking inside the *Stockroom* window. Next, select a round bottom flask and place it on the cork ring on the stockroom counter. On the reagent shelf you will find a single labeled bottle containing your unknown. When you are ready to analyze your unknown, click on the unknown bottle and add it to the round bottom flask. Click on the green *Return to Lab* arrow to return to the laboratory.

2. The round bottom flask containing the unknown should now be on the cork ring on the lab bench. The boiling point and C-H analysis for the unknown are listed on the chalkboard. If the unknown is a solid, the melting point can be measured by clicking on the melting point apparatus by the reagent shelf and dragging the melting point tube to the unknown in the flask. The melting point will be displayed on the red LED, which can be enlarged by mousing over the apparatus. It will also be useful to know the polarity of the unknown by performing a TLC measurement. Record all of this information in the data table below.

Data Table

C-H Analysis	Melting Point (°C)	Boiling Point (°C)	TLC (R_f)

3. To collect an IR spectrum of your unknown, click on the IR spectrometer located underneath the laboratory clock and drag the salt plate icon to the flask on the lab bench. A window containing the IR spectrum for your product should now open. Identify the relevant peaks in the IR spectrum and record the position and associated functional group for each in the IR table below. The IR spectrum can also be saved to the lab book for later analysis.

IR List position (cm^{-1}) & functional group	4.
1.	5.
2.	6.
3.	7.

4. To collect a ^{1}H NMR spectrum of your unknown, click on the NMR magnet located to the right of the chalkboard and drag the NMR sample tube to the flask on the lab bench. A window containing the NMR spectrum for your unknown should now open. You can zoom into various portions of the NMR spectrum by clicking and dragging over the desired area. The *Zoom Out* button is used to zoom back out to view the full spectrum. Identify all of the peaks in the NMR spectrum and record the chemical shift, the splitting, and the number of hydrogens for each peak in the NMR table on the reverse side. The NMR spectrum can also be saved to the lab book for later analysis.

^{1}H NMR	Peak	Chemical Shift (δ)	Multiplicity†	H‡	Peak	Chemical Shift (δ)	Multiplicity†	H‡
	1				7			
	2				8			
	3				9			
	4				10			
	5				11			
	6				12			

† Specify the multiplicity as a singlet (s), doublet (d), triplet (t), quartet (q), or multiplet (m).
‡ Specify the number of hydrogens associated with each peak.

5. To perform the functional group tests, pull down the TV by clicking on the handle located in the upper right-hand corner of the screen. Make sure the TV is in *Tutorial* mode. Next, click on the unknown and drag a test tube containing the unknown to the clamp over the stir plate. You should see a picture of your unknown in the TV. Now perform the bromine test by clicking on the reagent bottle labeled Br_2 and drag the pipet to the test tube. The results of the test are shown in the TV with either a picture or a short video clip. Record the results of the test as either positive or negative in the table below. (See your textbook for a description of the functional group tests.) Discard the test tube by dragging it to the red disposal bucket and repeat the procedure for the other functional group tests. Make sure to record all of your results in the table below.

Results for Functional Group Tests

Functional Group Test	+/–	Functional Group Test	+/–
Bromine Test		Iodoform Test	
Permanganate Test		Sodium Hydroxide	
Jones Oxidation Test		Hydroxamate Test	
Lucas Test		Hinsberg Test	
Periodic Acid		Hydrochloric Acid	
Tollens Test		Sodium Iodide/Acetone	
2,4-Dinitrophenylhydrazine		Sodium Iodide/Acetone + Heat	
Sodium Bisulfite Addition			

6. Using the data you have now collected, determine the structure of your unknown compound and report the name and structure below. Be sure to include your unknown number, which is shown on the chalkboard.

Unknown # _____   Name: _____

Structure:

VCL 8-1: Benzene Nitration – 1

For this assignment, the target compound that you should synthesize is **3-nitro-benzaldehyde.** This is an electrophilic aromatic substitution reaction. Examine the product carefully and determine the substitution pattern. Which group will already be present in the substrate? Keep in mind the mechanism and how that will control the selectivity of the process.

Synthesis Procedures

1. Start *Virtual ChemLab* and select *Benzene Nitration – 1* from the list of assignments in the electronic workbook. After entering the organic laboratory, go to the stockroom by clicking inside the *Stockroom* window. Next, select a round bottom flask and place it on the cork ring on the stockroom counter. Using the available reagents on the stockroom shelf, identify the appropriate starting materials required to synthesize the target compound and add them to the round bottom flask. Select the appropriate solvent and click on the green *Return to Lab* arrow to return to the laboratory.

2. The round bottom flask containing the starting materials should now be on the stir plate. Click on the handle located in the upper right corner of the laboratory to pull down the TV. The TV should already be in *Tutorial* mode and the starting materials and solvent should be listed. From the group of reagents found on the lab bench, select the correct reagent to synthesize the target compound and add it to the flask on the stir plate. Now attach the heater, condenser, and N_2 gas to the round bottom flask so the reaction mixture can be heated.

3. Start the reaction by clicking on the *Stir* button on the front of the stir plate. You should be able to observe the reaction mixture stirring in the flask. Monitor the progress of the reaction using TLC measurements as necessary until the product has formed and the starting materials have been consumed. You can advance the laboratory time using the clock on the wall. With the electronic lab book open (click on the lab book on the lab bench), you can also save your TLC plates by clicking *Save* on the TLC window.

4. When the reaction is complete, "work up" your reaction by first dragging and dropping the separatory funnel (located in a drawer) on the flask and then adding H_2O to the funnel. Extract the organic layer in the funnel by clicking on the top layer and dragging it to the cork ring on the lab bench. Your target compound should now be in this flask.

    List the starting materials, solvent, reagent, and products formed: _____

    _____

    How long did it take to finish the reaction? _____

    What are the TLC values (R$_f$) for (a) Starting Materials: _____ (b) Products: _____

    Write a mechanism for this reaction:

IR and NMR Spectra

After completing a reaction and working up the products, it is still necessary to confirm that the correct product was formed. The most common tools used for this analysis are Infrared (IR) and Nuclear Magnetic Resonance (NMR) spectroscopy. In the virtual laboratory, only ^{1}H NMR spectra are available. Details on interpreting IR and NMR spectra are found in your textbook. Your instructor may or may not ask you to perform this section depending on how your class is structured.

5. To collect an IR spectrum of your product, click on the IR spectrometer located underneath the laboratory clock and drag the salt plate icon to the flask on the lab bench. A window containing the IR spectrum for your product should now open. Identify the relevant peaks in the IR spectrum and record the position and associated functional group for each in the IR table below. The IR spectrum can also be saved to the lab book for later analysis.

IR List position (cm^{-1}) & functional group	4.
1.	5.
2.	6.
3.	7.

6. To collect a ^{1}H NMR spectrum of your product, click on the NMR magnet located to the right of the chalkboard and drag the NMR sample tube to the flask on the lab bench. A window containing the NMR spectrum for your product should now open. You can zoom into various portions of the NMR spectrum by clicking and dragging over the desired area. The *Zoom Out* button is used to zoom back out to view the full spectrum. Identify all of the peaks in the NMR spectrum and record the chemical shift, the splitting, and the number of hydrogens for each peak in the NMR table below. The NMR spectrum can also be saved to the lab book for later analysis.

^{1}H NMR	Peak	Chemical Shift (δ)	Multiplicity†	H‡	Peak	Chemical Shift (δ)	Multiplicity†	H‡
Structure:	1				7			
	2				8			
O₂N ... H	3				9			
	4				10			
3-Nitro-benzaldehyde	5				11			
	6				12			

† Specify the multiplicity as a singlet (s), doublet (d), triplet (t), quartet (q), or multiplet (m).
‡ Specify the number of hydrogens associated with each peak.

7. *Do the IR and NMR spectra you measured and recorded in the tables above confirm that you*

synthesized the assigned target compound? Explain. _____

_____

_____

VCL 8-2: Benzene Nitration – 2

For this assignment, the target compound that you should synthesize is **1-methyl-4-nitro-benzene.** This is an electrophilic aromatic substitution reaction. Examine the product carefully and determine the substitution pattern. Which group will already be present in the substrate? Keep in mind the mechanism and how that will control the selectivity of the process. Remember, you can easily separate ortho and para isomers.

Synthesis Procedures

1. Start *Virtual ChemLab* and select *Benzene Nitration – 2* from the list of assignments in the electronic workbook. After entering the organic laboratory, go to the stockroom by clicking inside the *Stockroom* window. Next, select a round bottom flask and place it on the cork ring on the stockroom counter. Using the available reagents on the stockroom shelf, identify the appropriate starting materials required to synthesize the target compound and add them to the round bottom flask. Select the appropriate solvent and click on the green *Return to Lab* arrow to return to the laboratory.

2. The round bottom flask containing the starting materials should now be on the stir plate. Click on the handle located in the upper right corner of the laboratory to pull down the TV. The TV should already be in *Tutorial* mode and the starting materials and solvent should be listed. From the group of reagents found on the lab bench, select the correct reagent to synthesize the target compound and add it to the flask on the stir plate. Now attach the heater, condenser, and N_2 gas to the round bottom flask so the reaction mixture can be heated.

3. Start the reaction by clicking on the *Stir* button on the front of the stir plate. You should be able to observe the reaction mixture stirring in the flask. Monitor the progress of the reaction using TLC measurements as necessary until the product has formed and the starting materials have been consumed. You can advance the laboratory time using the clock on the wall. With the electronic lab book open (click on the lab book on the lab bench), you can also save your TLC plates by clicking *Save* on the TLC window.

4. When the reaction is complete, "work up" your reaction by first dragging and dropping the separatory funnel (located in a drawer) on the flask and then adding H_2O to the funnel. Extract the organic layer in the funnel by clicking on the top layer and dragging it to the cork ring on the lab bench. Your target compound should now be in this flask.

    List the starting materials, solvent, reagent, and products formed: _____

    _____

    How long did it take to finish the reaction? _____

    What are the TLC values (R_f) for (a) Starting Materials: _____ *(b) Products:* _____

    Write a mechanism for this reaction:

IR and NMR Spectra

After completing a reaction and working up the products, it is still necessary to confirm that the correct product was formed. The most common tools used for this analysis are Infrared (IR) and Nuclear Magnetic Resonance (NMR) spectroscopy. In the virtual laboratory, only ^{1}H NMR spectra are available. Details on interpreting IR and NMR spectra are found in your textbook. Your instructor may or may not ask you to perform this section depending on how your class is structured.

5. To collect an IR spectrum of your product, click on the IR spectrometer located underneath the laboratory clock and drag the salt plate icon to the flask on the lab bench. A window containing the IR spectrum for your product should now open. Identify the relevant peaks in the IR spectrum and record the position and associated functional group for each in the IR table below. The IR spectrum can also be saved to the lab book for later analysis.

IR List position (cm^{-1}) & functional group	4.
1.	5.
2.	6.
3.	7.

6. To collect a ^{1}H NMR spectrum of your product, click on the NMR magnet located to the right of the chalkboard and drag the NMR sample tube to the flask on the lab bench. A window containing the NMR spectrum for your product should now open. You can zoom into various portions of the NMR spectrum by clicking and dragging over the desired area. The *Zoom Out* button is used to zoom back out to view the full spectrum. Identify all of the peaks in the NMR spectrum and record the chemical shift, the splitting, and the number of hydrogens for each peak in the NMR table below. The NMR spectrum can also be saved to the lab book for later analysis.

^{1}H NMR Structure: O$_2$N—⟨benzene ring⟩— 1-Methyl-4-nitro-benzene	Peak	Chemical Shift (δ)	Multiplicity[†]	H[‡]	Peak	Chemical Shift (δ)	Multiplicity[†]	H[‡]
	1				7			
	2				8			
	3				9			
	4				10			
	5				11			
	6				12			

[†] Specify the multiplicity as a singlet (s), doublet (d), triplet (t), quartet (q), or multiplet (m).
[‡] Specify the number of hydrogens associated with each peak.

7. *Do the IR and NMR spectra you measured and recorded in the tables above confirm that you synthesized the assigned target compound? Explain.* _____

_____

_____

_____

VCL 8-3: Benzene Nitration – 3

For this assignment, the target compound that you should synthesize is **1-methyl-2-nitro-benzene.** This is an electrophilic aromatic substitution reaction. Examine the product carefully and determine the substitution pattern. Which group will already be present in the substrate? Keep in mind the mechanism and how that will control the selectivity of the process. Remember, you can easily separate ortho and para isomers.

Synthesis Procedures

1. Start *Virtual ChemLab* and select *Benzene Nitration – 3* from the list of assignments in the electronic workbook. After entering the organic laboratory, go to the stockroom by clicking inside the *Stockroom* window. Next, select a round bottom flask and place it on the cork ring on the stockroom counter. Using the available reagents on the stockroom shelf, identify the appropriate starting materials required to synthesize the target compound and add them to the round bottom flask. Select the appropriate solvent and click on the green *Return to Lab* arrow to return to the laboratory.

2. The round bottom flask containing the starting materials should now be on the stir plate. Click on the handle located in the upper right corner of the laboratory to pull down the TV. The TV should already be in *Tutorial* mode and the starting materials and solvent should be listed. From the group of reagents found on the lab bench, select the correct reagent to synthesize the target compound and add it to the flask on the stir plate. Now attach the heater, condenser, and N_2 gas to the round bottom flask so the reaction mixture can be heated.

3. Start the reaction by clicking on the *Stir* button on the front of the stir plate. You should be able to observe the reaction mixture stirring in the flask. Monitor the progress of the reaction using TLC measurements as necessary until the product has formed and the starting materials have been consumed. You can advance the laboratory time using the clock on the wall. With the electronic lab book open (click on the lab book on the lab bench), you can also save your TLC plates by clicking *Save* on the TLC window.

4. When the reaction is complete, "work up" your reaction by first dragging and dropping the separatory funnel (located in a drawer) on the flask and then adding H_2O to the funnel. Extract the organic layer in the funnel by clicking on the top layer and dragging it to the cork ring on the lab bench. Your target compound should now be in this flask.

*List the starting materials, solvent, reagent, and products formed:*_____

_____

How long did it take to finish the reaction? _____

What are the TLC values (R_f) for (a) Starting Materials: _____ (b) Products: _____

Write a mechanism for this reaction:

IR and NMR Spectra

After completing a reaction and working up the products, it is still necessary to confirm that the correct product was formed. The most common tools used for this analysis are Infrared (IR) and Nuclear Magnetic Resonance (NMR) spectroscopy. In the virtual laboratory, only ^{1}H NMR spectra are available. Details on interpreting IR and NMR spectra are found in your textbook. Your instructor may or may not ask you to perform this section depending on how your class is structured.

5. To collect an IR spectrum of your product, click on the IR spectrometer located underneath the laboratory clock and drag the salt plate icon to the flask on the lab bench. A window containing the IR spectrum for your product should now open. Identify the relevant peaks in the IR spectrum and record the position and associated functional group for each in the IR table below. The IR spectrum can also be saved to the lab book for later analysis.

IR List position (cm^{-1}) & functional group	4.
1.	5.
2.	6.
3.	7.

6. To collect a ^{1}H NMR spectrum of your product, click on the NMR magnet located to the right of the chalkboard and drag the NMR sample tube to the flask on the lab bench. A window containing the NMR spectrum for your product should now open. You can zoom into various portions of the NMR spectrum by clicking and dragging over the desired area. The *Zoom Out* button is used to zoom back out to view the full spectrum. Identify all of the peaks in the NMR spectrum and record the chemical shift, the splitting, and the number of hydrogens for each peak in the NMR table below. The NMR spectrum can also be saved to the lab book for later analysis.

^{1}H NMR	Peak	Chemical Shift (δ)	Multiplicity[†]	H[‡]	Peak	Chemical Shift (δ)	Multiplicity[†]	H[‡]
	1				7			
Structure:	2				8			
	3				9			
1-Methyl-2-nitro-benzene	4				10			
	5				11			
	6				12			

[†] Specify the multiplicity as a singlet (s), doublet (d), triplet (t), quartet (q), or multiplet (m).
[‡] Specify the number of hydrogens associated with each peak.

7. *Do the IR and NMR spectra you measured and recorded in the tables above confirm that you synthesized the assigned target compound? Explain.* _____

_____

_____

_____

VCL 8-4: Friedel-Crafts – 1

For this assignment, the target compound that you should synthesize is **4-acetyltoluene.** This is an electrophilic aromatic substitution reaction. Examine the product carefully and determine the substitution pattern. Which group will already be present in the substrate? Keep in mind the mechanism and how that will control the selectivity of the process. Remember, you can easily separate ortho and para isomers.

Synthesis Procedures

1. Start *Virtual ChemLab* and select *Friedel-Crafts – 1* from the list of assignments in the electronic workbook. After entering the organic laboratory, go to the stockroom by clicking inside the *Stockroom* window. Next, select a round bottom flask and place it on the cork ring on the stockroom counter. Using the available reagents on the stockroom shelf, identify the appropriate starting materials required to synthesize the target compound and add them to the round bottom flask. Select the appropriate solvent and click on the green *Return to Lab* arrow to return to the laboratory.

2. The round bottom flask containing the starting materials should now be on the stir plate. Click on the handle located in the upper right corner of the laboratory to pull down the TV. The TV should already be in *Tutorial* mode and the starting materials and solvent should be listed. From the group of reagents found on the lab bench, select the correct reagent to synthesize the target compound and add it to the flask on the stir plate.

3. Start the reaction by clicking on the *Stir* button on the front of the stir plate. You should be able to observe the reaction mixture stirring in the flask. Monitor the progress of the reaction using TLC measurements as necessary until the product has formed and the starting materials have been consumed. You can advance the laboratory time using the clock on the wall. With the electronic lab book open (click on the lab book on the lab bench), you can also save your TLC plates by clicking *Save* on the TLC window.

4. When the reaction is complete, "work up" your reaction by first dragging and dropping the separatory funnel (located in a drawer) on the flask and then adding H_2O to the funnel. Extract the organic layer in the funnel by clicking on the top layer and dragging it to the cork ring on the lab bench. Your target compound should now be in this flask.

List the starting materials, solvent, reagent, and products formed: _____

_____

How long did it take to finish the reaction? _____

What are the TLC values (R_f) for (a) Starting Materials: _____ *(b) Products:* _____

Write a mechanism for this reaction:

IR and NMR Spectra

After completing a reaction and working up the products, it is still necessary to confirm that the correct product was formed. The most common tools used for this analysis are Infrared (IR) and Nuclear Magnetic Resonance (NMR) spectroscopy. In the virtual laboratory, only ^{1}H NMR spectra are available. Details on interpreting IR and NMR spectra are found in your textbook. Your instructor may or may not ask you to perform this section depending on how your class is structured.

5. To collect an IR spectrum of your product, click on the IR spectrometer located underneath the laboratory clock and drag the salt plate icon to the flask on the lab bench. A window containing the IR spectrum for your product should now open. Identify the relevant peaks in the IR spectrum and record the position and associated functional group for each in the IR table below. The IR spectrum can also be saved to the lab book for later analysis.

IR List position (cm^{-1}) & functional group	4.
1.	5.
2.	6.
3.	7.

6. To collect a ^{1}H NMR spectrum of your product, click on the NMR magnet located to the right of the chalkboard and drag the NMR sample tube to the flask on the lab bench. A window containing the NMR spectrum for your product should now open. You can zoom into various portions of the NMR spectrum by clicking and dragging over the desired area. The *Zoom Out* button is used to zoom back out to view the full spectrum. Identify all of the peaks in the NMR spectrum and record the chemical shift, the splitting, and the number of hydrogens for each peak in the NMR table below. The NMR spectrum can also be saved to the lab book for later analysis.

^{1}H NMR	Peak	Chemical Shift (δ)	Multiplicity†	H‡	Peak	Chemical Shift (δ)	Multiplicity†	H‡
Structure:	1				7			
	2				8			
	3				9			
4-Acetyltoluene	4				10			
	5				11			
	6				12			

† Specify the multiplicity as a singlet (s), doublet (d), triplet (t), quartet (q), or multiplet (m).
‡ Specify the number of hydrogens associated with each peak.

7. *Do the IR and NMR spectra you measured and recorded in the tables above confirm that you synthesized the assigned target compound? Explain.* _____

_____

_____

_____

VCL 8-5: Friedel-Crafts – 2

For this assignment, the target compound that you should synthesize is **2-acetyltoluene.** This is an electrophilic aromatic substitution reaction. Examine the product carefully and determine the substitution pattern. Which group will already be present in the substrate? Keep in mind the mechanism and how that will control the selectivity of the process. Remember, you can easily separate ortho and para isomers.

Synthesis Procedures

1. Start *Virtual ChemLab* and select *Friedel-Crafts – 2* from the list of assignments in the electronic workbook. After entering the organic laboratory, go to the stockroom by clicking inside the *Stockroom* window. Next, select a round bottom flask and place it on the cork ring on the stockroom counter. Using the available reagents on the stockroom shelf, identify the appropriate starting materials required to synthesize the target compound and add them to the round bottom flask. Select the appropriate solvent and click on the green *Return to Lab* arrow to return to the laboratory.

2. The round bottom flask containing the starting materials should now be on the stir plate. Click on the handle located in the upper right corner of the laboratory to pull down the TV. The TV should already be in *Tutorial* mode and the starting materials and solvent should be listed. From the group of reagents found on the lab bench, select the correct reagent to synthesize the target compound and add it to the flask on the stir plate.

3. Start the reaction by clicking on the *Stir* button on the front of the stir plate. You should be able to observe the reaction mixture stirring in the flask. Monitor the progress of the reaction using TLC measurements as necessary until the product has formed and the starting materials have been consumed. You can advance the laboratory time using the clock on the wall. With the electronic lab book open (click on the lab book on the lab bench), you can also save your TLC plates by clicking *Save* on the TLC window.

4. When the reaction is complete, "work up" your reaction by first dragging and dropping the separatory funnel (located in a drawer) on the flask and then adding H_2O to the funnel. Extract the organic layer in the funnel by clicking on the top layer and dragging it to the cork ring on the lab bench. Your target compound should now be in this flask.

   *List the starting materials, solvent, reagent, and products formed:*_____

   _____

   How long did it take to finish the reaction? _____

   What are the TLC values (R_f) for (a) Starting Materials: _____ *(b) Products:* _____

   Write a mechanism for this reaction:

IR and NMR Spectra

After completing a reaction and working up the products, it is still necessary to confirm that the correct product was formed. The most common tools used for this analysis are Infrared (IR) and Nuclear Magnetic Resonance (NMR) spectroscopy. In the virtual laboratory, only ^{1}H NMR spectra are available. Details on interpreting IR and NMR spectra are found in your textbook. Your instructor may or may not ask you to perform this section depending on how your class is structured.

5. To collect an IR spectrum of your product, click on the IR spectrometer located underneath the laboratory clock and drag the salt plate icon to the flask on the lab bench. A window containing the IR spectrum for your product should now open. Identify the relevant peaks in the IR spectrum and record the position and associated functional group for each in the IR table below. The IR spectrum can also be saved to the lab book for later analysis.

IR List position (cm^{-1}) & functional group	4.
1.	5.
2.	6.
3.	7.

6. To collect a ^{1}H NMR spectrum of your product, click on the NMR magnet located to the right of the chalkboard and drag the NMR sample tube to the flask on the lab bench. A window containing the NMR spectrum for your product should now open. You can zoom into various portions of the NMR spectrum by clicking and dragging over the desired area. The *Zoom Out* button is used to zoom back out to view the full spectrum. Identify all of the peaks in the NMR spectrum and record the chemical shift, the splitting, and the number of hydrogens for each peak in the NMR table below. The NMR spectrum can also be saved to the lab book for later analysis.

^{1}H NMR Structure: 2-Acetyltoluene	Peak	Chemical Shift (δ)	Multiplicity[†]	H[‡]	Peak	Chemical Shift (δ)	Multiplicity[†]	H[‡]
	1				7			
	2				8			
	3				9			
	4				10			
	5				11			
	6				12			

[†] Specify the multiplicity as a singlet (s), doublet (d), triplet (t), quartet (q), or multiplet (m).
[‡] Specify the number of hydrogens associated with each peak.

7. *Do the IR and NMR spectra you measured and recorded in the tables above confirm that you synthesized the assigned target compound? Explain.* _____

_____

_____

_____

VCL 8-6: Friedel-Crafts – 3

For this assignment, the target compound that you should synthesize is **2-methyl-benzophenone.** This is an electrophilic aromatic substitution reaction. Examine the product carefully and determine the substitution pattern. Which group will already be present in the substrate? Keep in mind the mechanism and how that will control the selectivity of the process. Remember, you can easily separate ortho and para isomers.

Synthesis Procedures

1. Start *Virtual ChemLab* and select *Friedel-Crafts – 3* from the list of assignments in the electronic workbook. After entering the organic laboratory, go to the stockroom by clicking inside the *Stockroom* window. Next, select a round bottom flask and place it on the cork ring on the stockroom counter. Using the available reagents on the stockroom shelf, identify the appropriate starting materials required to synthesize the target compound and add them to the round bottom flask. Select the appropriate solvent and click on the green *Return to Lab* arrow to return to the laboratory.

2. The round bottom flask containing the starting materials should now be on the stir plate. Click on the handle located in the upper right corner of the laboratory to pull down the TV. The TV should already be in *Tutorial* mode and the starting materials and solvent should be listed. From the group of reagents found on the lab bench, select the correct reagent to synthesize the target compound and add it to the flask on the stir plate.

3. Start the reaction by clicking on the *Stir* button on the front of the stir plate. You should be able to observe the reaction mixture stirring in the flask. Monitor the progress of the reaction using TLC measurements as necessary until the product has formed and the starting materials have been consumed. You can advance the laboratory time using the clock on the wall. With the electronic lab book open (click on the lab book on the lab bench), you can also save your TLC plates by clicking *Save* on the TLC window.

4. When the reaction is complete, "work up" your reaction by first dragging and dropping the separatory funnel (located in a drawer) on the flask and then adding H_2O to the funnel. Extract the organic layer in the funnel by clicking on the top layer and dragging it to the cork ring on the lab bench. Your target compound should now be in this flask.

   List the starting materials, solvent, reagent, and products formed: _____

   _____

   How long did it take to finish the reaction? _____

   What are the TLC values (R_f) for (a) Starting Materials: _____ *(b) Products:* _____

   Write a mechanism for this reaction:

IR and NMR Spectra

After completing a reaction and working up the products, it is still necessary to confirm that the correct product was formed. The most common tools used for this analysis are Infrared (IR) and Nuclear Magnetic Resonance (NMR) spectroscopy. In the virtual laboratory, only ^{1}H NMR spectra are available. Details on interpreting IR and NMR spectra are found in your textbook. Your instructor may or may not ask you to perform this section depending on how your class is structured.

5. To collect an IR spectrum of your product, click on the IR spectrometer located underneath the laboratory clock and drag the salt plate icon to the flask on the lab bench. A window containing the IR spectrum for your product should now open. Identify the relevant peaks in the IR spectrum and record the position and associated functional group for each in the IR table below. The IR spectrum can also be saved to the lab book for later analysis.

IR List position (cm^{-1}) & functional group	4.
1.	5.
2.	6.
3.	7.

6. To collect a ^{1}H NMR spectrum of your product, click on the NMR magnet located to the right of the chalkboard and drag the NMR sample tube to the flask on the lab bench. A window containing the NMR spectrum for your product should now open. You can zoom into various portions of the NMR spectrum by clicking and dragging over the desired area. The *Zoom Out* button is used to zoom back out to view the full spectrum. Identify all of the peaks in the NMR spectrum and record the chemical shift, the splitting, and the number of hydrogens for each peak in the NMR table below. The NMR spectrum can also be saved to the lab book for later analysis.

^{1}H NMR	Peak	Chemical Shift (δ)	Multiplicity†	H‡	Peak	Chemical Shift (δ)	Multiplicity†	H‡
	1				7			
Structure:	2				8			
	3				9			
	4				10			
2-Methyl-benzophenone	5				11			
	6				12			

† Specify the multiplicity as a singlet (s), doublet (d), triplet (t), quartet (q), or multiplet (m).
‡ Specify the number of hydrogens associated with each peak.

7. *Do the IR and NMR spectra you measured and recorded in the tables above confirm that you synthesized the assigned target compound? Explain.* _____

_____

_____

_____

VCL 8-7: Friedel-Crafts – 4

For this assignment, the target compound that you should synthesize is **4-methyl-benzophenone.** This is an electrophilic aromatic substitution reaction. Examine the product carefully and determine the substitution pattern. Which group will already be present in the substrate? Keep in mind the mechanism and how that will control the selectivity of the process. Remember, you can easily separate ortho and para isomers.

Synthesis Procedures

1. Start *Virtual ChemLab* and select *Friedel-Crafts – 4* from the list of assignments in the electronic workbook. After entering the organic laboratory, go to the stockroom by clicking inside the *Stockroom* window. Next, select a round bottom flask and place it on the cork ring on the stockroom counter. Using the available reagents on the stockroom shelf, identify the appropriate starting materials required to synthesize the target compound and add them to the round bottom flask. Select the appropriate solvent and click on the green *Return to Lab* arrow to return to the laboratory.

2. The round bottom flask containing the starting materials should now be on the stir plate. Click on the handle located in the upper right corner of the laboratory to pull down the TV. The TV should already be in *Tutorial* mode and the starting materials and solvent should be listed. From the group of reagents found on the lab bench, select the correct reagent to synthesize the target compound and add it to the flask on the stir plate.

3. Start the reaction by clicking on the *Stir* button on the front of the stir plate. You should be able to observe the reaction mixture stirring in the flask. Monitor the progress of the reaction using TLC measurements as necessary until the product has formed and the starting materials have been consumed. You can advance the laboratory time using the clock on the wall. With the electronic lab book open (click on the lab book on the lab bench), you can also save your TLC plates by clicking *Save* on the TLC window.

4. When the reaction is complete, "work up" your reaction by first dragging and dropping the separatory funnel (located in a drawer) on the flask and then adding H_2O to the funnel. Extract the organic layer in the funnel by clicking on the top layer and dragging it to the cork ring on the lab bench. Your target compound should now be in this flask.

*List the starting materials, solvent, reagent, and products formed:*_____

_____

How long did it take to finish the reaction? _____

What are the TLC values (R_f) for (a) Starting Materials: _____ (b) Products: _____

Write a mechanism for this reaction:

IR and NMR Spectra

After completing a reaction and working up the products, it is still necessary to confirm that the correct product was formed. The most common tools used for this analysis are Infrared (IR) and Nuclear Magnetic Resonance (NMR) spectroscopy. In the virtual laboratory, only ^{1}H NMR spectra are available. Details on interpreting IR and NMR spectra are found in your textbook. Your instructor may or may not ask you to perform this section depending on how your class is structured.

5. To collect an IR spectrum of your product, click on the IR spectrometer located underneath the laboratory clock and drag the salt plate icon to the flask on the lab bench. A window containing the IR spectrum for your product should now open. Identify the relevant peaks in the IR spectrum and record the position and associated functional group for each in the IR table below. The IR spectrum can also be saved to the lab book for later analysis.

IR List position (cm^{-1}) & functional group	4.
1.	5.
2.	6.
3.	7.

6. To collect a ^{1}H NMR spectrum of your product, click on the NMR magnet located to the right of the chalkboard and drag the NMR sample tube to the flask on the lab bench. A window containing the NMR spectrum for your product should now open. You can zoom into various portions of the NMR spectrum by clicking and dragging over the desired area. The *Zoom Out* button is used to zoom back out to view the full spectrum. Identify all of the peaks in the NMR spectrum and record the chemical shift, the splitting, and the number of hydrogens for each peak in the NMR table below. The NMR spectrum can also be saved to the lab book for later analysis.

^{1}**H NMR** Structure: 4-Methyl-benzophenone	Peak	Chemical Shift (δ)	Multiplicity[†]	H[‡]	Peak	Chemical Shift (δ)	Multiplicity[†]	H[‡]
	1				7			
	2				8			
	3				9			
	4				10			
	5				11			
	6				12			

[†] Specify the multiplicity as a singlet (s), doublet (d), triplet (t), quartet (q), or multiplet (m).
[‡] Specify the number of hydrogens associated with each peak.

7. *Do the IR and NMR spectra you measured and recorded in the tables above confirm that you synthesized the assigned target compound? Explain.* _____

_____

_____

_____

VCL 9-1: Ether Formation

For this assignment, the target compound that you should synthesize is **ethyl benzoate.** This is a carboxylic acid derivative transformation. Keep in mind the mechanism and the order of reactivity found in this series. Examine the product and determine the bond that will be formed.

Synthesis Procedures

1. Start *Virtual ChemLab* and select *Ether Formation* from the list of assignments in the electronic workbook. After entering the organic laboratory, go to the stockroom by clicking inside the *Stockroom* window. Next, select a round bottom flask and place it on the cork ring on the stockroom counter. Using the available reagents on the stockroom shelf, identify the appropriate starting materials required to synthesize the target compound and add them to the round bottom flask. Select the appropriate solvent and click on the green *Return to Lab* arrow to return to the laboratory.

2. The round bottom flask containing the starting materials should now be on the stir plate. Click on the handle located in the upper right corner of the laboratory to pull down the TV. The TV should already be in *Tutorial* mode and the starting materials and solvent should be listed. From the group of reagents found on the lab bench, select the correct reagent to synthesize the target compound and add it to the flask on the stir plate.

3. Start the reaction by clicking on the *Stir* button on the front of the stir plate. You should be able to observe the reaction mixture stirring in the flask. Monitor the progress of the reaction using TLC measurements as necessary until the product has formed and the starting materials have been consumed. You can advance the laboratory time using the clock on the wall. With the electronic lab book open (click on the lab book on the lab bench), you can also save your TLC plates by clicking *Save* on the TLC window.

4. When the reaction is complete, "work up" your reaction by first dragging and dropping the separatory funnel (located in a drawer) on the flask and then adding H_2O to the funnel. Extract the organic layer in the funnel by clicking on the top layer and dragging it to the cork ring on the lab bench. Your target compound should now be in this flask.

    *List the starting materials, solvent, reagent, and products formed:*_____

    _____

    How long did it take to finish the reaction? _____

    What are the TLC values (R_f) for (a) Starting Materials: _____ *(b) Products:* _____

    Write a mechanism for this reaction:

IR and NMR Spectra

After completing a reaction and working up the products, it is still necessary to confirm that the correct product was formed. The most common tools used for this analysis are Infrared (IR) and Nuclear Magnetic Resonance (NMR) spectroscopy. In the virtual laboratory, only ^{1}H NMR spectra are available. Details on interpreting IR and NMR spectra are found in your textbook. Your instructor may or may not ask you to perform this section depending on how your class is structured.

5. To collect an IR spectrum of your product, click on the IR spectrometer located underneath the laboratory clock and drag the salt plate icon to the flask on the lab bench. A window containing the IR spectrum for your product should now open. Identify the relevant peaks in the IR spectrum and record the position and associated functional group for each in the IR table below. The IR spectrum can also be saved to the lab book for later analysis.

IR List position (cm^{-1}) & functional group	4.
1.	5.
2.	6.
3.	7.

6. To collect a ^{1}H NMR spectrum of your product, click on the NMR magnet located to the right of the chalkboard and drag the NMR sample tube to the flask on the lab bench. A window containing the NMR spectrum for your product should now open. You can zoom into various portions of the NMR spectrum by clicking and dragging over the desired area. The *Zoom Out* button is used to zoom back out to view the full spectrum. Identify all of the peaks in the NMR spectrum and record the chemical shift, the splitting, and the number of hydrogens for each peak in the NMR table below. The NMR spectrum can also be saved to the lab book for later analysis.

^{1}H NMR Structure: Ethyl benzoate	Peak	Chemical Shift (δ)	Multiplicity[†]	H[‡]	Peak	Chemical Shift (δ)	Multiplicity[†]	H[‡]
	1				7			
	2				8			
	3				9			
	4				10			
	5				11			
	6				12			

[†] Specify the multiplicity as a singlet (s), doublet (d), triplet (t), quartet (q), or multiplet (m).
[‡] Specify the number of hydrogens associated with each peak.

7. *Do the IR and NMR spectra you measured and recorded in the tables above confirm that you synthesized the assigned target compound? Explain.* _____

_____

_____

_____

VCL 9-2: Amide Formation

For this assignment, the target compound that you should synthesize is **N,N-diisopropyl benzamide**. This is a carboxylic acid derivative transformation. Keep in mind the mechanism and the order of reactivity found in this series. Examine the product and determine the bond that will be formed.

Synthesis Procedures
1. Start *Virtual ChemLab* and select *Amide Formation* from the list of assignments in the electronic workbook. After entering the organic laboratory, go to the stockroom by clicking inside the *Stockroom* window. Next, select a round bottom flask and place it on the cork ring on the stockroom counter. Using the available reagents on the stockroom shelf, identify the appropriate starting materials required to synthesize the target compound and add them to the round bottom flask. Select the appropriate solvent and click on the green *Return to Lab* arrow to return to the laboratory.

2. The round bottom flask containing the starting materials should now be on the stir plate. Click on the handle located in the upper right corner of the laboratory to pull down the TV. The TV should already be in *Tutorial* mode and the starting materials and solvent should be listed. From the group of reagents found on the lab bench, select the correct reagent to synthesize the target compound and add it to the flask on the stir plate.

3. Start the reaction by clicking on the *Stir* button on the front of the stir plate. You should be able to observe the reaction mixture stirring in the flask. Monitor the progress of the reaction using TLC measurements as necessary until the product has formed and the starting materials have been consumed. You can advance the laboratory time using the clock on the wall. With the electronic lab book open (click on the lab book on the lab bench), you can also save your TLC plates by clicking *Save* on the TLC window.

4. When the reaction is complete, "work up" your reaction by first dragging and dropping the separatory funnel (located in a drawer) on the flask and then adding H_2O to the funnel. Extract the organic layer in the funnel by clicking on the top layer and dragging it to the cork ring on the lab bench. Your target compound should now be in this flask.

   List the starting materials, solvent, reagent, and products formed: _____

   _____

   How long did it take to finish the reaction? _____

   What are the TLC values (R_f) for (a) Starting Materials: _____ *(b) Products:* _____

   Write a mechanism for this reaction:

IR and NMR Spectra

After completing a reaction and working up the products, it is still necessary to confirm that the correct product was formed. The most common tools used for this analysis are Infrared (IR) and Nuclear Magnetic Resonance (NMR) spectroscopy. In the virtual laboratory, only ^{1}H NMR spectra are available. Details on interpreting IR and NMR spectra are found in your textbook. Your instructor may or may not ask you to perform this section depending on how your class is structured.

5. To collect an IR spectrum of your product, click on the IR spectrometer located underneath the laboratory clock and drag the salt plate icon to the flask on the lab bench. A window containing the IR spectrum for your product should now open. Identify the relevant peaks in the IR spectrum and record the position and associated functional group for each in the IR table below. The IR spectrum can also be saved to the lab book for later analysis.

IR List position (cm^{-1}) & functional group	4.
1.	5.
2.	6.
3.	7.

6. To collect a ^{1}H NMR spectrum of your product, click on the NMR magnet located to the right of the chalkboard and drag the NMR sample tube to the flask on the lab bench. A window containing the NMR spectrum for your product should now open. You can zoom into various portions of the NMR spectrum by clicking and dragging over the desired area. The *Zoom Out* button is used to zoom back out to view the full spectrum. Identify all of the peaks in the NMR spectrum and record the chemical shift, the splitting, and the number of hydrogens for each peak in the NMR table below. The NMR spectrum can also be saved to the lab book for later analysis.

^{1}H NMR	Peak	Chemical Shift (δ)	Multiplicity†	H‡	Peak	Chemical Shift (δ)	Multiplicity†	H‡
Structure:	1				7			
	2				8			
	3				9			
	4				10			
N,N-Diisopropyl-benzamide	5				11			
	6				12			

† Specify the multiplicity as a singlet (s), doublet (d), triplet (t), quartet (q), or multiplet (m).
‡ Specify the number of hydrogens associated with each peak.

7. *Do the IR and NMR spectra you measured and recorded in the tables above confirm that you*

   synthesized the assigned target compound? Explain. _____

   _____

   _____

   _____

VCL 9-3: Ester Hydrolysis

For this assignment, the target compound that you should synthesize is **propionic acid.** This is a carboxylic acid derivative transformation. Keep in mind the mechanism and the order of reactivity found in this series. Examine the product and determine the bond that will be formed.

Synthesis Procedures

1. Start *Virtual ChemLab* and select *Ester Hydrolysis* from the list of assignments in the electronic workbook. After entering the organic laboratory, go to the stockroom by clicking inside the *Stockroom* window. Next, select a round bottom flask and place it on the cork ring on the stockroom counter. Using the available reagents on the stockroom shelf, identify the appropriate starting materials required to synthesize the target compound and add them to the round bottom flask. Select the appropriate solvent and click on the green *Return to Lab* arrow to return to the laboratory.

2. The round bottom flask containing the starting materials should now be on the stir plate. Click on the handle located in the upper right corner of the laboratory to pull down the TV. The TV should already be in *Tutorial* mode and the starting materials and solvent should be listed. From the group of reagents found on the lab bench, select the correct reagent to synthesize the target compound and add it to the flask on the stir plate. Now attach the heater, condenser, and N_2 gas to the round bottom flask so the reaction mixture can be heated.

3. Start the reaction by clicking on the *Stir* button on the front of the stir plate. You should be able to observe the reaction mixture stirring in the flask. Monitor the progress of the reaction using TLC measurements as necessary until the product has formed and the starting materials have been consumed. You can advance the laboratory time using the clock on the wall. With the electronic lab book open (click on the lab book on the lab bench), you can also save your TLC plates by clicking *Save* on the TLC window.

4. When the reaction is complete, "work up" your reaction by first dragging and dropping the separatory funnel (located in a drawer) on the flask and then adding H_2O to the funnel. Extract the organic layer in the funnel by clicking on the top layer and dragging it to the cork ring on the lab bench. Your target compound should now be in this flask.

*List the starting materials, solvent, reagent, and products formed:*_____

_____

How long did it take to finish the reaction? _____

What are the TLC values (R_f) for (a) Starting Materials: _____ (b) Products: _____

Write a mechanism for this reaction:

IR and NMR Spectra

After completing a reaction and working up the products, it is still necessary to confirm that the correct product was formed. The most common tools used for this analysis are Infrared (IR) and Nuclear Magnetic Resonance (NMR) spectroscopy. In the virtual laboratory, only ^{1}H NMR spectra are available. Details on interpreting IR and NMR spectra are found in your textbook. Your instructor may or may not ask you to perform this section depending on how your class is structured.

5. To collect an IR spectrum of your product, click on the IR spectrometer located underneath the laboratory clock and drag the salt plate icon to the flask on the lab bench. A window containing the IR spectrum for your product should now open. Identify the relevant peaks in the IR spectrum and record the position and associated functional group for each in the IR table below. The IR spectrum can also be saved to the lab book for later analysis.

IR List position (cm^{-1}) & functional group	4.
1.	5.
2.	6.
3.	7.

6. To collect a ^{1}H NMR spectrum of your product, click on the NMR magnet located to the right of the chalkboard and drag the NMR sample tube to the flask on the lab bench. A window containing the NMR spectrum for your product should now open. You can zoom into various portions of the NMR spectrum by clicking and dragging over the desired area. The *Zoom Out* button is used to zoom back out to view the full spectrum. Identify all of the peaks in the NMR spectrum and record the chemical shift, the splitting, and the number of hydrogens for each peak in the NMR table below. The NMR spectrum can also be saved to the lab book for later analysis.

^{1}**H NMR**	Peak	Chemical Shift (δ)	Multiplicity†	H‡	Peak	Chemical Shift (δ)	Multiplicity†	H‡
	1				7			
Structure:	2				8			
	3				9			
Propionic acid	4				10			
	5				11			
	6				12			

† Specify the multiplicity as a singlet (s), doublet (d), triplet (t), quartet (q), or multiplet (m).
‡ Specify the number of hydrogens associated with each peak.

7. *Do the IR and NMR spectra you measured and recorded in the tables above confirm that you*

   synthesized the assigned target compound? Explain. _____

   _____

   _____

   _____

VCL 9-4: Transesterification

For this assignment, the target compound that you should synthesize is **ethyl propionate.** This is a carboxylic acid derivative transformation. Keep in mind the mechanism and the potential of reaction reversibility. Examine the product and determine the bond that will be formed.

Synthesis Procedures

1. Start *Virtual ChemLab* and select *Transesterification* from the list of assignments in the electronic workbook. After entering the organic laboratory, go to the stockroom by clicking inside the *Stockroom* window. Next, select a round bottom flask and place it on the cork ring on the stockroom counter. Using the available reagents on the stockroom shelf, identify the appropriate starting materials required to synthesize the target compound and add them to the round bottom flask. Select the appropriate solvent and click on the green *Return to Lab* arrow to return to the laboratory.

2. The round bottom flask containing the starting materials should now be on the stir plate. Click on the handle located in the upper right corner of the laboratory to pull down the TV. The TV should already be in *Tutorial* mode and the starting materials and solvent should be listed. From the group of reagents found on the lab bench, select the correct reagent to synthesize the target compound and add it to the flask on the stir plate. Now attach the heater, condenser, and N_2 gas to the round bottom flask so the reaction mixture can be heated.

3. Start the reaction by clicking on the *Stir* button on the front of the stir plate. You should be able to observe the reaction mixture stirring in the flask. Monitor the progress of the reaction using TLC measurements as necessary until the product has formed and the starting materials have been consumed. You can advance the laboratory time using the clock on the wall. With the electronic lab book open (click on the lab book on the lab bench), you can also save your TLC plates by clicking *Save* on the TLC window.

4. When the reaction is complete, "work up" your reaction by first dragging and dropping the separatory funnel (located in a drawer) on the flask and then adding H_2O to the funnel. Extract the organic layer in the funnel by clicking on the top layer and dragging it to the cork ring on the lab bench. Your target compound should now be in this flask.

   List the starting materials, solvent, reagent, and products formed: _____

   _____

   How long did it take to finish the reaction? _____

   What are the TLC values (R_f) for (a) Starting Materials: _____ *(b) Products:* _____

   Write a mechanism for this reaction:

IR and NMR Spectra

After completing a reaction and working up the products, it is still necessary to confirm that the correct product was formed. The most common tools used for this analysis are Infrared (IR) and Nuclear Magnetic Resonance (NMR) spectroscopy. In the virtual laboratory, only ^{1}H NMR spectra are available. Details on interpreting IR and NMR spectra are found in your textbook. Your instructor may or may not ask you to perform this section depending on how your class is structured.

5. To collect an IR spectrum of your product, click on the IR spectrometer located underneath the laboratory clock and drag the salt plate icon to the flask on the lab bench. A window containing the IR spectrum for your product should now open. Identify the relevant peaks in the IR spectrum and record the position and associated functional group for each in the IR table below. The IR spectrum can also be saved to the lab book for later analysis.

IR List position (cm^{-1}) & functional group	4.
1.	5.
2.	6.
3.	7.

6. To collect a ^{1}H NMR spectrum of your product, click on the NMR magnet located to the right of the chalkboard and drag the NMR sample tube to the flask on the lab bench. A window containing the NMR spectrum for your product should now open. You can zoom into various portions of the NMR spectrum by clicking and dragging over the desired area. The *Zoom Out* button is used to zoom back out to view the full spectrum. Identify all of the peaks in the NMR spectrum and record the chemical shift, the splitting, and the number of hydrogens for each peak in the NMR table below. The NMR spectrum can also be saved to the lab book for later analysis.

^{1}**H NMR** Structure: Ethyl propionate	Peak	Chemical Shift (δ)	Multiplicity[†]	H[‡]	Peak	Chemical Shift (δ)	Multiplicity[†]	H[‡]
	1				7			
	2				8			
	3				9			
	4				10			
	5				11			
	6				12			

[†] Specify the multiplicity as a singlet (s), doublet (d), triplet (t), quartet (q), or multiplet (m).
[‡] Specify the number of hydrogens associated with each peak.

7. *Do the IR and NMR spectra you measured and recorded in the tables above confirm that you*

synthesized the assigned target compound? Explain. _____

_____

_____

VCL 10-1: Grignard Addition – 1

For this assignment, the target compound that you should synthesize is **1-phenyl-1-propanol.** This is an organometallic addition reaction. Examine the product and identify potential bonds that may be formed. Keep in mind the mechanism and the need to quench the reaction with acid to liberate the neutral product.

Synthesis Procedures

1. Start *Virtual ChemLab* and select *Grignard Addition –1* from the list of assignments in the electronic workbook. After entering the organic laboratory, go to the stockroom by clicking inside the *Stockroom* window. Next, select a round bottom flask and place it on the cork ring on the stockroom counter. Using the available reagents on the stockroom shelf, identify the appropriate starting materials required to synthesize the target compound and add them to the round bottom flask. Select the appropriate solvent and click on the green *Return to Lab* arrow to return to the laboratory.

2. The round bottom flask containing the starting materials should now be on the stir plate. Click on the handle located in the upper right corner of the laboratory to pull down the TV. The TV should already be in *Tutorial* mode and the starting materials and solvent should be listed. From the group of reagents found on the lab bench, select the correct reagent to synthesize the target compound and add it to the flask on the stir plate.

3. Start the reaction by clicking on the *Stir* button on the front of the stir plate. You should be able to observe the reaction mixture stirring in the flask. Monitor the progress of the reaction using TLC measurements as necessary until the product has formed and the starting materials have been consumed. You can advance the laboratory time using the clock on the wall. With the electronic lab book open (click on the lab book on the lab bench), you can also save your TLC plates by clicking *Save* on the TLC window.

4. When the reaction is complete, "work up" your reaction by first dragging and dropping the separatory funnel (located in a drawer) on the flask and then adding H_2O to the funnel. Extract the organic layer in the funnel by clicking on the top layer and dragging it to the cork ring on the lab bench. Your target compound should now be in this flask.

    List the starting materials, solvent, reagent, and products formed: _____

    _____

    How long did it take to finish the reaction? _____

    What are the TLC values (R_f) for (a) Starting Materials: _____ (b) Products: _____

    Write a mechanism for this reaction:

IR and NMR Spectra

After completing a reaction and working up the products, it is still necessary to confirm that the correct product was formed. The most common tools used for this analysis are Infrared (IR) and Nuclear Magnetic Resonance (NMR) spectroscopy. In the virtual laboratory, only ^{1}H NMR spectra are available. Details on interpreting IR and NMR spectra are found in your textbook. Your instructor may or may not ask you to perform this section depending on how your class is structured.

5. To collect an IR spectrum of your product, click on the IR spectrometer located underneath the laboratory clock and drag the salt plate icon to the flask on the lab bench. A window containing the IR spectrum for your product should now open. Identify the relevant peaks in the IR spectrum and record the position and associated functional group for each in the IR table below. The IR spectrum can also be saved to the lab book for later analysis.

IR List position (cm^{-1}) & functional group	4.
1.	5.
2.	6.
3.	7.

6. To collect a ^{1}H NMR spectrum of your product, click on the NMR magnet located to the right of the chalkboard and drag the NMR sample tube to the flask on the lab bench. A window containing the NMR spectrum for your product should now open. You can zoom into various portions of the NMR spectrum by clicking and dragging over the desired area. The *Zoom Out* button is used to zoom back out to view the full spectrum. Identify all of the peaks in the NMR spectrum and record the chemical shift, the splitting, and the number of hydrogens for each peak in the NMR table below. The NMR spectrum can also be saved to the lab book for later analysis.

^{1}H NMR — Structure: 1-Phenyl-1-propanol	Peak	Chemical Shift (δ)	Multiplicity[†]	H[‡]	Peak	Chemical Shift (δ)	Multiplicity[†]	H[‡]
	1				7			
	2				8			
	3				9			
	4				10			
	5				11			
	6				12			

[†] Specify the multiplicity as a singlet (s), doublet (d), triplet (t), quartet (q), or multiplet (m).
[‡] Specify the number of hydrogens associated with each peak.

7. *Do the IR and NMR spectra you measured and recorded in the tables above confirm that you synthesized the assigned target compound? Explain.* _____

_____

_____

VCL 10-2: Grignard Addition – 2

For this assignment, the target compound that you should synthesize is **2-cyclohexyl-propan-2-ol.** This is an organometallic addition reaction. Examine the product and identify potential bonds that may be formed. Keep in mind the mechanism and the need to quench the reaction with acid to liberate the neutral product.

Synthesis Procedures

1. Start *Virtual ChemLab* and select *Grignard Addition –2* from the list of assignments in the electronic workbook. After entering the organic laboratory, go to the stockroom by clicking inside the *Stockroom* window. Next, select a round bottom flask and place it on the cork ring on the stockroom counter. Using the available reagents on the stockroom shelf, identify the appropriate starting materials required to synthesize the target compound and add them to the round bottom flask. Select the appropriate solvent and click on the green *Return to Lab* arrow to return to the laboratory.

2. The round bottom flask containing the starting materials should now be on the stir plate. Click on the handle located in the upper right corner of the laboratory to pull down the TV. The TV should already be in *Tutorial* mode and the starting materials and solvent should be listed. From the group of reagents found on the lab bench, select the correct reagent to synthesize the target compound and add it to the flask on the stir plate.

3. Start the reaction by clicking on the *Stir* button on the front of the stir plate. You should be able to observe the reaction mixture stirring in the flask. Monitor the progress of the reaction using TLC measurements as necessary until the product has formed and the starting materials have been consumed. You can advance the laboratory time using the clock on the wall. With the electronic lab book open (click on the lab book on the lab bench), you can also save your TLC plates by clicking *Save* on the TLC window.

4. When the reaction is complete, "work up" your reaction by first dragging and dropping the separatory funnel (located in a drawer) on the flask and then adding H_2O to the funnel. Extract the organic layer in the funnel by clicking on the top layer and dragging it to the cork ring on the lab bench. Your target compound should now be in this flask.

List the starting materials, solvent, reagent, and products formed: _____

_____

How long did it take to finish the reaction? _____

What are the TLC values (Rf) for (a) Starting Materials: _____ *(b) Products:* _____

Write a mechanism for this reaction:

IR and NMR Spectra

After completing a reaction and working up the products, it is still necessary to confirm that the correct product was formed. The most common tools used for this analysis are Infrared (IR) and Nuclear Magnetic Resonance (NMR) spectroscopy. In the virtual laboratory, only ^{1}H NMR spectra are available. Details on interpreting IR and NMR spectra are found in your textbook. Your instructor may or may not ask you to perform this section depending on how your class is structured.

5. To collect an IR spectrum of your product, click on the IR spectrometer located underneath the laboratory clock and drag the salt plate icon to the flask on the lab bench. A window containing the IR spectrum for your product should now open. Identify the relevant peaks in the IR spectrum and record the position and associated functional group for each in the IR table below. The IR spectrum can also be saved to the lab book for later analysis.

IR List position (cm^{-1}) & functional group	4.
1.	5.
2.	6.
3.	7.

6. To collect a ^{1}H NMR spectrum of your product, click on the NMR magnet located to the right of the chalkboard and drag the NMR sample tube to the flask on the lab bench. A window containing the NMR spectrum for your product should now open. You can zoom into various portions of the NMR spectrum by clicking and dragging over the desired area. The *Zoom Out* button is used to zoom back out to view the full spectrum. Identify all of the peaks in the NMR spectrum and record the chemical shift, the splitting, and the number of hydrogens for each peak in the NMR table below. The NMR spectrum can also be saved to the lab book for later analysis.

^{1}H NMR	Peak	Chemical Shift (δ)	Multiplicity†	H‡	Peak	Chemical Shift (δ)	Multiplicity†	H‡
Structure:	1				7			
	2				8			
OH	3				9			
2-Cyclohexyl-propan-2-ol	4				10			
	5				11			
	6				12			

† Specify the multiplicity as a singlet (s), doublet (d), triplet (t), quartet (q), or multiplet (m).
‡ Specify the number of hydrogens associated with each peak.

7. *Do the IR and NMR spectra you measured and recorded in the tables above confirm that you*

   synthesized the assigned target compound? Explain. _____

   _____

   _____

   _____

VCL 10-3: Grignard Addition – 3

For this assignment, the target compound that you should synthesize is **cyclohexane carboxylic acid.** This is an organometallic addition reaction. Examine the product and identify potential bonds that may be formed. Keep in mind the mechanism and the need to quench the reaction with acid to liberate the neutral product.

Synthesis Procedures

1. Start *Virtual ChemLab* and select *Grignard Addition –3* from the list of assignments in the electronic workbook. After entering the organic laboratory, go to the stockroom by clicking inside the *Stockroom* window. Next, select a round bottom flask and place it on the cork ring on the stockroom counter. Using the available reagents on the stockroom shelf, identify the appropriate starting materials required to synthesize the target compound and add them to the round bottom flask. Select the appropriate solvent and click on the green *Return to Lab* arrow to return to the laboratory.

2. The round bottom flask containing the starting materials should now be on the stir plate. Click on the handle located in the upper right corner of the laboratory to pull down the TV. The TV should already be in *Tutorial* mode and the starting materials and solvent should be listed. From the group of reagents found on the lab bench, select the correct reagent to synthesize the target compound and add it to the flask on the stir plate. Now attach the heater, condenser, and N_2 gas to the round bottom flask so the reaction mixture can be heated.

3. Start the reaction by clicking on the *Stir* button on the front of the stir plate. You should be able to observe the reaction mixture stirring in the flask. Monitor the progress of the reaction using TLC measurements as necessary until the product has formed and the starting materials have been consumed. You can advance the laboratory time using the clock on the wall. With the electronic lab book open (click on the lab book on the lab bench), you can also save your TLC plates by clicking *Save* on the TLC window.

4. When the reaction is complete, "work up" your reaction by first dragging and dropping the separatory funnel (located in a drawer) on the flask and then adding H_2O to the funnel. Extract the organic layer in the funnel by clicking on the top layer and dragging it to the cork ring on the lab bench. Your target compound should now be in this flask.

    List the starting materials, solvent, reagent, and products formed: _____

    _____

    How long did it take to finish the reaction? _____

    What are the TLC values (R_f) for (a) Starting Materials: _____ (b) Products: _____

    Write a mechanism for this reaction:

IR and NMR Spectra

After completing a reaction and working up the products, it is still necessary to confirm that the correct product was formed. The most common tools used for this analysis are Infrared (IR) and Nuclear Magnetic Resonance (NMR) spectroscopy. In the virtual laboratory, only ^{1}H NMR spectra are available. Details on interpreting IR and NMR spectra are found in your textbook. Your instructor may or may not ask you to perform this section depending on how your class is structured.

5. To collect an IR spectrum of your product, click on the IR spectrometer located underneath the laboratory clock and drag the salt plate icon to the flask on the lab bench. A window containing the IR spectrum for your product should now open. Identify the relevant peaks in the IR spectrum and record the position and associated functional group for each in the IR table below. The IR spectrum can also be saved to the lab book for later analysis.

IR List position (cm^{-1}) & functional group	4.
1.	5.
2.	6.
3.	7.

6. To collect a ^{1}H NMR spectrum of your product, click on the NMR magnet located to the right of the chalkboard and drag the NMR sample tube to the flask on the lab bench. A window containing the NMR spectrum for your product should now open. You can zoom into various portions of the NMR spectrum by clicking and dragging over the desired area. The *Zoom Out* button is used to zoom back out to view the full spectrum. Identify all of the peaks in the NMR spectrum and record the chemical shift, the splitting, and the number of hydrogens for each peak in the NMR table below. The NMR spectrum can also be saved to the lab book for later analysis.

^{1}H NMR	Peak	Chemical Shift (δ)	Multiplicity[†]	H[‡]	Peak	Chemical Shift (δ)	Multiplicity[†]	H[‡]
Structure:	1				7			
	2				8			
Cyclohexane carboxylic acid	3				9			
	4				10			
	5				11			
	6				12			

[†] Specify the multiplicity as a singlet (s), doublet (d), triplet (t), quartet (q), or multiplet (m).
[‡] Specify the number of hydrogens associated with each peak.

7. *Do the IR and NMR spectra you measured and recorded in the tables above confirm that you synthesized the assigned target compound? Explain.* _____

_____

_____

VCL 10-4: Carbonyl Reduction

For this assignment, the target compound that you should synthesize is **benzyl alcohol.** This is a hydride addition reaction. Examine the product and identify potential bonds that may be formed. Keep in mind the mechanism and the need to quench the reaction with acid to liberate the neutral product.

Synthesis Procedures

1. Start *Virtual ChemLab* and select *Carbonyl Reduction* from the list of assignments in the electronic workbook. After entering the organic laboratory, go to the stockroom by clicking inside the *Stockroom* window. Next, select a round bottom flask and place it on the cork ring on the stockroom counter. Using the available reagents on the stockroom shelf, identify the appropriate starting materials required to synthesize the target compound and add them to the round bottom flask. Select the appropriate solvent and click on the green *Return to Lab* arrow to return to the laboratory.

2. The round bottom flask containing the starting materials should now be on the stir plate. Click on the handle located in the upper right corner of the laboratory to pull down the TV. The TV should already be in *Tutorial* mode and the starting materials and solvent should be listed. From the group of reagents found on the lab bench, select the correct reagent to synthesize the target compound and add it to the flask on the stir plate. Now attach the heater, condenser, and N_2 gas to the round bottom flask so the reaction mixture can be heated.

3. Start the reaction by clicking on the *Stir* button on the front of the stir plate. You should be able to observe the reaction mixture stirring in the flask. Monitor the progress of the reaction using TLC measurements as necessary until the product has formed and the starting materials have been consumed. You can advance the laboratory time using the clock on the wall. With the electronic lab book open (click on the lab book on the lab bench), you can also save your TLC plates by clicking *Save* on the TLC window.

4. When the reaction is complete, "work up" your reaction by first dragging and dropping the separatory funnel (located in a drawer) on the flask and then adding H_2O to the funnel. Extract the organic layer in the funnel by clicking on the top layer and dragging it to the cork ring on the lab bench. Your target compound should now be in this flask.

List the starting materials, solvent, reagent, and products formed: _____

_____

How long did it take to finish the reaction? _____

What are the TLC values (R_f) for (a) Starting Materials: _____ *(b) Products:* _____

Write a mechanism for this reaction:

IR and NMR Spectra

After completing a reaction and working up the products, it is still necessary to confirm that the correct product was formed. The most common tools used for this analysis are Infrared (IR) and Nuclear Magnetic Resonance (NMR) spectroscopy. In the virtual laboratory, only ^{1}H NMR spectra are available. Details on interpreting IR and NMR spectra are found in your textbook. Your instructor may or may not ask you to perform this section depending on how your class is structured.

5. To collect an IR spectrum of your product, click on the IR spectrometer located underneath the laboratory clock and drag the salt plate icon to the flask on the lab bench. A window containing the IR spectrum for your product should now open. Identify the relevant peaks in the IR spectrum and record the position and associated functional group for each in the IR table below. The IR spectrum can also be saved to the lab book for later analysis.

IR List position (cm^{-1}) & functional group	4.
1.	5.
2.	6.
3.	7.

6. To collect a ^{1}H NMR spectrum of your product, click on the NMR magnet located to the right of the chalkboard and drag the NMR sample tube to the flask on the lab bench. A window containing the NMR spectrum for your product should now open. You can zoom into various portions of the NMR spectrum by clicking and dragging over the desired area. The *Zoom Out* button is used to zoom back out to view the full spectrum. Identify all of the peaks in the NMR spectrum and record the chemical shift, the splitting, and the number of hydrogens for each peak in the NMR table below. The NMR spectrum can also be saved to the lab book for later analysis.

^{1}H NMR Structure: Benzyl alcohol	Peak	Chemical Shift (δ)	Multiplicity†	H‡	Peak	Chemical Shift (δ)	Multiplicity†	H‡
	1				7			
	2				8			
	3				9			
	4				10			
	5				11			
	6				12			

† Specify the multiplicity as a singlet (s), doublet (d), triplet (t), quartet (q), or multiplet (m).
‡ Specify the number of hydrogens associated with each peak.

7. *Do the IR and NMR spectra you measured and recorded in the tables above confirm that you*

synthesized the assigned target compound? Explain. _____

_____

_____

_____

VCL 10-5: Acetal Formation

For this assignment, the target compound that you should synthesize is **1,1-diethoxy-cyclohexane.** This is a carbonyl addition reaction. Examine the product to determine the bonds that will be formed. Keep in mind the mechanism and how you might drive the reaction to completion.

Synthesis Procedures

1. Start *Virtual ChemLab* and select *Acetal Formation* from the list of assignments in the electronic workbook. After entering the organic laboratory, go to the stockroom by clicking inside the *Stockroom* window. Next, select a round bottom flask and place it on the cork ring on the stockroom counter. Using the available reagents on the stockroom shelf, identify the appropriate starting materials required to synthesize the target compound and add them to the round bottom flask. Select the appropriate solvent and click on the green *Return to Lab* arrow to return to the laboratory.

2. The round bottom flask containing the starting materials should now be on the stir plate. Click on the handle located in the upper right corner of the laboratory to pull down the TV. The TV should already be in *Tutorial* mode and the starting materials and solvent should be listed. From the group of reagents found on the lab bench, select the correct reagent to synthesize the target compound and add it to the flask on the stir plate.

3. Start the reaction by clicking on the *Stir* button on the front of the stir plate. You should be able to observe the reaction mixture stirring in the flask. Monitor the progress of the reaction using TLC measurements as necessary until the product has formed and the starting materials have been consumed. You can advance the laboratory time using the clock on the wall. With the electronic lab book open (click on the lab book on the lab bench), you can also save your TLC plates by clicking *Save* on the TLC window.

4. When the reaction is complete, "work up" your reaction by first dragging and dropping the separatory funnel (located in a drawer) on the flask and then adding H_2O to the funnel. Extract the organic layer in the funnel by clicking on the top layer and dragging it to the cork ring on the lab bench. Your target compound should now be in this flask.

List the starting materials, solvent, reagent, and products formed: _____

_____

How long did it take to finish the reaction? _____

What are the TLC values (R_f) for (a) Starting Materials: _____ (b) Products: _____

Write a mechanism for this reaction:

IR and NMR Spectra

After completing a reaction and working up the products, it is still necessary to confirm that the correct product was formed. The most common tools used for this analysis are Infrared (IR) and Nuclear Magnetic Resonance (NMR) spectroscopy. In the virtual laboratory, only ^{1}H NMR spectra are available. Details on interpreting IR and NMR spectra are found in your textbook. Your instructor may or may not ask you to perform this section depending on how your class is structured.

5. To collect an IR spectrum of your product, click on the IR spectrometer located underneath the laboratory clock and drag the salt plate icon to the flask on the lab bench. A window containing the IR spectrum for your product should now open. Identify the relevant peaks in the IR spectrum and record the position and associated functional group for each in the IR table below. The IR spectrum can also be saved to the lab book for later analysis.

IR List position (cm^{-1}) & functional group	4.
1.	5.
2.	6.
3.	7.

6. To collect a ^{1}H NMR spectrum of your product, click on the NMR magnet located to the right of the chalkboard and drag the NMR sample tube to the flask on the lab bench. A window containing the NMR spectrum for your product should now open. You can zoom into various portions of the NMR spectrum by clicking and dragging over the desired area. The *Zoom Out* button is used to zoom back out to view the full spectrum. Identify all of the peaks in the NMR spectrum and record the chemical shift, the splitting, and the number of hydrogens for each peak in the NMR table below. The NMR spectrum can also be saved to the lab book for later analysis.

^{1}H NMR	Peak	Chemical Shift (δ)	Multiplicity[†]	H[‡]	Peak	Chemical Shift (δ)	Multiplicity[†]	H[‡]
Structure:	1				7			
	2				8			
	3				9			
1,1-Diethoxy-cyclohexane	4				10			
	5				11			
	6				12			

[†] Specify the multiplicity as a singlet (s), doublet (d), triplet (t), quartet (q), or multiplet (m).
[‡] Specify the number of hydrogens associated with each peak.

7. *Do the IR and NMR spectra you measured and recorded in the tables above confirm that you*

    synthesized the assigned target compound? Explain. _____

    _____

    _____

    _____

VCL 11-1: α-Halogenation – 1

For this assignment, the target compound that you should synthesize is **2-bromo-butanal.** This is another electrophilic substitution reaction. Examine the product and determine which bonds may be formed. Consider the mechanism and how a nucleophilic intermediate may generated and used to form the new bond.

Synthesis Procedures

1. Start *Virtual ChemLab* and select *α-Halogenation – 1* from the list of assignments in the electronic workbook. After entering the organic laboratory, go to the stockroom by clicking inside the *Stockroom* window. Next, select a round bottom flask and place it on the cork ring on the stockroom counter. Using the available reagents on the stockroom shelf, identify the appropriate starting materials required to synthesize the target compound and add them to the round bottom flask. Select the appropriate solvent and click on the green *Return to Lab* arrow to return to the laboratory.

2. The round bottom flask containing the starting materials should now be on the stir plate. Click on the handle located in the upper right corner of the laboratory to pull down the TV. The TV should already be in *Tutorial* mode and the starting materials and solvent should be listed. From the group of reagents found on the lab bench, select the correct reagent to synthesize the target compound and add it to the flask on the stir plate. Now attach the heater, condenser, and N_2 gas to the round bottom flask so the reaction mixture can be heated.

3. Start the reaction by clicking on the *Stir* button on the front of the stir plate. You should be able to observe the reaction mixture stirring in the flask. Monitor the progress of the reaction using TLC measurements as necessary until the product has formed and the starting materials have been consumed. You can advance the laboratory time using the clock on the wall. With the electronic lab book open (click on the lab book on the lab bench), you can also save your TLC plates by clicking *Save* on the TLC window.

4. When the reaction is complete, "work up" your reaction by first dragging and dropping the separatory funnel (located in a drawer) on the flask and then adding H_2O to the funnel. Extract the organic layer in the funnel by clicking on the top layer and dragging it to the cork ring on the lab bench. Your target compound should now be in this flask.

   List the starting materials, solvent, reagent, and products formed: _____

   _____

   How long did it take to finish the reaction? _____

   What are the TLC values (R_f) for (a) Starting Materials: _____ (b) Products: _____

   Write a mechanism for this reaction:

IR and NMR Spectra

After completing a reaction and working up the products, it is still necessary to confirm that the correct product was formed. The most common tools used for this analysis are Infrared (IR) and Nuclear Magnetic Resonance (NMR) spectroscopy. In the virtual laboratory, only ^{1}H NMR spectra are available. Details on interpreting IR and NMR spectra are found in your textbook. Your instructor may or may not ask you to perform this section depending on how your class is structured.

5. To collect an IR spectrum of your product, click on the IR spectrometer located underneath the laboratory clock and drag the salt plate icon to the flask on the lab bench. A window containing the IR spectrum for your product should now open. Identify the relevant peaks in the IR spectrum and record the position and associated functional group for each in the IR table below. The IR spectrum can also be saved to the lab book for later analysis.

IR List position (cm^{-1}) & functional group	4.
1.	5.
2.	6.
3.	7.

6. To collect a ^{1}H NMR spectrum of your product, click on the NMR magnet located to the right of the chalkboard and drag the NMR sample tube to the flask on the lab bench. A window containing the NMR spectrum for your product should now open. You can zoom into various portions of the NMR spectrum by clicking and dragging over the desired area. The *Zoom Out* button is used to zoom back out to view the full spectrum. Identify all of the peaks in the NMR spectrum and record the chemical shift, the splitting, and the number of hydrogens for each peak in the NMR table below. The NMR spectrum can also be saved to the lab book for later analysis.

^{1}H NMR	Peak	Chemical Shift (δ)	Multiplicity[†]	H[‡]	Peak	Chemical Shift (δ)	Multiplicity[†]	H[‡]
Structure:	1				7			
	2				8			
	3				9			
	4				10			
2-Bromo-butanal	5				11			
	6				12			

[†] Specify the multiplicity as a singlet (s), doublet (d), triplet (t), quartet (q), or multiplet (m).
[‡] Specify the number of hydrogens associated with each peak.

7. *Do the IR and NMR spectra you measured and recorded in the tables above confirm that you synthesized the assigned target compound? Explain.* _____

_____

_____

_____

VCL 11-2: α-Halogenation – 2

For this assignment, the target compound that you should synthesize is **2-bromo-cyclohexanone**. This is another electrophilic substitution reaction. Examine the product and determine which bonds may be formed. Consider the mechanism and how a nucleophilic intermediate may generated and used to form the new bond.

Synthesis Procedures

1. Start *Virtual ChemLab* and select *α-Halogenation – 2* from the list of assignments in the electronic workbook. After entering the organic laboratory, go to the stockroom by clicking inside the *Stockroom* window. Next, select a round bottom flask and place it on the cork ring on the stockroom counter. Using the available reagents on the stockroom shelf, identify the appropriate starting materials required to synthesize the target compound and add them to the round bottom flask. Select the appropriate solvent and click on the green *Return to Lab* arrow to return to the laboratory.

2. The round bottom flask containing the starting materials should now be on the stir plate. Click on the handle located in the upper right corner of the laboratory to pull down the TV. The TV should already be in *Tutorial* mode and the starting materials and solvent should be listed. From the group of reagents found on the lab bench, select the correct reagent to synthesize the target compound and add it to the flask on the stir plate. Now attach the heater, condenser, and N_2 gas to the round bottom flask so the reaction mixture can be heated.

3. Start the reaction by clicking on the *Stir* button on the front of the stir plate. You should be able to observe the reaction mixture stirring in the flask. Monitor the progress of the reaction using TLC measurements as necessary until the product has formed and the starting materials have been consumed. You can advance the laboratory time using the clock on the wall. With the electronic lab book open (click on the lab book on the lab bench), you can also save your TLC plates by clicking *Save* on the TLC window.

4. When the reaction is complete, "work up" your reaction by first dragging and dropping the separatory funnel (located in a drawer) on the flask and then adding H_2O to the funnel. Extract the organic layer in the funnel by clicking on the top layer and dragging it to the cork ring on the lab bench. Your target compound should now be in this flask.

List the starting materials, solvent, reagent, and products formed: _____

_____

How long did it take to finish the reaction? _____

What are the TLC values (R_f) for (a) Starting Materials: _____ (b) Products: _____

Write a mechanism for this reaction:

IR and NMR Spectra

After completing a reaction and working up the products, it is still necessary to confirm that the correct product was formed. The most common tools used for this analysis are Infrared (IR) and Nuclear Magnetic Resonance (NMR) spectroscopy. In the virtual laboratory, only ^{1}H NMR spectra are available. Details on interpreting IR and NMR spectra are found in your textbook. Your instructor may or may not ask you to perform this section depending on how your class is structured.

5. To collect an IR spectrum of your product, click on the IR spectrometer located underneath the laboratory clock and drag the salt plate icon to the flask on the lab bench. A window containing the IR spectrum for your product should now open. Identify the relevant peaks in the IR spectrum and record the position and associated functional group for each in the IR table below. The IR spectrum can also be saved to the lab book for later analysis.

IR List position (cm^{-1}) & functional group	4.
1.	5.
2.	6.
3.	7.

6. To collect a ^{1}H NMR spectrum of your product, click on the NMR magnet located to the right of the chalkboard and drag the NMR sample tube to the flask on the lab bench. A window containing the NMR spectrum for your product should now open. You can zoom into various portions of the NMR spectrum by clicking and dragging over the desired area. The *Zoom Out* button is used to zoom back out to view the full spectrum. Identify all of the peaks in the NMR spectrum and record the chemical shift, the splitting, and the number of hydrogens for each peak in the NMR table below. The NMR spectrum can also be saved to the lab book for later analysis.

^{1}H NMR Structure: 2-Bromo-cyclohexanone	Peak	Chemical Shift (δ)	Multiplicity[†]	H[‡]	Peak	Chemical Shift (δ)	Multiplicity[†]	H[‡]
	1				7			
	2				8			
	3				9			
	4				10			
	5				11			
	6				12			

[†] Specify the multiplicity as a singlet (s), doublet (d), triplet (t), quartet (q), or multiplet (m).
[‡] Specify the number of hydrogens associated with each peak.

7. *Do the IR and NMR spectra you measured and recorded in the tables above confirm that you synthesized the assigned target compound? Explain.* _____

_____

_____

_____

VCL 11-3: α-Halogenation – 3

For this assignment, the target compound that you should synthesize is **bromo-phenyl-acetic acid.** This is another electrophilic substitution reaction. Examine the product and determine which bonds may be formed. Consider the mechanism and how a nucleophilic intermediate may generated and used to form the new bond.

Synthesis Procedures

1. Start *Virtual ChemLab* and select *α-Halogenation – 3* from the list of assignments in the electronic workbook. After entering the organic laboratory, go to the stockroom by clicking inside the *Stockroom* window. Next, select a round bottom flask and place it on the cork ring on the stockroom counter. Using the available reagents on the stockroom shelf, identify the appropriate starting materials required to synthesize the target compound and add them to the round bottom flask. Select the appropriate solvent and click on the green *Return to Lab* arrow to return to the laboratory.

2. The round bottom flask containing the starting materials should now be on the stir plate. Click on the handle located in the upper right corner of the laboratory to pull down the TV. The TV should already be in *Tutorial* mode and the starting materials and solvent should be listed. From the group of reagents found on the lab bench, select the correct reagent to synthesize the target compound and add it to the flask on the stir plate. Now attach the heater, condenser, and N_2 gas to the round bottom flask so the reaction mixture can be heated.

3. Start the reaction by clicking on the *Stir* button on the front of the stir plate. You should be able to observe the reaction mixture stirring in the flask. Monitor the progress of the reaction using TLC measurements as necessary until the product has formed and the starting materials have been consumed. You can advance the laboratory time using the clock on the wall. With the electronic lab book open (click on the lab book on the lab bench), you can also save your TLC plates by clicking *Save* on the TLC window.

4. When the reaction is complete, "work up" your reaction by first dragging and dropping the separatory funnel (located in a drawer) on the flask and then adding H_2O to the funnel. Extract the organic layer in the funnel by clicking on the top layer and dragging it to the cork ring on the lab bench. Your target compound should now be in this flask.

    List the starting materials, solvent, reagent, and products formed: _____

    _____

    How long did it take to finish the reaction? _____

    What are the TLC values (R_f) for (a) Starting Materials: _____ (b) Products: _____

    Write a mechanism for this reaction:

IR and NMR Spectra

After completing a reaction and working up the products, it is still necessary to confirm that the correct product was formed. The most common tools used for this analysis are Infrared (IR) and Nuclear Magnetic Resonance (NMR) spectroscopy. In the virtual laboratory, only ^{1}H NMR spectra are available. Details on interpreting IR and NMR spectra are found in your textbook. Your instructor may or may not ask you to perform this section depending on how your class is structured.

5. To collect an IR spectrum of your product, click on the IR spectrometer located underneath the laboratory clock and drag the salt plate icon to the flask on the lab bench. A window containing the IR spectrum for your product should now open. Identify the relevant peaks in the IR spectrum and record the position and associated functional group for each in the IR table below. The IR spectrum can also be saved to the lab book for later analysis.

IR List position (cm^{-1}) & functional group	4.
1.	5.
2.	6.
3.	7.

6. To collect a ^{1}H NMR spectrum of your product, click on the NMR magnet located to the right of the chalkboard and drag the NMR sample tube to the flask on the lab bench. A window containing the NMR spectrum for your product should now open. You can zoom into various portions of the NMR spectrum by clicking and dragging over the desired area. The *Zoom Out* button is used to zoom back out to view the full spectrum. Identify all of the peaks in the NMR spectrum and record the chemical shift, the splitting, and the number of hydrogens for each peak in the NMR table below. The NMR spectrum can also be saved to the lab book for later analysis.

^{1}H NMR Structure: Bromo-phenyl-acetic acid	Peak	Chemical Shift (δ)	Multiplicity[†]	H[‡]	Peak	Chemical Shift (δ)	Multiplicity[†]	H[‡]
	1				7			
	2				8			
	3				9			
	4				10			
	5				11			
	6				12			

[†] Specify the multiplicity as a singlet (s), doublet (d), triplet (t), quartet (q), or multiplet (m).
[‡] Specify the number of hydrogens associated with each peak.

7. *Do the IR and NMR spectra you measured and recorded in the tables above confirm that you*

   synthesized the assigned target compound? Explain. _____

   _____

   _____

   _____

VCL 11-4: Aldol – 1

For this assignment, the target compound that you should synthesize is **2-ethyl-3-hydroxy-hexanal.** This is a symmetric aldol reaction. Examine the product and determine which bond may be formed to link the two aldehydes. Keep in mind the mechanism and identify the nucleophile and the electrophile.

Synthesis Procedures
1. Start *Virtual ChemLab* and select *Aldol – 1* from the list of assignments in the electronic workbook. After entering the organic laboratory, go to the stockroom by clicking inside the *Stockroom* window. Next, select a round bottom flask and place it on the cork ring on the stockroom counter. Using the available reagents on the stockroom shelf, identify the appropriate starting materials required to synthesize the target compound and add them to the round bottom flask. Select the appropriate solvent and click on the green *Return to Lab* arrow to return to the laboratory.

2. The round bottom flask containing the starting materials should now be on the stir plate. Click on the handle located in the upper right corner of the laboratory to pull down the TV. The TV should already be in *Tutorial* mode and the starting materials and solvent should be listed. From the group of reagents found on the lab bench, select the correct reagent to synthesize the target compound and add it to the flask on the stir plate. Now put the mixture in an ice bath so the reaction mixture can be cooled.

3. Start the reaction by clicking on the *Stir* button on the front of the stir plate. You should be able to observe the reaction mixture stirring in the flask. Monitor the progress of the reaction using TLC measurements as necessary until the product has formed and the starting materials have been consumed. You can advance the laboratory time using the clock on the wall. With the electronic lab book open (click on the lab book on the lab bench), you can also save your TLC plates by clicking *Save* on the TLC window.

4. When the reaction is complete, "work up" your reaction by first dragging and dropping the separatory funnel (located in a drawer) on the flask and then adding H_2O to the funnel. Extract the organic layer in the funnel by clicking on the top layer and dragging it to the cork ring on the lab bench. Your target compound should now be in this flask.

List the starting materials, solvent, reagent, and products formed: _____

_____

How long did it take to finish the reaction? _____

What are the TLC values (R_f) for (a) Starting Materials: _____ *(b) Products:* _____

Write a mechanism for this reaction:

IR and NMR Spectra

After completing a reaction and working up the products, it is still necessary to confirm that the correct product was formed. The most common tools used for this analysis are Infrared (IR) and Nuclear Magnetic Resonance (NMR) spectroscopy. In the virtual laboratory, only ^{1}H NMR spectra are available. Details on interpreting IR and NMR spectra are found in your textbook. Your instructor may or may not ask you to perform this section depending on how your class is structured.

5. To collect an IR spectrum of your product, click on the IR spectrometer located underneath the laboratory clock and drag the salt plate icon to the flask on the lab bench. A window containing the IR spectrum for your product should now open. Identify the relevant peaks in the IR spectrum and record the position and associated functional group for each in the IR table below. The IR spectrum can also be saved to the lab book for later analysis.

IR List position (cm^{-1}) & functional group	4.
1.	5.
2.	6.
3.	7.

6. To collect a ^{1}H NMR spectrum of your product, click on the NMR magnet located to the right of the chalkboard and drag the NMR sample tube to the flask on the lab bench. A window containing the NMR spectrum for your product should now open. You can zoom into various portions of the NMR spectrum by clicking and dragging over the desired area. The *Zoom Out* button is used to zoom back out to view the full spectrum. Identify all of the peaks in the NMR spectrum and record the chemical shift, the splitting, and the number of hydrogens for each peak in the NMR table below. The NMR spectrum can also be saved to the lab book for later analysis.

^{1}H NMR Structure: 2-Ethyl-3-hydroxy-hexanal	Peak	Chemical Shift (δ)	Multiplicity†	H‡	Peak	Chemical Shift (δ)	Multiplicity†	H‡
	1				7			
	2				8			
	3				9			
	4				10			
	5				11			
	6				12			

† Specify the multiplicity as a singlet (s), doublet (d), triplet (t), quartet (q), or multiplet (m).
‡ Specify the number of hydrogens associated with each peak.

7. *Do the IR and NMR spectra you measured and recorded in the tables above confirm that you synthesized the assigned target compound? Explain.* _____

_____

_____

_____

VCL 11-5: Aldol – 2

For this assignment, the target compound that you should synthesize is **2-ethyl-hex-2-enal.** This is a symmetric aldol condensation reaction. Examine the product and determine which bond may be formed to link the two aldehydes. Keep in mind the mechanism and identify the nucleophile and the electrophile.

Synthesis Procedures

1. Start *Virtual ChemLab* and select *Aldol – 2* from the list of assignments in the electronic workbook. After entering the organic laboratory, go to the stockroom by clicking inside the *Stockroom* window. Next, select a round bottom flask and place it on the cork ring on the stockroom counter. Using the available reagents on the stockroom shelf, identify the appropriate starting materials required to synthesize the target compound and add them to the round bottom flask. Select the appropriate solvent and click on the green *Return to Lab* arrow to return to the laboratory.

2. The round bottom flask containing the starting materials should now be on the stir plate. Click on the handle located in the upper right corner of the laboratory to pull down the TV. The TV should already be in *Tutorial* mode and the starting materials and solvent should be listed. From the group of reagents found on the lab bench, select the correct reagent to synthesize the target compound and add it to the flask on the stir plate. Now attach the heater, condenser, and N_2 gas to the round bottom flask so the reaction mixture can be heated.

3. Start the reaction by clicking on the *Stir* button on the front of the stir plate. You should be able to observe the reaction mixture stirring in the flask. Monitor the progress of the reaction using TLC measurements as necessary until the product has formed and the starting materials have been consumed. You can advance the laboratory time using the clock on the wall. With the electronic lab book open (click on the lab book on the lab bench), you can also save your TLC plates by clicking *Save* on the TLC window.

4. When the reaction is complete, "work up" your reaction by first dragging and dropping the separatory funnel (located in a drawer) on the flask and then adding H_2O to the funnel. Extract the organic layer in the funnel by clicking on the top layer and dragging it to the cork ring on the lab bench. Your target compound should now be in this flask.

   List the starting materials, solvent, reagent, and products formed: _____

   _____

   How long did it take to finish the reaction? _____

   What are the TLC values (R_f) for (a) Starting Materials: _____ (b) Products: _____

   Write a mechanism for this reaction:

IR and NMR Spectra

After completing a reaction and working up the products, it is still necessary to confirm that the correct product was formed. The most common tools used for this analysis are Infrared (IR) and Nuclear Magnetic Resonance (NMR) spectroscopy. In the virtual laboratory, only ^{1}H NMR spectra are available. Details on interpreting IR and NMR spectra are found in your textbook. Your instructor may or may not ask you to perform this section depending on how your class is structured.

5. To collect an IR spectrum of your product, click on the IR spectrometer located underneath the laboratory clock and drag the salt plate icon to the flask on the lab bench. A window containing the IR spectrum for your product should now open. Identify the relevant peaks in the IR spectrum and record the position and associated functional group for each in the IR table below. The IR spectrum can also be saved to the lab book for later analysis.

IR List position (cm^{-1}) & functional group	4.
1.	5.
2.	6.
3.	7.

6. To collect a ^{1}H NMR spectrum of your product, click on the NMR magnet located to the right of the chalkboard and drag the NMR sample tube to the flask on the lab bench. A window containing the NMR spectrum for your product should now open. You can zoom into various portions of the NMR spectrum by clicking and dragging over the desired area. The *Zoom Out* button is used to zoom back out to view the full spectrum. Identify all of the peaks in the NMR spectrum and record the chemical shift, the splitting, and the number of hydrogens for each peak in the NMR table below. The NMR spectrum can also be saved to the lab book for later analysis.

^{1}H NMR Structure: 2-Ethyl-hex-2-enal	Peak	Chemical Shift (δ)	Multiplicity[†]	H[‡]	Peak	Chemical Shift (δ)	Multiplicity[†]	H[‡]
	1				7			
	2				8			
	3				9			
	4				10			
	5				11			
	6				12			

[†] Specify the multiplicity as a singlet (s), doublet (d), triplet (t), quartet (q), or multiplet (m).
[‡] Specify the number of hydrogens associated with each peak.

7. *Do the IR and NMR spectra you measured and recorded in the tables above confirm that you*

    synthesized the assigned target compound? Explain. _____

    _____

    _____

    _____

VCL 11-6: Aldol – 3

For this assignment, the target compound that you should synthesize is **3-phenyl-propenal.** This is a crossed aldol reaction. Examine the product and determine which bond may be formed to link the two aldehydes. Keep in mind the mechanism and identify the nucleophile and the electrophile.

Synthesis Procedures

1. Start *Virtual ChemLab* and select *Aldol – 3* from the list of assignments in the electronic workbook. After entering the organic laboratory, go to the stockroom by clicking inside the *Stockroom* window. Next, select a round bottom flask and place it on the cork ring on the stockroom counter. Using the available reagents on the stockroom shelf, identify the appropriate starting materials required to synthesize the target compound and add them to the round bottom flask. Select the appropriate solvent and click on the green *Return to Lab* arrow to return to the laboratory.

2. The round bottom flask containing the starting materials should now be on the stir plate. Click on the handle located in the upper right corner of the laboratory to pull down the TV. The TV should already be in *Tutorial* mode and the starting materials and solvent should be listed. From the group of reagents found on the lab bench, select the correct reagent to synthesize the target compound and add it to the flask on the stir plate. Now attach the heater, condenser, and N_2 gas to the round bottom flask so the reaction mixture can be heated.

3. Start the reaction by clicking on the *Stir* button on the front of the stir plate. You should be able to observe the reaction mixture stirring in the flask. Monitor the progress of the reaction using TLC measurements as necessary until the product has formed and the starting materials have been consumed. You can advance the laboratory time using the clock on the wall. With the electronic lab book open (click on the lab book on the lab bench), you can also save your TLC plates by clicking *Save* on the TLC window.

4. When the reaction is complete, "work up" your reaction by first dragging and dropping the separatory funnel (located in a drawer) on the flask and then adding H_2O to the funnel. Extract the organic layer in the funnel by clicking on the top layer and dragging it to the cork ring on the lab bench. Your target compound should now be in this flask.

   List the starting materials, solvent, reagent, and products formed: _____

   _____

   How long did it take to finish the reaction? _____

   What are the TLC values (R_f) for (a) Starting Materials: _____ *(b) Products:* _____

   Write a mechanism for this reaction:

IR and NMR Spectra

After completing a reaction and working up the products, it is still necessary to confirm that the correct product was formed. The most common tools used for this analysis are Infrared (IR) and Nuclear Magnetic Resonance (NMR) spectroscopy. In the virtual laboratory, only ^{1}H NMR spectra are available. Details on interpreting IR and NMR spectra are found in your textbook. Your instructor may or may not ask you to perform this section depending on how your class is structured.

5. To collect an IR spectrum of your product, click on the IR spectrometer located underneath the laboratory clock and drag the salt plate icon to the flask on the lab bench. A window containing the IR spectrum for your product should now open. Identify the relevant peaks in the IR spectrum and record the position and associated functional group for each in the IR table below. The IR spectrum can also be saved to the lab book for later analysis.

IR List position (cm^{-1}) & functional group	4.
1.	5.
2.	6.
3.	7.

6. To collect a ^{1}H NMR spectrum of your product, click on the NMR magnet located to the right of the chalkboard and drag the NMR sample tube to the flask on the lab bench. A window containing the NMR spectrum for your product should now open. You can zoom into various portions of the NMR spectrum by clicking and dragging over the desired area. The *Zoom Out* button is used to zoom back out to view the full spectrum. Identify all of the peaks in the NMR spectrum and record the chemical shift, the splitting, and the number of hydrogens for each peak in the NMR table below. The NMR spectrum can also be saved to the lab book for later analysis.

^{1}H NMR Structure: 3-Phenyl-propenal	Peak	Chemical Shift (δ)	Multiplicity†	H‡	Peak	Chemical Shift (δ)	Multiplicity†	H‡
	1				7			
	2				8			
	3				9			
	4				10			
	5				11			
	6				12			

† Specify the multiplicity as a singlet (s), doublet (d), triplet (t), quartet (q), or multiplet (m).
‡ Specify the number of hydrogens associated with each peak.

7. *Do the IR and NMR spectra you measured and recorded in the tables above confirm that you synthesized the assigned target compound? Explain.* _____

_____

_____

_____

VCL 11-7: Aldol – 4

For this assignment, the target compound that you should synthesize is **1-hydroxy-2,4,4-trimethyl-1-phenyl-pentan-3-one.** This is a crossed aldol reaction. Examine the product and determine which bond may be formed to link the two carbonyl compounds. Keep in mind the mechanism and identify the nucleophile and the electrophile. This is a closed, 6-atom transition state arrangement that controls the stereochemistry of the process. The geometry of the enolate must be taken into account.

Synthesis Procedures

1. Start *Virtual ChemLab* and select *Aldol –4* from the list of assignments in the electronic workbook. After entering the organic laboratory, go to the stockroom by clicking inside the *Stockroom* window. Next, select a round bottom flask and place it on the cork ring on the stockroom counter. Using the available reagents on the stockroom shelf, identify the appropriate starting materials required to synthesize the target compound and add them to the round bottom flask. Select the appropriate solvent and click on the green *Return to Lab* arrow to return to the laboratory.

2. The round bottom flask containing the starting materials should now be on the stir plate. Click on the handle located in the upper right corner of the laboratory to pull down the TV. The TV should already be in *Tutorial* mode and the starting materials and solvent should be listed. From the group of reagents found on the lab bench, select the correct reagent to synthesize the target compound and add it to the flask on the stir plate. Now put the mixture in an ice bath so the reaction mixture can be cooled.

3. Start the reaction by clicking on the *Stir* button on the front of the stir plate. You should be able to observe the reaction mixture stirring in the flask. Monitor the progress of the reaction using TLC measurements as necessary until the product has formed and the starting materials have been consumed. You can advance the laboratory time using the clock on the wall. With the electronic lab book open (click on the lab book on the lab bench), you can also save your TLC plates by clicking *Save* on the TLC window.

4. When the reaction is complete, "work up" your reaction by first dragging and dropping the separatory funnel (located in a drawer) on the flask and then adding HCl to the funnel. Extract the organic layer in the funnel by clicking on the top layer and dragging it to the cork ring on the lab bench. Your target compound should now be in this flask.

   List the starting materials, solvent, reagent, and products formed: _____

   _____

   How long did it take to finish the reaction? _____

   What are the TLC values (R_f) for (a) Starting Materials: _____ *(b) Products:* _____

   Write a mechanism for this reaction:

IR and NMR Spectra

After completing a reaction and working up the products, it is still necessary to confirm that the correct product was formed. The most common tools used for this analysis are Infrared (IR) and Nuclear Magnetic Resonance (NMR) spectroscopy. In the virtual laboratory, only ^{1}H NMR spectra are available. Details on interpreting IR and NMR spectra are found in your textbook. Your instructor may or may not ask you to perform this section depending on how your class is structured.

5. To collect an IR spectrum of your product, click on the IR spectrometer located underneath the laboratory clock and drag the salt plate icon to the flask on the lab bench. A window containing the IR spectrum for your product should now open. Identify the relevant peaks in the IR spectrum and record the position and associated functional group for each in the IR table below. The IR spectrum can also be saved to the lab book for later analysis.

IR List position (cm^{-1}) & functional group	4.
1.	5.
2.	6.
3.	7.

6. To collect a ^{1}H NMR spectrum of your product, click on the NMR magnet located to the right of the chalkboard and drag the NMR sample tube to the flask on the lab bench. A window containing the NMR spectrum for your product should now open. You can zoom into various portions of the NMR spectrum by clicking and dragging over the desired area. The *Zoom Out* button is used to zoom back out to view the full spectrum. Identify all of the peaks in the NMR spectrum and record the chemical shift, the splitting, and the number of hydrogens for each peak in the NMR table below. The NMR spectrum can also be saved to the lab book for later analysis.

^{1}H NMR	Peak	Chemical Shift (δ)	Multiplicity[†]	H[‡]	Peak	Chemical Shift (δ)	Multiplicity[†]	H[‡]
	1				7			
Structure:	2				8			
	3				9			
	4				10			
1-Hydroxy-2,4,4-trimethyl-1-phenyl-pentan-3-on	5				11			
	6				12			

[†] Specify the multiplicity as a singlet (s), doublet (d), triplet (t), quartet (q), or multiplet (m).
[‡] Specify the number of hydrogens associated with each peak.

7. *Do the IR and NMR spectra you measured and recorded in the tables above confirm that you synthesized the assigned target compound? Explain.* _____

_____

_____

_____

VCL 11-8: Claisen Condensation – 1

For this assignment, the target compound that you should synthesize is **methyl acetoacetate**. This is another carbonyl addition variation. Examine the product and determine which ester is the nucleophile and which is the electrophile. Keep in mind the mechanism and that you need to acidify the intermediate in order to isolate a neutral product.

Synthesis Procedures

1. Start *Virtual ChemLab* and select *Claisen Condensation –1* from the list of assignments in the electronic workbook. After entering the organic laboratory, go to the stockroom by clicking inside the *Stockroom* window. Next, select a round bottom flask and place it on the cork ring on the stockroom counter. Using the available reagents on the stockroom shelf, identify the appropriate starting materials required to synthesize the target compound and add them to the round bottom flask. Select the appropriate solvent and click on the green *Return to Lab* arrow to return to the laboratory.

2. The round bottom flask containing the starting materials should now be on the stir plate. Click on the handle located in the upper right corner of the laboratory to pull down the TV. The TV should already be in *Tutorial* mode and the starting materials and solvent should be listed. From the group of reagents found on the lab bench, select the correct reagent to synthesize the target compound and add it to the flask on the stir plate. Now attach the heater, condenser, and N_2 gas to the round bottom flask so the reaction mixture can be heated.

3. Start the reaction by clicking on the *Stir* button on the front of the stir plate. You should be able to observe the reaction mixture stirring in the flask. Monitor the progress of the reaction using TLC measurements as necessary until the product has formed and the starting materials have been consumed. You can advance the laboratory time using the clock on the wall. With the electronic lab book open (click on the lab book on the lab bench), you can also save your TLC plates by clicking *Save* on the TLC window.

4. When the reaction is complete, "work up" your reaction by first dragging and dropping the separatory funnel (located in a drawer) on the flask and then adding H_2O to the funnel. Extract the organic layer in the funnel by clicking on the top layer and dragging it to the cork ring on the lab bench. Your target compound should now be in this flask.

    List the starting materials, solvent, reagent, and products formed: _____

    _____

    How long did it take to finish the reaction? _____

    What are the TLC values (R_f) for (a) Starting Materials: _____ *(b) Products:* _____

    Write a mechanism for this reaction:

IR and NMR Spectra

After completing a reaction and working up the products, it is still necessary to confirm that the correct product was formed. The most common tools used for this analysis are Infrared (IR) and Nuclear Magnetic Resonance (NMR) spectroscopy. In the virtual laboratory, only ^{1}H NMR spectra are available. Details on interpreting IR and NMR spectra are found in your textbook. Your instructor may or may not ask you to perform this section depending on how your class is structured.

5.   To collect an IR spectrum of your product, click on the IR spectrometer located underneath the laboratory clock and drag the salt plate icon to the flask on the lab bench. A window containing the IR spectrum for your product should now open. Identify the relevant peaks in the IR spectrum and record the position and associated functional group for each in the IR table below. The IR spectrum can also be saved to the lab book for later analysis.

IR List position (cm^{-1}) & functional group	4.
1. 1750 C=O split	5.
2. 1300-1200 ester	6.
3. 1000 ester	7.

6.   To collect a ^{1}H NMR spectrum of your product, click on the NMR magnet located to the right of the chalkboard and drag the NMR sample tube to the flask on the lab bench. A window containing the NMR spectrum for your product should now open. You can zoom into various portions of the NMR spectrum by clicking and dragging over the desired area. The *Zoom Out* button is used to zoom back out to view the full spectrum. Identify all of the peaks in the NMR spectrum and record the chemical shift, the splitting, and the number of hydrogens for each peak in the NMR table below. The NMR spectrum can also be saved to the lab book for later analysis.

^{1}H NMR	Peak	Chemical Shift (δ)	Multiplicity[†]	H[‡]	Peak	Chemical Shift (δ)	Multiplicity[†]	H[‡]
Structure:	1	3.69	s	2	7			
	2	3.64	s	3	8			
(structure drawing) OMe	3	2.23	s	3	9			
Methyl acetoacetate	4				10			
	5				11			
	6				12			

[†] Specify the multiplicity as a singlet (s), doublet (d), triplet (t), quartet (q), or multiplet (m).
[‡] Specify the number of hydrogens associated with each peak.

7.   *Do the IR and NMR spectra you measured and recorded in the tables above confirm that you*

synthesized the assigned target compound? Explain. _____

_____

_____

_____

VCL 11-9: Claisen Condensation – 2

For this assignment, the target compound that you should synthesize is **methyl-3-oxopentanoate**. This is a crossed carbonyl addition variation. Examine the product and determine which ester is the nucleophile and which is the electrophile. Keep in mind the mechanism and that you need to acidify the intermediate in order to isolate a neutral product.

Synthesis Procedures

1. Start *Virtual ChemLab* and select *Claisen Condensation –2* from the list of assignments in the electronic workbook. After entering the organic laboratory, go to the stockroom by clicking inside the *Stockroom* window. Next, select a round bottom flask and place it on the cork ring on the stockroom counter. Using the available reagents on the stockroom shelf, identify the appropriate starting materials required to synthesize the target compound and add them to the round bottom flask. Select the appropriate solvent and click on the green *Return to Lab* arrow to return to the laboratory.

2. The round bottom flask containing the starting materials should now be on the stir plate. Click on the handle located in the upper right corner of the laboratory to pull down the TV. The TV should already be in *Tutorial* mode and the starting materials and solvent should be listed. From the group of reagents found on the lab bench, select the correct reagent to synthesize the target compound and add it to the flask on the stir plate. Now attach the heater, condenser, and N_2 gas to the round bottom flask so the reaction mixture can be heated.

3. Start the reaction by clicking on the *Stir* button on the front of the stir plate. You should be able to observe the reaction mixture stirring in the flask. Monitor the progress of the reaction using TLC measurements as necessary until the product has formed and the starting materials have been consumed. You can advance the laboratory time using the clock on the wall. With the electronic lab book open (click on the lab book on the lab bench), you can also save your TLC plates by clicking *Save* on the TLC window.

4. When the reaction is complete, "work up" your reaction by first dragging and dropping the separatory funnel (located in a drawer) on the flask and then adding H_2O to the funnel. Extract the organic layer in the funnel by clicking on the top layer and dragging it to the cork ring on the lab bench. Your target compound should now be in this flask.

   List the starting materials, solvent, reagent, and products formed: _____

   _____

   How long did it take to finish the reaction? _____

   What are the TLC values (R_f) for (a) Starting Materials: _____ *(b) Products:* _____

   Write a mechanism for this reaction:

IR and NMR Spectra

After completing a reaction and working up the products, it is still necessary to confirm that the correct product was formed. The most common tools used for this analysis are Infrared (IR) and Nuclear Magnetic Resonance (NMR) spectroscopy. In the virtual laboratory, only ^{1}H NMR spectra are available. Details on interpreting IR and NMR spectra are found in your textbook. Your instructor may or may not ask you to perform this section depending on how your class is structured.

5. To collect an IR spectrum of your product, click on the IR spectrometer located underneath the laboratory clock and drag the salt plate icon to the flask on the lab bench. A window containing the IR spectrum for your product should now open. Identify the relevant peaks in the IR spectrum and record the position and associated functional group for each in the IR table below. The IR spectrum can also be saved to the lab book for later analysis.

IR List position (cm^{-1}) & functional group	4.
1.	5.
2.	6.
3.	7.

6. To collect a ^{1}H NMR spectrum of your product, click on the NMR magnet located to the right of the chalkboard and drag the NMR sample tube to the flask on the lab bench. A window containing the NMR spectrum for your product should now open. You can zoom into various portions of the NMR spectrum by clicking and dragging over the desired area. The *Zoom Out* button is used to zoom back out to view the full spectrum. Identify all of the peaks in the NMR spectrum and record the chemical shift, the splitting, and the number of hydrogens for each peak in the NMR table below. The NMR spectrum can also be saved to the lab book for later analysis.

^{1}H NMR	Peak	Chemical Shift (δ)	Multiplicity†	H‡	Peak	Chemical Shift (δ)	Multiplicity†	H‡
	1				7			
Structure:	2				8			
	3				9			
Methyl-3-oxopentanoate	4				10			
	5				11			
	6				12			

† Specify the multiplicity as a singlet (s), doublet (d), triplet (t), quartet (q), or multiplet (m).
‡ Specify the number of hydrogens associated with each peak.

7. *Do the IR and NMR spectra you measured and recorded in the tables above confirm that you synthesized the assigned target compound? Explain.* _____

_____

_____

_____

VCL 11-10: Claisen Condensation – 3

For this assignment, the target compound that you should synthesize is **methyl-2-methyl-3-oxobutanoate.** This is a crossed carbonyl addition variation. Examine the product and determine which ester is the nucleophile and which is the electrophile. Keep in mind the mechanism and that you need to acidify the intermediate in order to isolate a neutral product.

Synthesis Procedures

1. Start *Virtual ChemLab* and select *Claisen Condensation –3* from the list of assignments in the electronic workbook. After entering the organic laboratory, go to the stockroom by clicking inside the *Stockroom* window. Next, select a round bottom flask and place it on the cork ring on the stockroom counter. Using the available reagents on the stockroom shelf, identify the appropriate starting materials required to synthesize the target compound and add them to the round bottom flask. Select the appropriate solvent and click on the green *Return to Lab* arrow to return to the laboratory.

2. The round bottom flask containing the starting materials should now be on the stir plate. Click on the handle located in the upper right corner of the laboratory to pull down the TV. The TV should already be in *Tutorial* mode and the starting materials and solvent should be listed. From the group of reagents found on the lab bench, select the correct reagent to synthesize the target compound and add it to the flask on the stir plate. Now attach the heater, condenser, and N_2 gas to the round bottom flask so the reaction mixture can be heated.

3. Start the reaction by clicking on the *Stir* button on the front of the stir plate. You should be able to observe the reaction mixture stirring in the flask. Monitor the progress of the reaction using TLC measurements as necessary until the product has formed and the starting materials have been consumed. You can advance the laboratory time using the clock on the wall. With the electronic lab book open (click on the lab book on the lab bench), you can also save your TLC plates by clicking *Save* on the TLC window.

4. When the reaction is complete, "work up" your reaction by first dragging and dropping the separatory funnel (located in a drawer) on the flask and then adding H_2O to the funnel. Extract the organic layer in the funnel by clicking on the top layer and dragging it to the cork ring on the lab bench. Your target compound should now be in this flask.

List the starting materials, solvent, reagent, and products formed: _____

_____

How long did it take to finish the reaction? _____

What are the TLC values (R_f) for (a) Starting Materials: _____ *(b) Products:* _____

Write a mechanism for this reaction:

IR and NMR Spectra

After completing a reaction and working up the products, it is still necessary to confirm that the correct product was formed. The most common tools used for this analysis are Infrared (IR) and Nuclear Magnetic Resonance (NMR) spectroscopy. In the virtual laboratory, only ^{1}H NMR spectra are available. Details on interpreting IR and NMR spectra are found in your textbook. Your instructor may or may not ask you to perform this section depending on how your class is structured.

5. To collect an IR spectrum of your product, click on the IR spectrometer located underneath the laboratory clock and drag the salt plate icon to the flask on the lab bench. A window containing the IR spectrum for your product should now open. Identify the relevant peaks in the IR spectrum and record the position and associated functional group for each in the IR table below. The IR spectrum can also be saved to the lab book for later analysis.

IR List position (cm^{-1}) & functional group	4.
1.	5.
2.	6.
3.	7.

6. To collect a ^{1}H NMR spectrum of your product, click on the NMR magnet located to the right of the chalkboard and drag the NMR sample tube to the flask on the lab bench. A window containing the NMR spectrum for your product should now open. You can zoom into various portions of the NMR spectrum by clicking and dragging over the desired area. The *Zoom Out* button is used to zoom back out to view the full spectrum. Identify all of the peaks in the NMR spectrum and record the chemical shift, the splitting, and the number of hydrogens for each peak in the NMR table below. The NMR spectrum can also be saved to the lab book for later analysis.

^{1}H NMR	Peak	Chemical Shift (δ)	Multiplicity†	H‡	Peak	Chemical Shift (δ)	Multiplicity†	H‡
Structure:	1				7			
	2				8			
(Methyl-2-methyl-3-oxobutanoate, OMe)	3				9			
	4				10			
Methyl-2-methyl-3-oxobutanoate	5				11			
	6				12			

† Specify the multiplicity as a singlet (s), doublet (d), triplet (t), quartet (q), or multiplet (m).
‡ Specify the number of hydrogens associated with each peak.

7. *Do the IR and NMR spectra you measured and recorded in the tables above confirm that you synthesized the assigned target compound? Explain.* _____

_____

_____

VCL 11-11: Dieckmann Reaction

For this assignment, the target compound that you should synthesize is **2-oxo-cyclohexane carboxylic acid methyl ester.** This is an intramolecular carbonyl addition variation. Examine the product and determine which ester is the nucleophile and which is the electrophile. Keep in mind the mechanism and that you need to acidify the intermediate in order to isolate a neutral product.

Synthesis Procedures

1. Start *Virtual ChemLab* and select *Dieckmann Reaction* from the list of assignments in the electronic workbook. After entering the organic laboratory, go to the stockroom by clicking inside the *Stockroom* window. Next, select a round bottom flask and place it on the cork ring on the stockroom counter. Using the available reagents on the stockroom shelf, identify the appropriate starting materials required to synthesize the target compound and add them to the round bottom flask. Select the appropriate solvent and click on the green *Return to Lab* arrow to return to the laboratory.

2. The round bottom flask containing the starting materials should now be on the stir plate. Click on the handle located in the upper right corner of the laboratory to pull down the TV. The TV should already be in *Tutorial* mode and the starting materials and solvent should be listed. From the group of reagents found on the lab bench, select the correct reagent to synthesize the target compound and add it to the flask on the stir plate. Now attach the heater, condenser, and N_2 gas to the round bottom flask so the reaction mixture can be heated.

3. Start the reaction by clicking on the *Stir* button on the front of the stir plate. You should be able to observe the reaction mixture stirring in the flask. Monitor the progress of the reaction using TLC measurements as necessary until the product has formed and the starting materials have been consumed. You can advance the laboratory time using the clock on the wall. With the electronic lab book open (click on the lab book on the lab bench), you can also save your TLC plates by clicking *Save* on the TLC window.

4. When the reaction is complete, "work up" your reaction by first dragging and dropping the separatory funnel (located in a drawer) on the flask and then adding H_2O to the funnel. Extract the organic layer in the funnel by clicking on the top layer and dragging it to the cork ring on the lab bench. Your target compound should now be in this flask.

   List the starting materials, solvent, reagent, and products formed: _____

   _____

   How long did it take to finish the reaction? _____

   What are the TLC values (R_f) for (a) Starting Materials: _____ (b) Products: _____

   Write a mechanism for this reaction:

IR and NMR Spectra

After completing a reaction and working up the products, it is still necessary to confirm that the correct product was formed. The most common tools used for this analysis are Infrared (IR) and Nuclear Magnetic Resonance (NMR) spectroscopy. In the virtual laboratory, only ^{1}H NMR spectra are available. Details on interpreting IR and NMR spectra are found in your textbook. Your instructor may or may not ask you to perform this section depending on how your class is structured.

5. To collect an IR spectrum of your product, click on the IR spectrometer located underneath the laboratory clock and drag the salt plate icon to the flask on the lab bench. A window containing the IR spectrum for your product should now open. Identify the relevant peaks in the IR spectrum and record the position and associated functional group for each in the IR table below. The IR spectrum can also be saved to the lab book for later analysis.

IR List position (cm^{-1}) & functional group	4.
1.	5.
2.	6.
3.	7.

6. To collect a ^{1}H NMR spectrum of your product, click on the NMR magnet located to the right of the chalkboard and drag the NMR sample tube to the flask on the lab bench. A window containing the NMR spectrum for your product should now open. You can zoom into various portions of the NMR spectrum by clicking and dragging over the desired area. The *Zoom Out* button is used to zoom back out to view the full spectrum. Identify all of the peaks in the NMR spectrum and record the chemical shift, the splitting, and the number of hydrogens for each peak in the NMR table below. The NMR spectrum can also be saved to the lab book for later analysis.

^{1}**H NMR** Structure: 2-Oxo-cyclohexane carboxylic acid methyl ester	Peak	Chemical Shift (δ)	Multiplicity†	H‡	Peak	Chemical Shift (δ)	Multiplicity†	H‡
	1				7			
	2				8			
	3				9			
	4				10			
	5				11			
	6				12			

† Specify the multiplicity as a singlet (s), doublet (d), triplet (t), quartet (q), or multiplet (m).
‡ Specify the number of hydrogens associated with each peak.

7. *Do the IR and NMR spectra you measured and recorded in the tables above confirm that you*

   synthesized the assigned target compound? Explain. _____

   _____

   _____

   _____

VCL 11-12: Aldol – 5

For this assignment, the target compound that you should synthesize is ***anti*-3-hydroxy-2-methyl-hexanoic acid-2,6-dimethyl-phenyl ester.** This is a crossed aldol reaction. Examine the product and determine which bond may be formed to link the two carbonyl compounds. Keep in mind the mechanism and identify the nucleophile and the electrophile. This is a closed, 6-atom transition state arrangement that controls the stereochemistry of the process. The geometry of the enolate must be considered.

Synthesis Procedures
1. Start *Virtual ChemLab* and select *Aldol –5* from the list of assignments in the electronic workbook. After entering the organic laboratory, go to the stockroom by clicking inside the *Stockroom* window. Next, select a round bottom flask and place it on the cork ring on the stockroom counter. Using the available reagents on the stockroom shelf, identify the appropriate starting materials required to synthesize the target compound and add them to the round bottom flask. Select the appropriate solvent and click on the green *Return to Lab* arrow to return to the laboratory.

2. The round bottom flask containing the starting materials should now be on the stir plate. Click on the handle located in the upper right corner of the laboratory to pull down the TV. The TV should already be in *Tutorial* mode and the starting materials and solvent should be listed. From the group of reagents found on the lab bench, select the correct reagent to synthesize the target compound and add it to the flask on the stir plate. Now put the mixture in an ice bath so the reaction mixture can be cooled.

3. Start the reaction by clicking on the *Stir* button on the front of the stir plate. You should be able to observe the reaction mixture stirring in the flask. Monitor the progress of the reaction using TLC measurements as necessary until the product has formed and the starting materials have been consumed. You can advance the laboratory time using the clock on the wall. With the electronic lab book open (click on the lab book on the lab bench), you can also save your TLC plates by clicking *Save* on the TLC window.

4. When the reaction is complete, "work up" your reaction by first dragging and dropping the separatory funnel (located in a drawer) on the flask and then adding HCl to the funnel. Extract the organic layer in the funnel by clicking on the top layer and dragging it to the cork ring on the lab bench. Your target compound should now be in this flask.

List the starting materials, solvent, reagent, and products formed: _____

_____

_____

How long did it take to finish the reaction? _____

What are the TLC values (R_f) for (a) Starting Materials: _____ (b) Products: _____

Write a mechanism for this reaction:

IR and NMR Spectra

After completing a reaction and working up the products, it is still necessary to confirm that the correct product was formed. The most common tools used for this analysis are Infrared (IR) and Nuclear Magnetic Resonance (NMR) spectroscopy. In the virtual laboratory, only ^{1}H NMR spectra are available. Details on interpreting IR and NMR spectra are found in your textbook. Your instructor may or may not ask you to perform this section depending on how your class is structured.

5. To collect an IR spectrum of your product, click on the IR spectrometer located underneath the laboratory clock and drag the salt plate icon to the flask on the lab bench. A window containing the IR spectrum for your product should now open. Identify the relevant peaks in the IR spectrum and record the position and associated functional group for each in the IR table below. The IR spectrum can also be saved to the lab book for later analysis.

IR List position (cm^{-1}) & functional group	4.
1.	5.
2.	6.
3.	7.

6. To collect a ^{1}H NMR spectrum of your product, click on the NMR magnet located to the right of the chalkboard and drag the NMR sample tube to the flask on the lab bench. A window containing the NMR spectrum for your product should now open. You can zoom into various portions of the NMR spectrum by clicking and dragging over the desired area. The *Zoom Out* button is used to zoom back out to view the full spectrum. Identify all of the peaks in the NMR spectrum and record the chemical shift, the splitting, and the number of hydrogens for each peak in the NMR table below. The NMR spectrum can also be saved to the lab book for later analysis.

^{1}H NMR Structure: *anti*-3-hydroxy-2-methyl-hexanoic acid-2,6-dimethyl-phenyl ester	Peak	Chemical Shift (δ)	Multiplicity†	H‡	Peak	Chemical Shift (δ)	Multiplicity†	H‡
	1				7			
	2				8			
	3				9			
	4				10			
	5				11			
	6				12			

† Specify the multiplicity as a singlet (s), doublet (d), triplet (t), quartet (q), or multiplet (m).
‡ Specify the number of hydrogens associated with each peak.

7. *Do the IR and NMR spectra you measured and recorded in the tables above confirm that you synthesized the assigned target compound? Explain.* _____

_____

_____

_____

VCL 12-1: Alcohol Oxidation – 1

For this assignment, the target compound that you should synthesize is **benzoic acid.** This is an oxidation reaction. Examine the product and determine a lower oxidation state functional group that may be present in the starting material.

Synthesis Procedures

1. Start *Virtual ChemLab* and select *Alcohol Oxidation – 1* from the list of assignments in the electronic workbook. After entering the organic laboratory, go to the stockroom by clicking inside the *Stockroom* window. Next, select a round bottom flask and place it on the cork ring on the stockroom counter. Using the available reagents on the stockroom shelf, identify the appropriate starting materials required to synthesize the target compound and add them to the round bottom flask. Select the appropriate solvent and click on the green *Return to Lab* arrow to return to the laboratory.

2. The round bottom flask containing the starting materials should now be on the stir plate. Click on the handle located in the upper right corner of the laboratory to pull down the TV. The TV should already be in *Tutorial* mode and the starting materials and solvent should be listed. From the group of reagents found on the lab bench, select the correct reagent to synthesize the target compound and add it to the flask on the stir plate. Now attach the heater, condenser, and N_2 gas to the round bottom flask so the reaction mixture can be heated.

3. Start the reaction by clicking on the *Stir* button on the front of the stir plate. You should be able to observe the reaction mixture stirring in the flask. Monitor the progress of the reaction using TLC measurements as necessary until the product has formed and the starting materials have been consumed. You can advance the laboratory time using the clock on the wall. With the electronic lab book open (click on the lab book on the lab bench), you can also save your TLC plates by clicking *Save* on the TLC window.

4. When the reaction is complete, "work up" your reaction by first dragging and dropping the separatory funnel (located in a drawer) on the flask and then adding H_2O to the funnel. Extract the organic layer in the funnel by clicking on the top layer and dragging it to the cork ring on the lab bench. Your target compound should now be in this flask.

List the starting materials, solvent, reagent, and products formed: _____

_____

How long did it take to finish the reaction? _____

What are the TLC values (R_f) for (a) Starting Materials: _____ *(b) Products:* _____

Write a mechanism for this reaction:

Chapter 12

IR and NMR Spectra

After completing a reaction and working up the products, it is still necessary to confirm that the correct product was formed. The most common tools used for this analysis are Infrared (IR) and Nuclear Magnetic Resonance (NMR) spectroscopy. In the virtual laboratory, only ^{1}H NMR spectra are available. Details on interpreting IR and NMR spectra are found in your textbook. Your instructor may or may not ask you to perform this section depending on how your class is structured.

5. To collect an IR spectrum of your product, click on the IR spectrometer located underneath the laboratory clock and drag the salt plate icon to the flask on the lab bench. A window containing the IR spectrum for your product should now open. Identify the relevant peaks in the IR spectrum and record the position and associated functional group for each in the IR table below. The IR spectrum can also be saved to the lab book for later analysis.

IR List position (cm^{-1}) & functional group	4.
1.	5.
2.	6.
3.	7.

6. To collect a ^{1}H NMR spectrum of your product, click on the NMR magnet located to the right of the chalkboard and drag the NMR sample tube to the flask on the lab bench. A window containing the NMR spectrum for your product should now open. You can zoom into various portions of the NMR spectrum by clicking and dragging over the desired area. The *Zoom Out* button is used to zoom back out to view the full spectrum. Identify all of the peaks in the NMR spectrum and record the chemical shift, the splitting, and the number of hydrogens for each peak in the NMR table below. The NMR spectrum can also be saved to the lab book for later analysis.

^{1}H NMR Structure: Benzoic acid	Peak	Chemical Shift (δ)	Multiplicity†	H‡	Peak	Chemical Shift (δ)	Multiplicity†	H‡
	1				7			
	2				8			
	3				9			
	4				10			
	5				11			
	6				12			

† Specify the multiplicity as a singlet (s), doublet (d), triplet (t), quartet (q), or multiplet (m).
‡ Specify the number of hydrogens associated with each peak.

7. *Do the IR and NMR spectra you measured and recorded in the tables above confirm that you synthesized the assigned target compound? Explain.* _____

_____

_____

_____

VCL 12-2: Alcohol Oxidation – 2

For this assignment, the target compound that you should synthesize is **benzaldehyde.** This is an oxidation reaction. Examine the product and determine a lower oxidation state functional group that may be present in the starting material. Keep in mind that you need to stop at the aldehyde oxidation state and prevent carboxylic acid formation.

Synthesis Procedures

1. Start *Virtual ChemLab* and select *Alcohol Oxidation – 2* from the list of assignments in the electronic workbook. After entering the organic laboratory, go to the stockroom by clicking inside the *Stockroom* window. Next, select a round bottom flask and place it on the cork ring on the stockroom counter. Using the available reagents on the stockroom shelf, identify the appropriate starting materials required to synthesize the target compound and add them to the round bottom flask. Select the appropriate solvent and click on the green *Return to Lab* arrow to return to the laboratory.

2. The round bottom flask containing the starting materials should now be on the stir plate. Click on the handle located in the upper right corner of the laboratory to pull down the TV. The TV should already be in *Tutorial* mode and the starting materials and solvent should be listed. From the group of reagents found on the lab bench, select the correct reagent to synthesize the target compound and add it to the flask on the stir plate. Now attach the heater, condenser, and N_2 gas to the round bottom flask so the reaction mixture can be heated.

3. Start the reaction by clicking on the *Stir* button on the front of the stir plate. You should be able to observe the reaction mixture stirring in the flask. Monitor the progress of the reaction using TLC measurements as necessary until the product has formed and the starting materials have been consumed. You can advance the laboratory time using the clock on the wall. With the electronic lab book open (click on the lab book on the lab bench), you can also save your TLC plates by clicking *Save* on the TLC window.

4. When the reaction is complete, "work up" your reaction by first dragging and dropping the separatory funnel (located in a drawer) on the flask and then adding HCl the funnel. Extract the organic layer in the funnel by clicking on the top layer and dragging it to the cork ring on the lab bench. Your target compound should now be in this flask.

   List the starting materials, solvent, reagent, and products formed: _____

   _____

   How long did it take to finish the reaction? _____

   What are the TLC values (R_f) for (a) Starting Materials: _____   (b) Products: _____

   Write a mechanism for this reaction:

IR and NMR Spectra

After completing a reaction and working up the products, it is still necessary to confirm that the correct product was formed. The most common tools used for this analysis are Infrared (IR) and Nuclear Magnetic Resonance (NMR) spectroscopy. In the virtual laboratory, only ^{1}H NMR spectra are available. Details on interpreting IR and NMR spectra are found in your textbook. Your instructor may or may not ask you to perform this section depending on how your class is structured.

5. To collect an IR spectrum of your product, click on the IR spectrometer located underneath the laboratory clock and drag the salt plate icon to the flask on the lab bench. A window containing the IR spectrum for your product should now open. Identify the relevant peaks in the IR spectrum and record the position and associated functional group for each in the IR table below. The IR spectrum can also be saved to the lab book for later analysis.

IR List position (cm⁻¹) & functional group	4.
1.	5.
2.	6.
3.	7.

6. To collect a ^{1}H NMR spectrum of your product, click on the NMR magnet located to the right of the chalkboard and drag the NMR sample tube to the flask on the lab bench. A window containing the NMR spectrum for your product should now open. You can zoom into various portions of the NMR spectrum by clicking and dragging over the desired area. The *Zoom Out* button is used to zoom back out to view the full spectrum. Identify all of the peaks in the NMR spectrum and record the chemical shift, the splitting, and the number of hydrogens for each peak in the NMR table below. The NMR spectrum can also be saved to the lab book for later analysis.

^{1}H NMR	Peak	Chemical Shift (δ)	Multiplicity†	H‡	Peak	Chemical Shift (δ)	Multiplicity†	H‡
	1				7			
Structure:	2				8			
Benzaldehyde	3				9			
	4				10			
	5				11			
	6				12			

† Specify the multiplicity as a singlet (s), doublet (d), triplet (t), quartet (q), or multiplet (m).
‡ Specify the number of hydrogens associated with each peak.

7. *Do the IR and NMR spectra you measured and recorded in the tables above confirm that you synthesized the assigned target compound? Explain.* _____

_____

_____

_____

VCL 12-3: Alcohol Oxidation – 3

For this assignment, the target compound that you should synthesize is **3-methyl-cyclohex-2-enone.** This is an oxidation reaction. Examine the product and determine a lower oxidation state functional group that may be present in the starting material. Keep in mind the mechanism and the possibility of a rearrangement.

Synthesis Procedures
1. Start *Virtual ChemLab* and select *Alcohol Oxidation – 3* from the list of assignments in the electronic workbook. After entering the organic laboratory, go to the stockroom by clicking inside the *Stockroom* window. Next, select a round bottom flask and place it on the cork ring on the stockroom counter. Using the available reagents on the stockroom shelf, identify the appropriate starting materials required to synthesize the target compound and add them to the round bottom flask. Select the appropriate solvent and click on the green *Return to Lab* arrow to return to the laboratory.

2. The round bottom flask containing the starting materials should now be on the stir plate. Click on the handle located in the upper right corner of the laboratory to pull down the TV. The TV should already be in *Tutorial* mode and the starting materials and solvent should be listed. From the group of reagents found on the lab bench, select the correct reagent to synthesize the target compound and add it to the flask on the stir plate. Now attach the heater, condenser, and N_2 gas to the round bottom flask so the reaction mixture can be heated.

3. Start the reaction by clicking on the *Stir* button on the front of the stir plate. You should be able to observe the reaction mixture stirring in the flask. Monitor the progress of the reaction using TLC measurements as necessary until the product has formed and the starting materials have been consumed. You can advance the laboratory time using the clock on the wall. With the electronic lab book open (click on the lab book on the lab bench), you can also save your TLC plates by clicking *Save* on the TLC window.

4. When the reaction is complete, "work up" your reaction by first dragging and dropping the separatory funnel (located in a drawer) on the flask and then adding HCl the funnel. Extract the organic layer in the funnel by clicking on the top layer and dragging it to the cork ring on the lab bench. Your target compound should now be in this flask.

List the starting materials, solvent, reagent, and products formed: _____

_____

How long did it take to finish the reaction? _____

What are the TLC values (R_f) for (a) Starting Materials: _____ *(b) Products:* _____

Write a mechanism for this reaction:

IR and NMR Spectra

After completing a reaction and working up the products, it is still necessary to confirm that the correct product was formed. The most common tools used for this analysis are Infrared (IR) and Nuclear Magnetic Resonance (NMR) spectroscopy. In the virtual laboratory, only ^{1}H NMR spectra are available. Details on interpreting IR and NMR spectra are found in your textbook. Your instructor may or may not ask you to perform this section depending on how your class is structured.

5. To collect an IR spectrum of your product, click on the IR spectrometer located underneath the laboratory clock and drag the salt plate icon to the flask on the lab bench. A window containing the IR spectrum for your product should now open. Identify the relevant peaks in the IR spectrum and record the position and associated functional group for each in the IR table below. The IR spectrum can also be saved to the lab book for later analysis.

IR List position (cm^{-1}) & functional group	4.
1.	5.
2.	6.
3.	7.

6. To collect a ^{1}H NMR spectrum of your product, click on the NMR magnet located to the right of the chalkboard and drag the NMR sample tube to the flask on the lab bench. A window containing the NMR spectrum for your product should now open. You can zoom into various portions of the NMR spectrum by clicking and dragging over the desired area. The *Zoom Out* button is used to zoom back out to view the full spectrum. Identify all of the peaks in the NMR spectrum and record the chemical shift, the splitting, and the number of hydrogens for each peak in the NMR table below. The NMR spectrum can also be saved to the lab book for later analysis.

^{1}H NMR Structure: 3-Methyl-cyclohex-2-enone	Peak	Chemical Shift (δ)	Multiplicity[†]	H[‡]	Peak	Chemical Shift (δ)	Multiplicity[†]	H[‡]
	1				7			
	2				8			
	3				9			
	4				10			
	5				11			
	6				12			

[†] Specify the multiplicity as a singlet (s), doublet (d), triplet (t), quartet (q), or multiplet (m).
[‡] Specify the number of hydrogens associated with each peak.

7. *Do the IR and NMR spectra you measured and recorded in the tables above confirm that you*

   synthesized the assigned target compound? Explain. _____

   _____

   _____

   _____

VCL 12-4: Aldehyde Oxidation

For this assignment, the target compound that you should synthesize is **butanoic acid.** This is an oxidation reaction. Examine the product and determine a lower oxidation state functional group that may be present in the starting material.

Synthesis Procedures

1. Start *Virtual ChemLab* and select *Aldehyde Oxidation* from the list of assignments in the electronic workbook. After entering the organic laboratory, go to the stockroom by clicking inside the *Stockroom* window. Next, select a round bottom flask and place it on the cork ring on the stockroom counter. Using the available reagents on the stockroom shelf, identify the appropriate starting materials required to synthesize the target compound and add them to the round bottom flask. Select the appropriate solvent and click on the green *Return to Lab* arrow to return to the laboratory.

2. The round bottom flask containing the starting materials should now be on the stir plate. Click on the handle located in the upper right corner of the laboratory to pull down the TV. The TV should already be in *Tutorial* mode and the starting materials and solvent should be listed. From the group of reagents found on the lab bench, select the correct reagent to synthesize the target compound and add it to the flask on the stir plate. Now attach the heater, condenser, and N_2 gas to the round bottom flask so the reaction mixture can be heated.

3. Start the reaction by clicking on the *Stir* button on the front of the stir plate. You should be able to observe the reaction mixture stirring in the flask. Monitor the progress of the reaction using TLC measurements as necessary until the product has formed and the starting materials have been consumed. You can advance the laboratory time using the clock on the wall. With the electronic lab book open (click on the lab book on the lab bench), you can also save your TLC plates by clicking *Save* on the TLC window.

4. When the reaction is complete, "work up" your reaction by first dragging and dropping the separatory funnel (located in a drawer) on the flask and then adding H_2O the funnel. Extract the organic layer in the funnel by clicking on the top layer and dragging it to the cork ring on the lab bench. Your target compound should now be in this flask.

List the starting materials, solvent, reagent, and products formed: _____

_____

How long did it take to finish the reaction? _____

What are the TLC values (R_f) for (a) Starting Materials: _____ *(b) Products:* _____

Write a mechanism for this reaction:

IR and NMR Spectra

After completing a reaction and working up the products, it is still necessary to confirm that the correct product was formed. The most common tools used for this analysis are Infrared (IR) and Nuclear Magnetic Resonance (NMR) spectroscopy. In the virtual laboratory, only ^{1}H NMR spectra are available. Details on interpreting IR and NMR spectra are found in your textbook. Your instructor may or may not ask you to perform this section depending on how your class is structured.

5. To collect an IR spectrum of your product, click on the IR spectrometer located underneath the laboratory clock and drag the salt plate icon to the flask on the lab bench. A window containing the IR spectrum for your product should now open. Identify the relevant peaks in the IR spectrum and record the position and associated functional group for each in the IR table below. The IR spectrum can also be saved to the lab book for later analysis.

IR List position (cm^{-1}) & functional group	4. **900 OH dimer**
1.	5.
2.	6.
3.	7.

6. To collect a ^{1}H NMR spectrum of your product, click on the NMR magnet located to the right of the chalkboard and drag the NMR sample tube to the flask on the lab bench. A window containing the NMR spectrum for your product should now open. You can zoom into various portions of the NMR spectrum by clicking and dragging over the desired area. The *Zoom Out* button is used to zoom back out to view the full spectrum. Identify all of the peaks in the NMR spectrum and record the chemical shift, the splitting, and the number of hydrogens for each peak in the NMR table below. The NMR spectrum can also be saved to the lab book for later analysis.

^{1}H NMR Structure: Butanoic acid	Peak	Chemical Shift (δ)	Multiplicity†	H‡	Peak	Chemical Shift (δ)	Multiplicity†	H‡
	1				7			
	2				8			
	3				9			
	4				10			
	5				11			
	6				12			

† Specify the multiplicity as a singlet (s), doublet (d), triplet (t), quartet (q), or multiplet (m).
‡ Specify the number of hydrogens associated with each peak.

7. *Do the IR and NMR spectra you measured and recorded in the tables above confirm that you synthesized the assigned target compound? Explain.* _____

_____

_____

_____

VCL 12-5: Baeyer-Villiger Oxidation

For this assignment, the target compound that you should synthesize is **propanoic acid, 1,1-dimethylethyl ester.** This is an oxidation reaction. Examine the product and determine a lower oxidation state functional group that may be present in the starting material. Keep in mind the mechanism and the potential for a migration in the process. Why does one group migrate in preference to the other?

Synthesis Procedures

1. Start *Virtual ChemLab* and select *Baeyer-Villiger Oxidation* from the list of assignments in the electronic workbook. After entering the organic laboratory, go to the stockroom by clicking inside the *Stockroom* window. Next, select a round bottom flask and place it on the cork ring on the stockroom counter. Using the available reagents on the stockroom shelf, identify the appropriate starting materials required to synthesize the target compound and add them to the round bottom flask. Select the appropriate solvent and click on the green *Return to Lab* arrow to return to the laboratory.

2. The round bottom flask containing the starting materials should now be on the stir plate. Click on the handle located in the upper right corner of the laboratory to pull down the TV. The TV should already be in *Tutorial* mode and the starting materials and solvent should be listed. From the group of reagents found on the lab bench, select the correct reagent to synthesize the target compound and add it to the flask on the stir plate. Now attach the heater, condenser, and N_2 gas to the round bottom flask so the reaction mixture can be heated.

3. Start the reaction by clicking on the *Stir* button on the front of the stir plate. You should be able to observe the reaction mixture stirring in the flask. Monitor the progress of the reaction using TLC measurements as necessary until the product has formed and the starting materials have been consumed. You can advance the laboratory time using the clock on the wall. With the electronic lab book open (click on the lab book on the lab bench), you can also save your TLC plates by clicking *Save* on the TLC window.

4. When the reaction is complete, "work up" your reaction by first dragging and dropping the separatory funnel (located in a drawer) on the flask and then adding NaOH the funnel. Extract the organic layer in the funnel by clicking on the top layer and dragging it to the cork ring on the lab bench. Your target compound should now be in this flask.

List the starting materials, solvent, reagent, and products formed: _____

_____

How long did it take to finish the reaction? _____

What are the TLC values (R_f) for (a) Starting Materials: _____ (b) Products: _____

Write a mechanism for this reaction:

IR and NMR Spectra

After completing a reaction and working up the products, it is still necessary to confirm that the correct product was formed. The most common tools used for this analysis are Infrared (IR) and Nuclear Magnetic Resonance (NMR) spectroscopy. In the virtual laboratory, only ^{1}H NMR spectra are available. Details on interpreting IR and NMR spectra are found in your textbook. Your instructor may or may not ask you to perform this section depending on how your class is structured.

5. To collect an IR spectrum of your product, click on the IR spectrometer located underneath the laboratory clock and drag the salt plate icon to the flask on the lab bench. A window containing the IR spectrum for your product should now open. Identify the relevant peaks in the IR spectrum and record the position and associated functional group for each in the IR table below. The IR spectrum can also be saved to the lab book for later analysis.

IR List position (cm^{-1}) & functional group	4. 1000 ester
1.	5.
2.	6.
3.	7.

6. To collect a ^{1}H NMR spectrum of your product, click on the NMR magnet located to the right of the chalkboard and drag the NMR sample tube to the flask on the lab bench. A window containing the NMR spectrum for your product should now open. You can zoom into various portions of the NMR spectrum by clicking and dragging over the desired area. The *Zoom Out* button is used to zoom back out to view the full spectrum. Identify all of the peaks in the NMR spectrum and record the chemical shift, the splitting, and the number of hydrogens for each peak in the NMR table below. The NMR spectrum can also be saved to the lab book for later analysis.

^{1}**H NMR** Structure: Propanoic acid, 1,1-dimethylethyl ester	Peak	Chemical Shift (δ)	Multiplicity†	H‡	Peak	Chemical Shift (δ)	Multiplicity†	H‡
	1				7			
	2				8			
	3				9			
	4				10			
	5				11			
	6				12			

† Specify the multiplicity as a singlet (s), doublet (d), triplet (t), quartet (q), or multiplet (m).
‡ Specify the number of hydrogens associated with each peak.

7. *Do the IR and NMR spectra you measured and recorded in the tables above confirm that you*

   synthesized the assigned target compound? Explain. _____

   _____

   _____

   _____

VCL 12-6: Alkene Dihydroxylation

For this assignment, the target compound that you should synthesize is **cis-octahydro-naphthalene-4a,8a-diol.** This is an oxidation reaction. Examine the product and determine a lower oxidation state functional group that may be present in the starting material. Keep in mind the mechanism and how it controls the stereochemistry of the process.

Synthesis Procedures

1. Start *Virtual ChemLab* and select *Alkene Dihydroxylation* from the list of assignments in the electronic workbook. After entering the organic laboratory, go to the stockroom by clicking inside the *Stockroom* window. Next, select a round bottom flask and place it on the cork ring on the stockroom counter. Using the available reagents on the stockroom shelf, identify the appropriate starting materials required to synthesize the target compound and add them to the round bottom flask. Select the appropriate solvent and click on the green *Return to Lab* arrow to return to the laboratory.

2. The round bottom flask containing the starting materials should now be on the stir plate. Click on the handle located in the upper right corner of the laboratory to pull down the TV. The TV should already be in *Tutorial* mode and the starting materials and solvent should be listed. From the group of reagents found on the lab bench, select the correct reagent to synthesize the target compound and add it to the flask on the stir plate. Now attach the heater, condenser, and N_2 gas to the round bottom flask so the reaction mixture can be heated.

3. Start the reaction by clicking on the *Stir* button on the front of the stir plate. You should be able to observe the reaction mixture stirring in the flask. Monitor the progress of the reaction using TLC measurements as necessary until the product has formed and the starting materials have been consumed. You can advance the laboratory time using the clock on the wall. With the electronic lab book open (click on the lab book on the lab bench), you can also save your TLC plates by clicking *Save* on the TLC window.

4. When the reaction is complete, "work up" your reaction by first dragging and dropping the separatory funnel (located in a drawer) on the flask and then adding H_2O the funnel. Extract the organic layer in the funnel by clicking on the top layer and dragging it to the cork ring on the lab bench. Your target compound should now be in this flask.

   List the starting materials, solvent, reagent, and products formed: _____

   _____

   How long did it take to finish the reaction? _____

   What are the TLC values (R_f) for (a) Starting Materials: _____ *(b) Products:* _____

   Write a mechanism for this reaction:

IR and NMR Spectra

After completing a reaction and working up the products, it is still necessary to confirm that the correct product was formed. The most common tools used for this analysis are Infrared (IR) and Nuclear Magnetic Resonance (NMR) spectroscopy. In the virtual laboratory, only ^{1}H NMR spectra are available. Details on interpreting IR and NMR spectra are found in your textbook. Your instructor may or may not ask you to perform this section depending on how your class is structured.

5. To collect an IR spectrum of your product, click on the IR spectrometer located underneath the laboratory clock and drag the salt plate icon to the flask on the lab bench. A window containing the IR spectrum for your product should now open. Identify the relevant peaks in the IR spectrum and record the position and associated functional group for each in the IR table below. The IR spectrum can also be saved to the lab book for later analysis.

IR List position (cm^{-1}) & functional group		4.
1.		5.
2.		6.
3.		7.

6. To collect a ^{1}H NMR spectrum of your product, click on the NMR magnet located to the right of the chalkboard and drag the NMR sample tube to the flask on the lab bench. A window containing the NMR spectrum for your product should now open. You can zoom into various portions of the NMR spectrum by clicking and dragging over the desired area. The *Zoom Out* button is used to zoom back out to view the full spectrum. Identify all of the peaks in the NMR spectrum and record the chemical shift, the splitting, and the number of hydrogens for each peak in the NMR table below. The NMR spectrum can also be saved to the lab book for later analysis.

^{1}H NMR Structure: OH / OH *cis*-Octahydro-naphthalene-4a,8a-diol	Peak	Chemical Shift (δ)	Multiplicity†	H‡	Peak	Chemical Shift (δ)	Multiplicity†	H‡
	1				7			
	2				8			
	3				9			
	4				10			
	5				11			
	6				12			

† Specify the multiplicity as a singlet (s), doublet (d), triplet (t), quartet (q), or multiplet (m).
‡ Specify the number of hydrogens associated with each peak.

7. *Do the IR and NMR spectra you measured and recorded in the tables above confirm that you*

   synthesized the assigned target compound? Explain. _____

   _____

   _____

   _____

VCL 12-7: Quinone Reduction

For this assignment, the target compound that you should synthesize is **benzene-1,4-diol.** This is an oxidation reaction. Examine the product and determine a lower oxidation state functional group that may be present in the starting material.

Synthesis Procedures

1. Start *Virtual ChemLab* and select *Quinone Reduction* from the list of assignments in the electronic workbook. After entering the organic laboratory, go to the stockroom by clicking inside the *Stockroom* window. Next, select a round bottom flask and place it on the cork ring on the stockroom counter. Using the available reagents on the stockroom shelf, identify the appropriate starting materials required to synthesize the target compound and add them to the round bottom flask. Select the appropriate solvent and click on the green *Return to Lab* arrow to return to the laboratory.

2. The round bottom flask containing the starting materials should now be on the stir plate. Click on the handle located in the upper right corner of the laboratory to pull down the TV. The TV should already be in *Tutorial* mode and the starting materials and solvent should be listed. From the group of reagents found on the lab bench, select the correct reagent to synthesize the target compound and add it to the flask on the stir plate. Now attach the heater, condenser, and N_2 gas to the round bottom flask so the reaction mixture can be heated.

3. Start the reaction by clicking on the *Stir* button on the front of the stir plate. You should be able to observe the reaction mixture stirring in the flask. Monitor the progress of the reaction using TLC measurements as necessary until the product has formed and the starting materials have been consumed. You can advance the laboratory time using the clock on the wall. With the electronic lab book open (click on the lab book on the lab bench), you can also save your TLC plates by clicking *Save* on the TLC window.

4. When the reaction is complete, "work up" your reaction by first dragging and dropping the separatory funnel (located in a drawer) on the flask and then adding H_2O the funnel. Extract the organic layer in the funnel by clicking on the top layer and dragging it to the cork ring on the lab bench. Your target compound should now be in this flask.

List the starting materials, solvent, reagent, and products formed: _____

_____

How long did it take to finish the reaction? _____

What are the TLC values (Rf) for (a) Starting Materials: _____ *(b) Products:* _____

Write a mechanism for this reaction:

177

IR and NMR Spectra

After completing a reaction and working up the products, it is still necessary to confirm that the correct product was formed. The most common tools used for this analysis are Infrared (IR) and Nuclear Magnetic Resonance (NMR) spectroscopy. In the virtual laboratory, only ^{1}H NMR spectra are available. Details on interpreting IR and NMR spectra are found in your textbook. Your instructor may or may not ask you to perform this section depending on how your class is structured.

5. To collect an IR spectrum of your product, click on the IR spectrometer located underneath the laboratory clock and drag the salt plate icon to the flask on the lab bench. A window containing the IR spectrum for your product should now open. Identify the relevant peaks in the IR spectrum and record the position and associated functional group for each in the IR table below. The IR spectrum can also be saved to the lab book for later analysis.

IR List position (cm^{-1}) & functional group	4.
1.	5.
2.	6.
3.	7.

6. To collect a ^{1}H NMR spectrum of your product, click on the NMR magnet located to the right of the chalkboard and drag the NMR sample tube to the flask on the lab bench. A window containing the NMR spectrum for your product should now open. You can zoom into various portions of the NMR spectrum by clicking and dragging over the desired area. The *Zoom Out* button is used to zoom back out to view the full spectrum. Identify all of the peaks in the NMR spectrum and record the chemical shift, the splitting, and the number of hydrogens for each peak in the NMR table below. The NMR spectrum can also be saved to the lab book for later analysis.

^{1}H NMR Structure: HO—⟨benzene ring⟩—OH Benzene-1,4-diol	Peak	Chemical Shift (δ)	Multiplicity†	H‡	Peak	Chemical Shift (δ)	Multiplicity†	H‡
	1				7			
	2				8			
	3				9			
	4				10			
	5				11			
	6				12			

† Specify the multiplicity as a singlet (s), doublet (d), triplet (t), quartet (q), or multiplet (m).
‡ Specify the number of hydrogens associated with each peak.

7. *Do the IR and NMR spectra you measured and recorded in the tables above confirm that you synthesized the assigned target compound? Explain.* _____

_____

_____

_____

VCL 13-1: Epoxidation – 3

For this assignment, the target compound that you should synthesize is **2,3-epoxy-cyclohexanol.** This is a epoxidation reaction, an electrophilic process. Notice the *cis* relationship between the epoxide and the hydroxyl group. Keep in mind the mechanism and how that may control the *cis* selectivity of the process.

Synthesis Procedures

1. Start *Virtual ChemLab* and select *Amine Formation* from the list of assignments in the electronic workbook. After entering the organic laboratory, go to the stockroom by clicking inside the *Stockroom* window. Next, select a round bottom flask and place it on the cork ring on the stockroom counter. Using the available reagents on the stockroom shelf, identify the appropriate starting materials required to synthesize the target compound and add them to the round bottom flask. Select the appropriate solvent and click on the green *Return to Lab* arrow to return to the laboratory.

2. The round bottom flask containing the starting materials should now be on the stir plate. Click on the handle located in the upper right corner of the laboratory to pull down the TV. The TV should already be in *Tutorial* mode and the starting materials and solvent should be listed. From the group of reagents found on the lab bench, select the correct reagent to synthesize the target compound and add it to the flask on the stir plate. Now attach the heater, condenser, and N_2 gas to the round bottom flask so the reaction mixture can be heated.

3. Start the reaction by clicking on the *Stir* button on the front of the stir plate. You should be able to observe the reaction mixture stirring in the flask. Monitor the progress of the reaction using TLC measurements as necessary until the product has formed and the starting materials have been consumed. You can advance the laboratory time using the clock on the wall. With the electronic lab book open (click on the lab book on the lab bench), you can also save your TLC plates by clicking *Save* on the TLC window.

4. When the reaction is complete, "work up" your reaction by first dragging and dropping the separatory funnel (located in a drawer) on the flask and then adding NaOH the funnel. Extract the organic layer in the funnel by clicking on the top layer and dragging it to the cork ring on the lab bench. Your target compound should now be in this flask.

List the starting materials, solvent, reagent, and products formed: _____

_____

How long did it take to finish the reaction? _____

What are the TLC values (R_f) for (a) Starting Materials: _____ *(b) Products:* _____

Write a mechanism for this reaction:

179

IR and NMR Spectra

After completing a reaction and working up the products, it is still necessary to confirm that the correct product was formed. The most common tools used for this analysis are Infrared (IR) and Nuclear Magnetic Resonance (NMR) spectroscopy. In the virtual laboratory, only ^{1}H NMR spectra are available. Details on interpreting IR and NMR spectra are found in your textbook. Your instructor may or may not ask you to perform this section depending on how your class is structured.

5. To collect an IR spectrum of your product, click on the IR spectrometer located underneath the laboratory clock and drag the salt plate icon to the flask on the lab bench. A window containing the IR spectrum for your product should now open. Identify the relevant peaks in the IR spectrum and record the position and associated functional group for each in the IR table below. The IR spectrum can also be saved to the lab book for later analysis.

IR List position (cm^{-1}) & functional group	4.
1.	5.
2.	6.
3.	7.

6. To collect a ^{1}H NMR spectrum of your product, click on the NMR magnet located to the right of the chalkboard and drag the NMR sample tube to the flask on the lab bench. A window containing the NMR spectrum for your product should now open. You can zoom into various portions of the NMR spectrum by clicking and dragging over the desired area. The *Zoom Out* button is used to zoom back out to view the full spectrum. Identify all of the peaks in the NMR spectrum and record the chemical shift, the splitting, and the number of hydrogens for each peak in the NMR table below. The NMR spectrum can also be saved to the lab book for later analysis.

^{1}H NMR	Peak	Chemical Shift (δ)	Multiplicity†	H‡	Peak	Chemical Shift (δ)	Multiplicity†	H‡
	1				7			
Structure:	2				8			
OH	3				9			
(2,3-Epoxy-cyclohexanol)	4				10			
2,3-Epoxy-cyclohexanol	5				11			
	6				12			

† Specify the multiplicity as a singlet (s), doublet (d), triplet (t), quartet (q), or multiplet (m).
‡ Specify the number of hydrogens associated with each peak.

7. *Do the IR and NMR spectra you measured and recorded in the tables above confirm that you synthesized the assigned target compound? Explain.* _____

_____

_____

_____

Woodfield/Andrus
Virtual ChemLab Organic Chemistry Laboratory CD v.2.5
0-13-222129-2
© 2007 Pearson Education, Inc.
Pearson Prentice Hall
Pearson Education, Inc.
Upper Saddle River, NJ 07458
Pearson Prentice Hall™ is a trademark of Pearson Education, Inc.